Table of s

1 Definitions and formalities

1.1 What is land?

Law of Property Act 1925 s 205(1)(ix):
'Land' includes land of any tenure, and mines and minerals, whether or not held apart from the surface, buildings or parts of buildings (whether the division is horizontal, vertical or made in any other way) and other corporeal hereditaments; also a manor, an advowson, and a rent and other incorporeal hereditaments, and an easement, right, privilege, or benefit in, over, or derived from land; but not an undivided share in land; and 'mines and minerals' includes any strata or seam of minerals or substances in or under any land, and powers of working and getting the same but not an undivided share thereof; and 'manor' includes a lordship, and reputed manor or lordship; and 'hereditament' means any real property which on an intestacy occurring before the commencement of this Act might have devolved upon an heir.

Interpretation Act 1978 Schedule 1:
'Land' includes buildings and other structures, land covered with water, and any estate, interest, easement, servitude or right in or over land.

1.1.1 How far does it extend? *Cuius est solum eius est usque ad coelum et ad inferos.*

Ad coelum *(to the heavens)*?

Bernstein v Skyviews & General Ltd (1978)
The defendants flew over B's land and took aerial photographs of his country house. They offered to sell the photographs to B who claimed, *inter alia*, damages for trespass.

Held that B's rights in the airspace above his land were limited to such height as was necessary for the ordinary use and enjoyment of the land, and such rights had not been infringed. It was further stated *per curiam* that the protection given by s 40(1) of the Civil Aviation Act 1949 (now s 76(1) Civil Aviation Act 1982 below) applied to all flights at a reasonable height.

Civil Aviation Act 1982 s 76(1):
No action shall lie in respect of nuisance, by reason only of the flight of
an aircraft over any property at a height above the ground which,
having regard to wind, weather and all the circumstances of the case is
reasonable ...

Ad inferos *(to the depths of the earth)?*

> Note
>
> Minerals belong to the landowner, except: gold and silver – *Case of Mines*
> (1568); coal – Coal Act 1938 s 3; petroleum and natural gas – Petroleum
> (Production) Act 1934 s 1(1).

*If the original owner is unknown, chattels discovered in the land
belong to the landowner unless they are treasure trove*

**Attorney-General of the Duchy of Lancaster v G E Overton (Farms) Ltd
(1982) CA**
A large hoard of Roman coins was found buried in a field belonging to the
defendants. The plaintiff claimed the find as treasure trove because: (i) the
coins contained some silver; and (ii) it could be inferred that they had been
buried by somebody who later intended to reclaim them. The defendants
contended that, as the coins contained only a small amount of silver, they
were base metal and therefore could not be treasure trove. A coroner's
inquest found for the plaintiff, but the appeal was allowed by Dillon J. The
plaintiff appealed.
    Held that in order for the coins to be treasure trove they should contain
a 'substantial' amount of gold or silver. The coins were therefore the property of the defendants.

Q In order to claim property as treasure trove the items concerned must
contain a 'substantial' amount of gold or silver and the Crown must establish that the property has been hidden with the intention of being recovered. Is this satisfactory? See the reforms proposed in the Earl of Perth's
Treasure Bill 1994 and the Law Commission's Treasure trove: *Law Reform
Issues* (HMSO, 1987).

Q If the article is found on, as opposed to in, the ground and the owner is
unknown it will only become the property of the landowner if it is found
in a place over which the landowner exercises control, for example a private building. What if the chattel is found in a place to which the public
have access? See *Parker v British Airways Board* (1982). Or in a public park?
See *Waverley BC v Fletcher* (1995).

1.1.2   Chattels may become part of the land – *quicquid plantatur*

solo, solo cedit (whatever is attached to the land becomes part of it
– ie it becomes a fixture)

Note
If an article is a fixture it should, unless otherwise agreed, be sold as part
of the land. Fittings, on the other hand, may be removed by the vendor.

The degree of annexation test

Holland v Hodgson (1872)
The owner of a mill mortgaged it to the plaintiffs. When he became bankrupt the owner executed a deed of arrangement assigning all of his property to the defendants as trustees. The latter seized certain looms in the
mill in order to satisfy creditors. The plaintiffs claimed that the looms,
being nailed into beams which were built into the stone floor, were fixtures
rather than fittings and that as such they were part of the mortgaged
realty.
Held that the looms were fixtures. Blackburn J stated that when an
article is attached to the land 'even slightly', the presumption is that it is a
fixture, 'the onus lying on those who contend that it is a chattel'.

The purpose of annexation test

Leigh v Taylor (1902) HL
A tenant for life mounted valuable tapestries on to the walls of a house by
attaching them to canvas and then nailing them to the wall. After the
tenant for life died a summons was taken out on behalf of the infant
remaindermen claiming that the tapestries were fixtures and should pass
with the realty. At first instance the tapestries were found to be fixtures,
but the Court of Appeal allowed the appeal.
Held that the tapestries 'remained chattels from first to last' (*per* Lord
Lindley) because they were affixed to the walls as ornaments for the better
enjoyment of them as chattels.

Re Whaley (1908)
A testator owned a house in which there was an Elizabethan dining room,
on the walls of which there hung a painting and a tapestry, both of which
were screwed to the wall. By will he left to his wife all of the furniture and
chattels in the house absolutely and gave her a life interest in the house
itself. The question was whether the picture and the tapestry were fixtures,
in which case the widow had a life interest in them, or whether they were
merely fittings, in which case she took them absolutely.
Held that they were fixtures because they were not placed in the room
in order to display them as chattels but as part of the overall Elizabethan
scheme of decoration.

Berkley v Poulett (1976) CA

P sold a mansion to property to developers who in turn sold it to B. Before conveyance, P removed: (i) a number of pictures which had been affixed by screws to panelling; (ii) a statue weighing half a ton; and (iii) a sundial. B claimed the items as fixtures.

Held that the items were not fixtures. Scarman LJ applied both tests. The pictures, he stated 'were not fixtures. They were in place on the wall to be enjoyed as pictures'. The sundial had been removed many years previously and could not be a fixture. Similarly the statue, being unattached to the land, could not be a fixture, 'but even if it were attached the application of the second test (ie the purpose of annexation test would lead to the same conclusion'. The plinth, however, upon which the statue (and previously the sundial) had rested, being part of the general architectural design, was a fixture.

TSB Bank plc v Botham (1995)

The plaintiff bank, as mortgagee in possession, wished to sell the mortgaged property, a purpose-built flat. Inside the flat there were certain items which the bank wished to include in the sale of the flat as fixtures. The defendant wished to remove these items, claiming that they were merely chattels, and not part of the mortgaged realty. The items included fitted carpets, light fittings, gas fires, curtains and blinds, bathroom fittings, kitchen 'white goods' (freezer, dishwasher etc), and a sink unit. The bank sought a declaration that the items concerned were fixtures.

Held that the items were fixtures. Jacob J cited *Leigh v Taylor* (1902) before applying the purpose of annexation test to the facts. The carpets, being fitted, were fixtures despite the fact they were easily removable; the light fittings were attached to the realty and became part of it; the gas fires were the appropriate size for the apertures and were in place to be enjoyed as fires in the rooms rather than as chattels in themselves; the pelmets on the curtains were fixtures and the curtains and blinds, though removable, were specifically designed for the windows in question and were therefore fixtures; the bathroom fittings and mirror were clearly attached and were fixtures; the sink and kitchen units were similarly attached, and the 'white goods' were all physically fixed, plumbed or wired in and were part of the overall kitchen design.

Note ───

Although this case is not remarkable *per se*, it shows that the issue of annexation is relevant to everyday items and not merely to antique tapestries and marble statues.

1.2 Who is a purchaser?

Law of Property Act 1925 s 205(1)(xxi):
'Purchaser' means a purchaser in good faith for valuable consideration and includes a lessee, mortgagee, or other person who for valuable consideration acquires an interest in property ... and in reference to a legal estate includes a charge by way of legal mortgage; and where the context so requires 'purchaser' includes an intending purchaser; 'purchase' has a meaning corresponding to with that of 'purchaser'; and 'valuable consideration' includes marriage but does not include a nominal consideration in money.

Note
There are similar definitions in the Settled Land Act 1925 s 117(1)(xxi); the Land Registration Act 1925 s 3(xxi) and (xxxi); and the Law of Property (Miscellaneous Provisions) Act 1989 s 1(6).

Land Charges Act 1972 s 17(1):
'purchaser' means any person (including a mortgagee or lessee) who, for valuable consideration, takes any interest in land, and 'purchase' has a corresponding meaning.

Note
There is no requirement that the purchaser should be *bona fide*; for the implications of this see *Midland Bank Trust Co Ltd v Green* (1981) at 2.2.2.

1.3 Who is in possession?

Law of Property Act 1925 s 205(1)(xix):
'Possession' includes receipt of rents and profits or the right to secure the same, if any; and 'income' includes rents and profits.

Note
A lessor and a lessee may both be in possession simultaneously. The lessor because he or she is in receipt of rent, and the lessee because he or she is in occupation.

1.4 Legal estates and interests in land

1.4.1 Legal estates

Law of Property Act 1925 s 1(1):
The only estates in land which are capable of subsisting or of being created at law are –

(a) An estate in fee simple absolute in possession;

(b) A term of years absolute.

1.4.2 Legal interests

Law of Property Act 1925 s 1(2) and (3):

(2) The only interests or charges in or over land which are capable of subsisting or of being created at law are –

(a) An easement, right or privilege in or over land for an interest equivalent to an estate in fee simple absolute in possession or a term of years absolute;

(b) A rentcharge in possession issuing out of or charged on land being either perpetual or for a term of years absolute;

(c) A charge by way of legal mortgage; ...

(e) Rights of entry exercisable over or in respect of a legal term of years absolute, or annexed ... to a legal rentcharge.

(3) All other estates, interests, and charges in or over land take effect as equitable interests.

1.5 Formalities

1.5.1 Conveyances to be by deed

Law of Property Act 1925 s 52(1):

All conveyances of land or of any interest therein are void for the purpose of conveying or creating a legal estate unless made by deed.

Law of Property (Miscellaneous Provisions) Act 1989 s 1:

(2) An instrument shall not be a deed unless –

(a) it makes it clear on its face that it is intended to be a deed by the person making it or ... by the parties to it ... ; and

(b) it is validly executed as a deed by that person or ... one or more of those parties.

(3) An instrument is validly executed as a deed by an individual if, and only if –

(a) it is signed-

(i) by him in the presence of a witness who attests the signature; or

(ii) at his direction and in his presence and in the presence of two witnesses who each attest the signature; and

(b) it is delivered as a deed by him or by a person authorised to do so on his behalf.

1.5.2 Creation and disposition of interests in land

Law of Property Act 1925 s 53:

(1) Subject to the provisions ... with respect to the creation of interests by parol –

(a) no interest in land can be created or disposed of except by writing signed by the person creating or conveying the same, or by his agent thereunto lawfully authorised in writing, or by will, or by operation of law;

(b) a declaration of trust respecting any land or any interest therein must be manifested and proved by some writing signed by the person who is able to declare such trust or by his will;

(c) a disposition of an equitable interest or trust subsisting at the time of the disposition, must be in writing signed the person disposing of the same, or by his agent ... or by will.

(2) This section does not affect the creation or operation of resulting, implied or constructive trusts.

1.5.3 Contracts

Before 27 September 1989

Law of Property Act 1925 s 40:

(1) No action may be brought upon any contract for the sale or other disposition of land, unless the agreement upon which such action is brought, or some memorandum or note thereof, is in writing, and signed by the party to be charged or by some other person thereunto by him lawfully authorised.

(2) This section applies to contracts whether made before or after the commencement of this Act and does not affect the law relating to part performance, or sales by the court.

After 26 September 1989

Law of Property (Miscellaneous Provisions) Act 1989 s 2:

(1) A contract for the sale or other disposition of an interest in land can only be made in writing and only by incorporating all the terms which the parties have expressly agreed in one document, or, where contracts are exchanged, in each.

(2) The terms may be incorporated in a document either by being set out in it or by reference to some other document.

(3) The document incorporating the terms or, where documents are exchanged, one of the documents (but not necessarily the same one) must be signed by or on behalf of each party to the contract.

Q Since the 1989 Act came into force it has no longer been possible to use part performance in order to enforce a contract which does not comply with the formality requirements. To what extent is it possible to use estoppel to achieve a similar result? See Davis (1993) 13 OJLS 99.

1.5.4   Options to purchase

Spiro v Glencrown Properties Ltd (1991)

S granted an option to purchase land to G Ltd, who sought to exercise the option within the stipulated time limit. G then failed to complete the purchase. The grant of the option complied with s 2 of the 1989 Act (see above), but the exercise of the option, being signed only by G, did not. S sued for breach of contract, but G argued that, as the exercise of the option did not comply with s 2, there was no valid contract for sale.

Held that G was in breach of contract. The grant of the option had to comply with s 2; the exercise of that option could be a unilateral act. The grant was a conditional contract (*per* Hoffman J) and the condition was fulfilled when the option was exercised.

> Note ───
> This case is unusual because it is usually the party seeking to exercise the option who wishes to enforce the agreement.

Q If the exercise of an option had to comply with s 2 would the granting of an option be worth anything at all? It could certainly not be seen as 'an equitable interest ... or estate' (*London & South Western Railway Co v Gomm* (1882) *per* Jessel MR).

Armstrong & Holmes Ltd v Holmes (1993)

In 1986 H granted to A & H Ltd a five-year option to purchase land for the open market price, or, if the parties could not agree, for a price to be determined by arbitration. As the land was unregistered land, A & H Ltd registered the estate contract as a class C (iv) land charge in the Land Charges Register. They purported to exercise the option in October 1988 but H did not co-operate in fixing a price. H then sold part of the option land, subject to the option agreement, to a third party in December 1988. The third party sold the land to the second defendant, D, who was registered as the legal proprietor at the Land Registry by way of first registration, subject to the option agreement. A & H Ltd claimed specific performance against each defendant and were successful at first instance. The second defendant, D, appealed, claiming that the option was void as against him because the agreement resulting from the exercise of the option had not been registered.

Held, applying *Spiro v Glencrown Properties Ltd* (above), that the exercise of the option did not have to be registered. The option itself had been registered as an estate contract and that was sufficient to make it enforceable against third parties, even if they were purchasers for value.

1.5.5 Rights of pre-emption (rights of first refusal)

Pritchard v Briggs (1980) CA

Mr and Mrs L, the owners of land, granted B's predecessor in title a right of pre-emption. They then granted a lease, which contained an option to purchase the land after their deaths, to P. Both the right of pre-emption and the option were registered as estate contracts in the Land Charges Register. After Mr and Mrs L died, Mr L's personal representatives sold the land to B. P claimed that the right of pre-emption which had been granted to B's predecessor was a personal right only and could not be assigned to B. He sought to exercise his option but was unsuccessful at first instance, the judge deciding that B's right of pre-emption should take priority because of its prior registration. P appealed.

Held, allowing the appeal, that 'the grant of the right of pre-emption creates a mere *spes*' (*per* Templeman J), but that *spes* becomes an option when the owner decides to sell the land. It was therefore capable of binding third parties if registered under the Land Charges Act 1972 as a class C (iv) land charge. In the present case, however, the grant of the option to the plaintiff was not a condition upon which the right of pre-emption became exercisable. The option therefore took priority over the right of pre-emption and the conveyance of the land to B was made subject to P's option.

Q Is a right of pre-emption a mere *spes*, or is it an interest in land by virtue of the LCA 1972 s 2 (4)? (see 2.2.2)

1.5.6 'Lock-out' agreements

Pitt v PHH Asset Management Ltd (1994) CA

The defendants, as agents for the mortgagees in possession, offered a property for sale. They accepted an offer made by the plaintiff, but then withdrew their acceptance in favour of a higher offer from B. The plaintiff then increased his offer, and the increased offer was initially accepted by the defendants before being once again rejected in favour of a higher offer made by B. After the plaintiff threatened to seek an injunction, the defendant agreed to an oral 'lock out' agreement, which was later confirmed in writing, by which the property would be sold to the plaintiff if he exchanged contracts within two weeks. Before the plaintiff was able to exchange contracts the defendant's principal accepted B's offer and sold the property to her. The plaintiff claimed damages for breach of the 'lock-out' agreement, and the defendants argued that there was no valid contract which complied with s 2 of the Law of Property Act (Miscellaneous Provisions) Act 1989. The judge at first instance found for the plaintiff. The defendants appealed.

Held that the agreement did not have to comply with s 2. As there were no further matters to be agreed between the parties, the agreement was capable of subsisting independently of the negotiations for the sale of the land. The agreement was seen not as a contract for the sale of land but as a separate agreement which would bind the defendants.

2 Unregistered land

2.1 Before 1926

2.1.1 Legal rights are rights *in rem* and bind the whole world; equitable rights are rights *in personam* and are subject to the doctrine of notice

Pilcher v Rawlins (1872) Ch App

R mortgaged his property to the trustees of JP's family settlement. Five years later he wished to secure a further advance on the property from S and L. He colluded with the surviving trustee of the settlement, WP, who reconveyed the property to R despite the fact that only part of the initial advance had been repaid. R then mortgaged the property to S and L, who were unaware of the reconveyance and the prior mortgage. R defaulted and the beneficiaries of the settlement brought an action claiming that they were entitled to the property because the mortgage in their favour took priority over the later mortgage in favour of S and L.

Held that S and L were *bona fide* purchasers of a legal estate for value without notice of the interest of the beneficiaries. Once a purchaser has proved that he is Equity's darling, that fact 'is an absolute, unqualified unanswerable defence' (*per* James LJ).

Hunt v Luck (1902) CA

Mrs H believed that certain conveyances purportedly made by her late husband to G were forgeries. She took action against Miss L, G's representative, who did not defend the action. The people to whom G had mortgaged the properties did defend the proceedings, however, claiming to be *bona fide* purchasers without notice. Mrs H claimed that the mortgagees were under a duty to make such enquiries as a prudent, careful and reasonable man would have made. They made no enquiries of the tenants in occupation of the properties and therefore they should be fixed with constructive notice. Farwell J found for the mortgagees at first instance and Mrs H appealed.

Held that the mortgagees were purchasers for value without notice and that their title must prevail over that of the plaintiff. A purchaser will be fixed with constructive notice of the rights of any person in occupation of the land, but not of the rights of any other person. A tenant in occupation cannot serve notice of the rights of his landlord.

Wilkes v Spooner (1911) CA

S was the tenant of two shops, 137 and 170 High Street. At No 170 he conducted his business as a general butcher, and at No 137, which was leased from a different landlord, he covenanted not to use the premises for any trade other than that of a pork butcher. He assigned the lease of No 170 to W and covenanted with him not to carry on the trade of a general butcher at No 137. S then surrendered the lease of No 137 to the landlord, who knew nothing of S's covenant with W. The landlord accepted surrender and granted a new lease to S's son free from the covenant in the earlier lease. S's son then opened a business as a general butcher in competition with W, even though he knew about the covenant which his father had entered into with W. W sued to restrain the breach of covenant and was successful at first instance. S's son appealed.

Held that the covenant was not binding upon S's son. The landlord was a *bona fide* purchaser for value without notice of the covenant, and the covenant was in effect extinguished upon conveyance of the legal estate to him. Once the covenant had been extinguished, it could not be revived even if the new lessee had knowledge of it.

Q Could S himself have taken the lease free from the covenant? See *Barrow's Case* (1880) – 'The only exception ... is that which prevents a trustee buying back trust property which he has sold, or, a fraudulent man who has acquired property by fraud saying he sold it to a *bona fide* purchaser without notice and has got it back again' (*per* Jessel MR).

2.2 After 1925

2.2.1 Family equitable interests may be overreached

Law of Property Act 1925 ss 2(1) and 2(2):

(1) A conveyance to a purchaser of a legal estate in land shall overreach any equitable interest or power affecting that estate, whether or not he has notice thereof, if –

(i) the conveyance is made under the powers conferred by the Settled Land Act 1925, or any additional powers conferred by a settlement, and the equitable interest or power is capable of being overreached thereby, and the statutory requirements respecting the payment of capital money arising under the settlement are complied with;

(ii) the conveyance is made by trustees for sale and the equitable interest or power is at the date of the conveyance capable of being overreached by such trustees under the provisions of subsection (2) of this section ... and the statutory requirements respecting the payment of capital money arising under a disposition upon trust for sale are complied with;

(iii) the conveyance is made by a mortgagee or personal representative in the exercise of his paramount powers; ...

(iv) the conveyance is made under an order of the court; ...

(2) Where the legal estate affected is subject to a trust for sale, then if ... the trustees ... are either –

(a) two or more individuals ... or

(b) a trust corporation ...

any equitable interest or power having priority to the trust for sale shall ... be overreached by the conveyance and shall, according to its priority, take effect as if created or arising by means of a primary trust affecting the proceeds of sale and the income of the land until sale.

Note ————————————————————————————
See 2.2.3 for the effect of non-overreachable family equitable interests.

2.2.2 Commercial equitable interests should be registered in the Land Charges Register

Land Charges Act 1972 s 2:
(1) If a charge on or obligation affecting land falls into one of the classes described in this section, it may be registered in the register of land charges as a land charge of that class ...

(4) A Class C land charge is any of the following ... namely –

(i) a puisne mortgage;

(ii) a limited owners charge;

(iii) a general equitable charge;

(iv) an estate contract;

and for this purpose –

(i) a puisne mortgage is a legal mortgage not protected by a deposit of documents relating to the legal estate affected ...

(iii) a general equitable charge is any equitable charge which –

(a) is not secured by a deposit of documents relating to the legal estate affected; and

(b) does not arise or affect an interest arising under a trust for sale or settlement ...

(iv) an estate contract is a contract by an absolute owner or by a person entitled at the date of the contract to have a legal estate conveyed to him to convey or create a legal estate, including a contract conferring ... a valid option to purchase, a right of pre-emption or any other like right.

(5) A Class D land charge is any of the following, namely –

(i) an Inland Revenue charge;

(ii) a restrictive covenant;

(iii) an equitable easement;

and for this purpose –

(i) ...

(ii) a restrictive covenant is a covenant or agreement (other than a covenant or agreement between lessor and lessee) restrictive of the user of land and entered into on or after 1 January 1926;

(iii) an equitable easement is an easement, right or privilege over or affecting land created or arising on or after 1 January 1926, and being merely an equitable interest ...

(7) A Class F land charge is a charge affecting any land by virtue of the Matrimonial Homes Act 1983.

Note ——————————————————————————————————

For rights acquired under the Matrimonial Homes Acts, see 6.4.

The effect of registration

Law of Property Act 1925 s 198(1):

The registration of any instrument or matter in any register kept under the Land Charges Act 1972 or any local land charges register, shall be deemed to constitute actual notice of such instrument or matter, and the fact of such registration, to all persons and for all purposes connected with the land affected, as from the date of registration or other prescribed date and so long as the registration continues in force.

The effect of non-registration

Land Charges Act 1972 s 4:

(5) A land charge of Class B and a land charge of Class C (other than an estate contract) created or arising on or after 1 January 1926 shall be void as against a purchaser of the land charged with it, or of any interest in such land, unless the land charge is registered in the appropriate register before the completion of the purchase.

(6) An estate contract and a land charge of Class D created or entered into on or after 1 January 1926 shall be void as against a purchaser for money or money's worth of a legal estate in the land charged with it, unless the land charge is registered in the appropriate register before completion of the purchase.

(8) A land charge of Class F shall be void as against a purchaser of the land charged with it, or of any interest in such land, unless the land charge is registered in the appropriate register before completion of the purchase.

Note ——————————————————————————————————

(i) A purchaser of the legal estate (and of any interest therein for all apart from class C (iv) and D charges) who gives money or money's worth will take free from all unregistered land charges.

(ii) A purchaser of the legal estate, or of any interest therein, for marriage or nominal consideration will take free from all unregistered land charges apart from those in classes C (iv) and D.

(iii) Donees and beneficiaries under a will or intestacy are bound by all land charges whether registered or not.

Midland Bank Trust Co Ltd v Green (1981) HL

In 1961 a father granted to his son a 10-year option to purchase a farm. The son did not register the option as a class C (iv) land charge. In order to deprive his son of the option the father sold the farm, which was worth about £40,000, to his wife for £500. The son then registered his option and purported to exercise it.

Held that the option was void as against the mother. She had notice of the option and she was certainly not a *bona fide* purchaser, but she was nevertheless a purchaser for money or money's worth and that was sufficient for the purposes of the Land Charges Act 1972 s 4(6) (above). There was in the Act no requirement that a purchaser should be *bona fide* (see 1.2 above). According to Lord Wilberforce, 'the Act itself provides a simple and effective protection for persons in Geoffrey's (ie the son's) position – *viz* – by registration.'

Q Considering the maxim 'Equity will not permit a statute to be used as an instrument of fraud', could not equity have intervened to prevent the son falling victim to the fraud perpetrated by his parents? Lord Wilberforce was of the opinion that 'it is not 'fraud' to rely on legal rights conferred by Act of Parliament'. See 3.10 for comparable situations in registered land.

The effect of an official search certificate

Land Charges Act 1972 s 10(4):
In favour of a purchaser or an intending purchaser, as against persons interested under or in respect of matters or documents entries of which are required or allowed as aforesaid, the certificate, according to its tenor, shall be conclusive, affirmatively or negatively, as the case may be.

Registration in the name of the estate owner

Land Charges Act 1972 s 3(1):
A land charge shall be registered in the name of the estate owner whose estate is intended to be affected.

Oak Co-operative Building Society v Blackburn (1968) CA

In 1958 B granted to C an option to purchase property. He then mortgaged the property to a building society in 1959. The mortgage was registered in the Land Charges Register under his full name, Francis David Blackburn. Shortly afterwards C registered her option as a class C (iv) land charge under the name of Frank David Blackburn, the name B used for business purposes. In 1962 B applied for a mortgage to the plaintiff building society, who searched the Land Charges Register under the name of Francis Davis Blackburn. They obtained a certificate showing no entries under the name searched, but attention was drawn to the previous mortgage under the name of Francis David Blackburn. After B became bankrupt, the building society sought possession free from the option and were successful at first instance. C appealed.

Held, allowing the appeal, that had the building society searched under the correct full name the certificate obtained would have been conclusive. However they searched under the wrong name and could not rely upon the certificate. The option was also registered under the wrong name, but the name used was a recognised version of B's full name and therefore it was not a nullity. It was effective against either a purchaser who did not search the register, or, as in the present case, a purchaser who searched under the wrong name.

Diligent Finance Co Ltd v Alleyne (1972)

Mr A, the legal proprietor of the matrimonial home, left his wife, who registered her right of occupation as a Class F land charge against Erskine Alleyne. Mr A then took out a mortgage with D Ltd and left the country with the money. D Ltd, who had searched the Land Charges Register under A's full name, Erskine Owen Alleyne, and received a certificate showing no entries, sought to possess the property free from Mrs Alleyne's right of occupation.

Held that the Class F land charge did not did not bind the finance company because it was not registered under the correct full name. Foster J declared that Erskine Alleyne was neither Mr A's full name nor the name that had been used on the conveyancing documents.

2.2.3 Some interests are neither registrable nor overreachable. Such residual interests remain subject to the doctrine of notice

Law of Property Act 1925 s 199(1):

A purchaser shall not be prejudicially affected by notice of –

(i) any instrument or matter capable of registration under the Land Charges Act 1925, or any enactment which it replaces, which is void or not enforceable as against him under that Act or enactment, by reason of the non-registration thereof;

(ii) any other instrument or matter or any fact or thing unless –

(a) it is within his own knowledge, or would have come to his knowledge if such inquiries and inspections had been made as ought reasonably to have been made by him; or

(b) ... it has come to the knowledge of his counsel, as such, or his solicitor or other agent, as such, or would have come to the knowledge of his solicitor or other agent, as such, if such inquiries and inspections had been made as ought reasonably have been made by the solicitor or other agent.

Beneficial interests under a trust when there is only one trustee

Kingsnorth Finance Co Ltd v Tizard (1986)

In 1979 Mr and Mrs T purchased a house using the proceeds from the sale of a former matrimonial home. The property was conveyed to Mr T as sole legal proprietor. In 1982 the marriage broke down and Mrs T eventually moved to her sister's house, returning daily to look after the children and sleeping in the house during her husband's frequent absences on business. Mr and Mrs T agreed between themselves that, because of Mrs T's contributions to the purchase, the property should eventually be sold and the proceeds divided equally between them. She therefore had a beneficial interest under a resulting or constructive trust (see 6.1). In 1983 Mr T negotiated a loan with K Ltd, who sent a surveyor to inspect the property. Mr T ensured that the inspection occurred when his wife was not in the house and he removed all obvious traces of her presence. The surveyor was told that Mrs T had left the property and was living nearby, but no further enquiries were made. After obtaining the mortgage Mr T emigrated and K Ltd sought possession of the house.

Held that K were bound by Mrs T's interest because, although Mr T had removed all trace of his wife from the house on the day of the surveyor's visit, the presence of the children in the house was sufficient to fix the surveyor with constructive notice. Mrs T was in occupation for some portion of every day, and her clothes were still stored on the premises. As the surveyor was K Ltd's agent, this notice could be imputed to K Ltd who were under a duty to make further enquiries.

In the absence of further inquiries or inspections, I do not think that it is open to the plaintiffs to say that if they had made further inspection they would still not have found Mrs Tizard in occupation (*per* Judge John Finlay QC).

Note ───────────────────────────────

This decision was little more than an application of the rule in *Hunt v Luck* (see above at 2.1.1).

Interests arising under the doctrine of mutual benefit and burden

Halsall v Brizell (1957)

In 1851 the original owners of seafront properties covenanted to pay for the maintenance of sewers, a road, a sea wall, and a promenade. The covenants were expressed to be for themselves, their heirs, executors and assigns. In 1950 the executors of one of the subsequent owners refused to comply with the terms of the covenants. They argued that, as the covenants were positive in nature (ie they involved expenditure on the

17

part of the covenantor – see 9.3.1 below), they were incapable of running
with the land.

Held that if the occupiers wished to benefit from the covenants by using
the road and sewers etc, they must also be bound by the burden. The parties had executed a deed which stated the terms of the covenant and 'it is
ancient law that a man cannot take benefit under a covenant without sub-
scribing to the obligations thereunder' (*per* Upjohn J).

Rights arising under proprietary estoppel

ER Ives Investment Ltd v High (1967) CA

In 1949 H bought a plot of land and began to build a house on it. At about
the same time W began to build on an adjoining site. The foundations of
W's block of flats encroached about one foot on to H's land below ground
level. H objected but came to an oral agreement with W that, if the foundations were allowed to remain, H could have a right of way across W's
land. There was evidence of the agreement in the letters which passed
between the parties. In 1950 W sold his site to the W's.

In 1959 H, relying upon his right of way, built a garage, the only access
to which was via the right of way. In 1960 the W's got H to resurface the
yard over which he had a right of way, and H paid one-fifth of the cost of
resurfacing. In 1963 the W's sold the site to I, the property being conveyed
subject to the right of way. I claimed an injunction and damages for
trespass because the right of way was not binding on them for want of
registration as either a class C (iv) or a class D (iii) land charge. H counterclaimed that, if the plaintiff's claim succeeded, he should be entitled to an
injunction ordering the removal of the foundations from his land.

Held that H was entitled to use the right of way. Lord Denning MR
thought this was the case, for two reasons. First, under the doctrine of
mutual benefit and burden (see *Halsall v Brizell* above); and second,
because of proprietary estoppel. H had relied to his detriment upon a
promise made by the Ws, and the Ws had acquiesced in the knowledge of
that reliance. The Ws 'created in Mr High's mind reasonable expectation
that his access over the yard would not be disturbed. That gives rise to an
'equity arising out of acquiescence'. It is available not only against the
Wrights but also against their successors in title.' The right arising out of
estoppel was not capable of registration either as a class C (iv) land charge
(estate contract) or as a class D (iii) charge (equitable easement); it was
therefore subject to the doctrine of notice.

Equitable rights of entry

Shiloh Spinners Ltd v Harding (1973) HL

SS assigned their leasehold interest to T in 1961. T covenanted to perform
certain fencing and repairing obligations and gave SS a right to re-enter the
premises in the event of breach of covenant. In 1965 T assigned their

interest to H who defaulted on the covenants. SS sought possession for default but H claimed that the right of re-entry was void as against them because they were purchasers for 'money or money's worth' and the right was registered neither as a class C (iv) nor as a class D (iii) land charge.

Held that the right of re-entry was neither an estate contract (Class C (iv)) nor an equitable easement (Class D (iii)). It was therefore not capable of registration and was subject to the doctrine of notice. H had notice of the covenant and was bound by it.

There is no doubt that if it was capable of registration under that Act (ie the Land Charges Act 1972), it would be unenforceable if not registered ... the consequence of equitable rights of entry not being registrable is that they are subject to the doctrine of notice, as preserved by section 199 of the Law of Property Act (*per* Lord Wilberforce).

Note

In addition to the interests listed in 2.2.3, equitable easements and restrictive covenants created before 1926 (see the LCA 1972 s 2 at 2.2.2 above) are subject to the doctrine of notice, as are equitable mortgages created by the deposit of title deeds. Leasehold covenants are not registrable, and mortgages of an equitable interest are subject to the rule in *Dearle v Hall* (1823) (see 10.4.3).

3 Registered land

3.1 Definition of registered land

Land Registration Act 1925 s 3(xxiv):
'Registered land' means land or any estate or interest in land the title to which is registered under this Act or any enactment replaced by this Act, and includes any easement, right, privilege, or benefit which is appurtenant or appendant thereto, and any mines and minerals within or under the same and held therewith ...

3.2 The extent of registered land

Land Registration, England and Wales: Registration of Title Order 1989 SI 1989 No 1347:
By this order the remaining areas of England and Wales which were still subject to unregistered conveyancing were made areas of compulsory first registration on conveyance. The whole of England and Wales has been subject to compulsory registration since 1 January 1990.

3.3 The register

Land Registration Act 1925 s 1:
(1) The Chief Land Registrar shall continue to keep a register of title to freehold and leasehold land.
(2) The register need not be kept in documentary form.

Land Registration Rules 1925, SR & O 1925 No 1093 rr 2 and 8:
(2) ... The register shall consist of three parts, called the Property Register, the Proprietorship Register, and the Charges Register. The title to each registered property shall bear a distinguishing number ...
(8) Index Map and Parcels Index. – (1) Index Maps shall be kept in the Registry which shall show the position and extent of every registered estate ...

3.4 Registrable interests

Land Registration Act 1925 s 2(1):
After the commencement of this Act, estates capable of subsisting as legal estates shall be the only interests in land in respect of which a proprietor can be registered and all other interests in registered land (except overriding interests and interests entered on the register at or before such commencement) shall take effect in equity as minor interests, but all interests (except undivided shares in land) entered on the register at such commencement which are not legal estates shall be capable of being dealt with under this Act.

3.4.1 Absolute title

Land Registration Act 1925 s 5:
Where the registered land is a freehold estate, the registration of any person as first proprietor thereof with an absolute title shall vest in the person so registered an estate in fee simple in possession in the land, together with all rights, privileges, and appurtenances belonging to or appurtenant thereto, subject to the following rights and interests, that is to say –

(a) Subject to the incumbrances, and other entries, if any, appearing on the register; and

(b) Unless the contrary is expressed on the register, subject to such overriding interests, if any, as affect the registered land; and

(c) Where the first proprietor is not entitled for his own benefit to the registered land subject, as between himself and the persons entitled to minor interests, to any minor interests of such persons of which he has notice,

but free from all other estates and interests whatsoever, including estates and interests of His Majesty.

> Note
> There is similar provision made for absolute leasehold title in s 9; the difference being that the leasehold title is subject to all implied and express covenants, obligations etc.

3.4.2 Good leasehold title

Land Registration Act 1925 s 10:
Where the registered land is a leasehold interest, the registration of a person as first proprietor thereof with good leasehold title shall not affect or prejudice the enforcement of any estate, right or interest affecting or in derogation of the title of the lessor to grant the lease, but, save as aforesaid, shall have the same effect as registration with absolute title.

3.4.3 Possessory title

Land Registration Act 1925 s 6:
Where the registered land is a freehold estate, the registration of any person as first proprietor thereof with a possessory title only shall not affect or prejudice the enforcement of any estate, right or interest adverse to or in derogation of the title of the first proprietor, and subsisting or capable of arising at the time of registration of that proprietor; but save as aforesaid, shall have the same effect as registration of a person with absolute title.

Note

There is similar provision made for possessory leasehold title in s 11; the difference being that it could be either the title of the lessor or the title of the lessee which is in dispute.

3.4.4 Qualified title

Land Registration Act 1925 s 7(1):
Where an absolute title is required, and on the examination of the title it appears to the registrar that the title can be established only for a limited period, or only subject to certain reservations, the registrar may, on the application of the party applying to be registered, by an entry made in the register, except from the effect of registration any estate, right, or interest ... and a title registered subject to such excepted estate, right, or interest shall be called a qualified title.

Note

1 There is similar provision made for qualified leasehold title in s 12; the difference being that the qualification may relate either to the title of the lessor or to the title of the lessee.

2 Section 77 provides that if the registrar is later satisfied as to one of the lesser titles he may upgrade it to title absolute. In case there are any adverse claims (see 6.5) a possessory title may be converted to title absolute after being registered for 12 years.

3.4.5 Land and charge certificates

Land Registration Act 1925 ss 63–68:
Section 63(1)
On the first registration of a freehold or leasehold interest in land, and on registration of a charge, a land certificate, or charge certificate, as the case may be, shall be prepared in the prescribed form: it shall state whether the title is absolute, good leasehold, qualified or possessory, and shall be either delivered to the proprietor or deposited in the registry as the proprietor may prefer ...

Section 64(1)
(1) So long as a land certificate or charge certificate is outstanding, it shall be produced to the registrar –
(a) on every entry in the register of a disposition by the proprietor ...
(b) on every registered transmission; and
(c) in every case ... where under this Act or otherwise notice of any estate right or claim or a restriction is entered or placed on the register, adversely affecting the title of the proprietor of the registered land or charge, but not in the case of the lodgement of a caution or of an inhibition or of a creditor's notice, or of entry of a notice of a lease at a rent without taking a fine ...

Section 68
Any land certificate or charge certificate shall be admissible as evidence of the several matters therein contained.

3.4.6   The effect of a transfer

Land Registration Act 1925 s 19(1):
The transfer of the registered estate in the land or part thereof shall be completed by the registrar entering on the register the transferee as the proprietor of the estate transferred, but until such entry is made the transferor shall be deemed to remain proprietor of the registered estate; and, where part only of the land is transferred, notice thereof shall also be noted on the register.

Note
It is therefore the entry on the register which transfers the legal estate. Until the proprietorship register has been altered the transferee's title remains equitable only, even after completion of the purchase.

3.5   Minor interests

Land Registration Act 1925 s 3(xv):
'Minor interests' mean the interests not capable of being disposed of or created by registered dispositions and capable of being overridden (whether or not a purchaser has notice thereof) by the proprietors unless protected as provided by this Act, and all rights and interests which are not registered or protected on the register and are not overriding interests, and include –
(a) in the case of land on trust for sale, all interests and powers which are ... capable of being overridden by the trustees for sale, whether or not such interests and powers are so protected; and

(b) in the case of settled land, all interests and powers which are ... capable of being overridden by the tenant for life or statutory owner, whether or not such interests and powers are so protected as aforesaid.

3.5.1 Notices

Land Registration Act 1925 s 52:
(1) A disposition by the proprietor shall take effect subject to all estates, rights and claims which are protected by way of notice on the register at the date of registration or entry of notice of the disposition, but only if and so far as such estates, rights and claims may be valid and are not (independently of this Act) overridden by the disposition.
(2) Where notice of a claim is entered on the register, such entry shall operate by way of notice only, and shall not operate to render the claim valid whether made adversely to or for the benefit of the registered land or charge.

Note

For the order of priority of notices *inter se* see *Mortgage Corporation Ltd v Nationwide Credit Corporation Ltd* (1993) at 10.5.1 below.

3.5.2 Cautions

Land Registration Act 1925 s 55(1):
After any such caution against dealings has been lodged in respect of any registered land or charge, the registrar shall not, without the consent of the cautioner, register any dealing or make any entry on the register for protecting the rights acquired under a deposit of a land or charge certificate or other dealing by the proprietor with such land or charge until he has served notice on the cautioner, warning him that his caution will cease to have any effect after the expiration of the prescribed number of days next following the date at which such notice is served; and after the expiration of such time as aforesaid the caution shall cease unless an order to the contrary is made by the registrar, and upon the caution so ceasing the registered land or charge may be dealt with in the same manner as if no caution had been lodged.

Parkash v Irani Finance Ltd (1970)
K agreed to sell property of which he was the registered proprietor to P. No formal contract was ever signed, but on 2 July 1967 P went into possession. On 7 July I Ltd obtained a charging order on the property to secure a judgment debt against K, and they lodged a caution three days later. On 27 July P received an official search certificate which did not show the caution and he went ahead with the purchase, applying for registration on 14 August. I Ltd, upon receiving notice of P's application, objected, and the Chief

Land Registrar applied to the court on the question of whether the caution should continue to have effect or be cancelled.

Held that the caution was to continue to have effect.

> **Note**
> The plaintiff, however, may have been able to obtain an indemnity (see 3.8 below).

Barclays Bank Ltd v Taylor (1974) CA

The registered proprietors of land were in debt to the plaintiff bank. They agreed to deposit the land certificate with the bank and agreed to execute a legal charge when called upon to do so. The bank entered a notice of deposit against the title and called upon the proprietors to execute the charge, but they did not attempt to register the charge until one year after execution. In the meantime, T entered into a contract to purchase the land. He paid the purchase price and lodged a caution against dealings, but did not obtain a transfer of the land. When the bank came to register their charge, T claimed priority by virtue of his caution.

Held that both the unregistered charge and the contract for sale were minor interests; they therefore took effect in equity only. The general rule is that the first in time should prevail and therefore the bank's mortgage should take priority. Had T managed to obtain a transfer of the land (which would not have been possible because the bank held the land certificate) he would have taken free from the unregistered charge, but a caution alone does not affect the priority of interests.

Clark v Chief Land Registrar (1994) CA

Two judgment debtors owned land which was subject to a mortgage. C, the judgment creditor, protected his charging order by lodging a caution against dealings against the registered title of the debtors. A second defendant advanced a sum of money to the debtors and secured the loan by way of legal charge. The Registrar did not inform C of the application to register the charge, and C claimed that, as a cautioner, he was entitled to be given notice prior to registration. He further claimed that his caution took priority over the charge. The judge held that the caution did not give C priority, but that he should be indemnified by the defendant. The Chief Land Registrar appealed.

Held, dismissing the appeal, that the caution did not affect the priority afforded to the legal charge. However, C had been denied the opportunity of objecting to the registration of the charge and he was therefore entitled to an indemnity from the Chief Land Registrar.

3.5.3 Inhibitions

Land Registration Act 1925 s 57(1):
The court, or, subject to an appeal to the court, the registrar, upon application of any person interested ... in relation to any registered land or charge, may ... issue an order or make an entry inhibiting for a time, or until the occurrence of an event to be named in such order or entry, or generally until further order or entry, the registration of or entry of any dealing with any registered land or registered charge.

3.5.4 Restrictions

Land Registration Act 1925 s 58(1):
Where the proprietor of any registered land or charge desires to place restrictions on transferring or charging the land or on disposing of or dealing with the land or charge in any manner in which he is by this Act authorised to dispose of or deal with it, or on the deposit by way of security of any certificate, the proprietor may apply to the registrar to make an entry in the register that no transaction to which the application relates shall be effected, unless the following things, or such of them as the proprietor may determine, are done –

(a) unless notice of any application for the transaction is transmitted by post to such address as he may specify to the registrar;

(b) unless the consent of some person or persons, to be named by the proprietor, is given to the transaction;

(c) unless some such other matter or thing is done as may be required by the applicant and approved by the registrar:

Provided that no restriction under this section shall extend or apply to dispositions of or dealings with minor interests.

> Note ───
>
> In the event of a strict settlement or a trust for sale, a restriction may be entered on the register to ensure that capital monies are paid to at least two trustees or to a trust corporation in compliance with the overreaching provisions (see 2.2.1 and 3.9).

3.6 Overriding interests

Land Registration Act 1925 s 3(xvi):
'Overriding interests' mean all the incumbrances, interests, rights, and powers not entered on the register but subject to which registered dispositions are by this Act to take effect, and in regard to land registered at the commencement of this Act include the matters which are by any enactment repealed by this Act declared not to be incumbrances ...

Land Registration Act 1925 s 70(1):
All registered land shall, unless under the provisions of this Act the contrary is expressed on the register, be deemed to be subject to such of the following overriding interests as may be for the time being subsisting in reference thereto, and such interests shall not be treated as incumbrances within the meaning of this Act, (that is to say):

(a) Rights of common, drainage rights, customary rights (until extinguished), public rights, profits *à prendre*, rights of sheepwalk, rights of way, watercourses, rights of water, and other easements not being equitable easements required to be protected by notice on the register;

(b) Liability to repair highways by reason of tenure, quit-rents, crown rents, heriots, and other rents and charges (until extinguished) having their origin in tenure;

(c) Liability to repair the chancel of any church;

(d) Liability in respect of embankments, and sea and river walls;

(e) ... payments in lieu of tithe, and charges or annuities payable for the redemption of tithe rentcharges;

(f) Subject to the provisions of this Act, rights acquired or in the course of being acquired under the Limitation Acts;

(g) The rights of every person in actual occupation of the land or in receipt of rents and profits thereof, save where enquiry is made of such person and the rights are not disclosed;

(h) In the case of possessory, qualified or good leasehold title, all estates, rights, interests and powers excepted from the effect of registration;

(i) Rights under local land charges unless and until registered or protected on the register in the prescribed manner;

(j) Rights of fishing and sporting, seigniorial and manorial rights of all descriptions (until extinguished), and franchises;

(k) Leases granted for a term not exceeding twenty-one years;

(l) In respect of land registered before the commencement of this Act rights to mines and minerals, and rights of entry, search, and user ...

Land Registration Rules 1925 SR & O 1925 No 1093 r 197:
(1) Where any person desires to have an entry made in the register of the freedom from or the existence of an overriding interest mentioned in Section 70 of the Act, the application shall be made in writing and shall state the particulars of the entry required to be made ...

(6) Any entry showing that the registered land is free from any one or more of the liabilities, rights, or interests, mentioned in Section 70 of the Act, shall be made in the Property Register.

3.6.1   Section 70(1)(a)

Celsteel Ltd v Alton House Holdings Ltd (1986) CA
A Ltd was the fee simple owner of a block of flats. The plaintiff was a tenant of one of the flats and of a garage under a contract for a lease made

with A Ltd's predecessor in title. The contract gave a right of way to the plaintiff in order to give him access to the garage. The lease itself was never granted and the agreement for the lease (see 7.2.2) was not registered, and therefore both the leasehold interest and the easement took effect only in equity. A Ltd granted a lease of part of the land over which the plaintiff had a right of way to an oil company, who planned to build on the land. The plaintiff claimed to have an easement, but the problem was that the right of way had not been entered on the register, and s 70(1)(a) appears to exclude specifically equitable easements from those interests which are capable of being overriding.

Held that the right of way was an overriding interest. Scott J interpreted r 258 of the Land Registration Rules 1925 as meaning that any equitable easement openly exercised and enjoyed at the time of the transfer of the land could qualify as an overriding interest.

Note
The Law Commission have recommended that equitable easements should no longer capable of being be overriding interests (Report No 158, 1987).

3.6.2 Section 70(1)(f)

Bridges v Mees (1957)
In 1939, B, who lived in an area of compulsory registration, contracted to purchase a strip of unregistered land adjoining his house. He went into possession and finished paying the purchase money by instalments in 1940. The land was never transferred to him however, and he did not enter a caution against first registration. In 1955 the owner conveyed the land to M, who was registered as the legal proprietor by way of first registration. B claimed to be the beneficial owner of the land and sought rectification of the register (see 3.7 below for rectification).

Held that the plaintiff was entitled to have the legal estate transferred to him. Harman J thought that B's rights were overriding either by virtue of his actual occupation under s 70(1)(g) or because of his title acquired by adverse possession for 12 years under s 70(1)(f) (see 6.2 for adverse possession). The legal estate was held by M as trustee for B and he should transfer it to him; or, alternatively B was entitled to rectification of the register.

Note
See also *Chowood Ltd v Lyall (No 2)* (1930) below at 3.7.

3.6.3 Section 70(1)(g)

Strand Securities Ltd v Caswell (1965) CA
X was the registered proprietor with good leasehold title of a house. She granted a sublease of a flat for 39 and a quarter years to C in 1949, but he

did not register his lease. In 1952 X sold the house, subject to the sublease, to P, who in turn sold it to the plaintiffs in 1962. C applied to register his sublease on 5 April 1962, and the plaintiffs applied for registration of the transfer on 24 April. The land registry gave the plaintiff's claim preference, mistakenly believing that the head lessor's land certificate had to be produced in order to register a sublease. Once registered as the legal proprietors, the plaintiffs objected to the registration of the sublease and they issued a writ seeking a declaration that the sublease was void for want of registration.

C claimed first that the registry's interpretation of the Land Registration Act 1925 s 64(1) was mistaken; and alternatively that his interest was overriding by virtue of s 70(1)(g). In order to take advantage of that subsection, however, he had to be in 'actual occupation' or 'in receipt of rents and profits', and he did not in fact live in the flat himself but allowed his daughter to live there rent-free. The judge at first instance found for the plaintiffs and C appealed.

Held, allowing the appeal, that the registry were mistaken in their interpretation of the Land Registration Act 1925 and that C's sublease should take priority. Lord Denning MR, however, ruled that C could not take advantage of subsection 70(1)(g). His daughter was in actual occupation but she, being a mere licensee, had no rights in the land. C himself would have to be in occupation to take advantage of that provision.

For it is quite clear that if the second defendant (ie the daughter) had paid a token sum as rent ... to the first defendant, he would be 'in receipt of rents and profits' and his rights would be protected in s 70(1)(g). Again if the first defendant put his servant or caretaker into the flat, rent free, he would be protected because his agent would have actual occupation on his behalf.

Note ───
As Lord Denning pointed out, the proviso in s 70(1)(g) is little more than a statutory application of the rule in *Hunt v Luck* (1902) (see 2.1.1 above) to registered land.
──

Q Would the decision in *Hunt v Luck* itself have been the same in registered land, or would Mrs H's husband have been in receipt of rents and profits for the purposes of s 70(1)(g)?

Webb v Pollmount Ltd (1966)

P's predecessor in title granted their tenant, W, an option to purchase the freehold. W did not protect the option by means of a notice or caution. P acquired the freehold in 1962 when W was in occupation of the premises, and shortly afterwards W purported to exercise the option. P claimed that they were not bound by the option because it had not been entered on the register.

Held by Ungoed-Thomas J that the option was an overriding interest. It was an interest in the land and W was in actual occupation at the time of the transfer to P, who therefore took the land subject to the option.

Q Would the outcome have been the same had title to the land been un-registered? What are the consequences of failure to register a C (iv) land charge as against a purchaser for money or money's worth?

Williams and Glyn's Bank Ltd v Boland (1981) HL

Mr B was the sole registered proprietor of the matrimonial home. Mrs B had made substantial contributions to the purchase price and she claimed an interest, which had not been entered on the register, by way of result-ing trust. Mr B, without the consent of Mrs B, charged the property to secure his business debts. The bank made no enquiry as to whether Mrs B had any interest in the property, and when Mr B defaulted they sought possession. Mrs B claimed to have an overriding interest which was bind-ing upon the bank.

The bank claimed firstly that Mrs B's interest in the property was in effect a right to a share in the proceeds of sale (see 5.5 for the doctrine of conversion) and could not be protected as an overriding interest; and secondly that, whether Mrs B had an interest in the land or not, she was not in actual occupation. At first instance Templeman J found in favour of the bank, but the decision was reversed by the Court of Appeal. Lord Denning MR declared that 'a wife who has a share in the house has an equitable interest in the land' and 'actual occupation is a matter of fact, not a matter of law'. It was further stated *per curiam* that mortgagees should make enquiries of spouses in order to avoid the consequences of s 70(1)(g). The bank appealed.

Held that Mrs Boland had an overriding interest. Lord Wilberforce agreed that Mrs Boland had an interest in the land and 'actual occupation' are 'ordinary words of plain English and ... should be interpreted as such ... If there is actual occupation, and the occupier has rights, the purchaser takes subject to them. If not, he does not. No further element is material.'

Note ————————————————————————————

1 This decision shows how important it is for purchasers to make enquiries of, and if necessary obtain waivers from, all persons of full age in occupation of land. The Law Society estimated that the additional cost of such enquiries to consumers of domestic conveyancing services after Boland was about £7 million per annum.

2 For a similar situation in unregistered land see *Kingsnorth Finance Co Ltd v Tizard* (1986) (above at 2.2.3), which brought unregistered con-veyancing into line with registered conveyancing.

Q Would it have made any difference if there had been two trustees holding the legal estate (ie two registered proprietors)? See 3.9 below.

Note ───

Although the following case concerned unregistered land, the same principles apply to registered land (see *Paddington Building Society v Mendelsohn* (1985)).

Bristol & West Building Society v Henning (1985) CA

A cohabiting couple who called themselves Mr and Mrs H agreed to buy a house together with the aid of a mortgage in 1975. The house was conveyed into Mr H's sole name but Mrs H made contributions to the purchase price. In 1978 they agreed to buy a villa in Devon for £12,900, borrowing £11,000 from the plaintiff building society, and using the proceeds from the former 'matrimonial' home for the balance. The property, title to which was unregistered, was similarly conveyed solely to Mr H. In 1981 Mr H left Mrs H and the children in the property, and he initiated possession proceedings against her which concluded with a consent order stating that he had at all times intended that she should have a one-half beneficial interest in the property. Mr H defaulted on the mortgage repayments and the building society brought possession proceedings against both Mr and Mrs H. In the county court it was held that Mrs H had an irrevocable interest, of which the building society had constructive notice, and possession was accordingly refused.

Held, allowing the appeal, that the building society was entitled to possession. As there was no express declaration of trust any beneficial interest would have to be imputed. Mrs H must have authorised Mr H to raise the purchase money by means of a mortgage in favour of the plaintiff society. She must have known about the loan, otherwise the property could not have been purchased in the first place. Although she might have a beneficial interest, she could not claim priority for that interest as against the plaintiffs.

Note ───

Henning effectively limited the application of *Boland* to cases where the party claiming to have an overriding interest against a mortgagee either had not consented to the mortgage or had no knowledge of it.

Abbey National Building Society v Cann (1991) HL

Mr C obtained a mortgage loan of £25,000 from the plaintiff building society. He stated that he was to be the sole occupier of the house but he really intended that his elderly mother and her husband-to-be should live there. His mother had previously made a substantial contribution to a property previously owned by Mr C, the proceeds of which were to be used for the present purchase. She therefore claimed an interest by way of resulting trust. Mr C used £4,000 of the mortgage money to purchase the house, using the balance to pay his creditors. At 10.00 am on 13 August 1984, Mr C and Mrs C's husband-to-be arrived at the house, followed at

11.45 am by carpet fitters, acting on behalf of Mrs C with the consent of the vendors. Completion of both the purchase and of the charge took place at 12.30 pm and thereafter the house was occupied by Mrs C and her husband-to-be. On 13 September both the transfer and the charge were registered at the land registry. Mr C defaulted and the building society sought possession.

Mrs C claimed to have an overriding interest by virtue of an implied trust evidenced by her contributions, coupled with her actual occupation. She had no part in obtaining the mortgage and, by the time the legal estate was transferred (ie 13 September, when the transfer was registered) she was in occupation. Even if the relevant date for determining the existence of an overriding interest is the date of completion, logically there must be some *scintilla temporis*, or minute particle of time, between completion and the execution of the charge (you have to own the property before you can mortgage it!); Mrs C was in occupation at the time of completion and therefore she had an overriding interest which was capable of binding the building society. The Court of Appeal found for the building society and Mrs C appealed.

Held: (1) Applying *Henning* (above) and upholding the Court of Appeal, that Mrs C had impliedly authorised Mr C to obtain the mortgage because she was aware that the shortfall in the purchase price was to be met by means of a mortgage loan. Lord Oliver, having declared that this fact alone was sufficient to defeat Mrs C's claim, went on to examine the other issues raised by the case because 'it is desirable that they should be decided'.

(2) The relevant date for determining the existence of an overriding interest is the date of registration, but the relevant date for determining actual occupation for the purposes of s 70(1)(g) is the date of completion.

(3) There is no *scintilla temporis* between completion and charge, both acts forming a part of what is in effect a single transaction.

(4) Mrs C was not in actual occupation at the time of completion in any case. Indeed, she was not even in the country. Her clothes were in the property and both her son and her husband-to-be were on the premises, as were the carpet fitters. It may be possible to occupy property via an agent (see Lord Denning's comment in *Strand Securities v Caswell*, above) but that does not apply to this case. Even if Mrs C had been on the premises herself, Lord Oliver thought, she would not have been in actual occupation: 'A prospective tenant or purchaser who is allowed, as a matter of indulgence, to go into property in order to plan decorations or measure for furnishings would not, in ordinary parlance, be said to be occupying it, even though he might be there for hours at a time.'

Lloyds Bank plc v Rosset (1991) HL

Mr and Mrs R decided to purchase a semi-derelict farmhouse. The purchase was financed by Mr R's family trust fund and the property was registered in his sole name. It was said to be their common intention that Mrs R was to have a beneficial interest in the property. On 7 November

1982 builders were allowed into the property and Mrs R spent nearly every day on the site, supervising the builders, delivering building materials, and decorating the house. Contracts were exchanged on 23 November and the sale was completed on 17 December. Unknown to Mrs R, her husband had taken out a mortgage with the plaintiff bank. He left his wife in May 1984 and defaulted on the mortgage repayments. The bank sought possession. Mrs R claimed to have an interest by way of constructive trust which, as no enquiries had been made of her, was overriding because of her actual occupation. The Court of Appeal agreed that Mrs R had an overriding interest by virtue of s 70(1)(g) and the bank appealed.

Held, allowing the appeal, that Mrs R had no interest in the property. The issue of actual occupation was therefore irrelevant because she had no rights which could bind the bank. Lord Bridge considered that, in order to give rise to a resulting trust or a presumed constructive trust, Mrs R must have made a substantial contribution to the acquisition of the realty: 'On any view the monetary value of Mrs Rosset's work expressed as a contribution to the property acquired at a cost exceeding £70,000 must have been so trifling as to be almost *de minimis*.' Similarly;

> it is necessary for the party asserting a claim to a beneficial interest against the partner entitled to the legal estate to show that he or she has acted to his or her detriment or significantly altered his or her position in reliance on the agreement in order to give rise to a constructive trust or proprietary estoppel.

Lord Bridge examined the cases of *Eves v Eves* (1975) and *Grant v Edwards* (1986) (see 6.1.3 for both cases) where little detriment was required in order to give rise to constructive trusts after express promises or representations had been made by the legal proprietor. In this case there was indeed an express agreement, but there were two important differences. First, there was no evidence that Mr R deliberately made a false representation regarding Mrs R's beneficial interest in the property; and, as there was no fraud for a constructive trust to work upon, he should have confirmed Mrs R's interest either by a declaration of trust or by ensuring that the property was registered in both of their names. Second, Mrs R had not altered her position in reliance upon the agreement because:

> in these circumstances it would seem to be the most natural thing in the world for any wife, in the absence of her husband abroad, to spend all the time she could spare and to employ any skills she might have ... in doing all she could to accelerate progress of the work quite irrespective of any expectation she might have of enjoying a beneficial interest in the property.

Equity and Law Home Loans Ltd v Prestidge (1992) CA

P and Mrs B purchased a house together. Of the purchase money, £10,000 was provided by Mrs B, the remaining £30,000 being raised by way of a mortgage with the Britannia Building Society. The property was conveyed into the sole name of P, who was also responsible for the mortgage repayments. One year later P decided to remortgage the property for £43,000 with the plaintiffs. He repaid the original mortgage and kept the balance for his own use. The plaintiffs knew that Mrs B was in occupation but made no inquiries of her, nor did they inform her that they had granted a mortgage to P. P left the property and made no mortgage repayments. The plaintiffs sought possession and Mrs B claimed that she had an interest by way of resulting trust in the property and that the mortgage was void as against her because she had no knowledge of it. At first instance the recorder found for the plaintiffs and Mrs B appealed.

Held, dismissing the appeal, that, in spite of the fact that Mrs B undoubtedly had an interest in the property and that she had no knowledge of the second mortgage, the plaintiffs were entitled to possession. Mrs B knew about and approved of the first mortgage loan for £30,000. The second mortgage should therefore take priority over her interest, not for the full amount of £43,000, but to the extent of the £30,000 to which she had consented.

Note ──

At first sight this might appear to be a harsh decision, but Mrs B's interest would have been subject to the first mortgage in any case. Had the subsequent mortgage not been given priority to the extent of £30,000 she would in effect have received the unencumbered property as a windfall because of the repayment of the first mortgage at the plaintiffs' expense. The case is notable because it extends the *Henning* principle to remortgages.

Q It is not clear from the law reports whether this case concerned registered or unregistered land, though the authorities cited and the location of the property concerned make it most likely to be unregistered land. Does it matter?

3.7 Rectification

Land Registration Act 1925 s 82:

(1) the register may be rectified pursuant to an order of the court or by the registrar, subject to an appeal to the court, in any of the following cases, but subject to the provisions of this section –

(a) ... where a court of competent jurisdiction has decided that any person is entitled to any estate right or interest in or to any registered land or charge, and as a consequence of such decision such court is of opinion that a rectification of the register is required, and makes an order to that effect;

(b) ... where the court, on the application in the prescribed manner of any person who is aggrieved by any entry made in, or by the omission of any entry from, the register, or by default being made, or unnecessary delay taking place, in the making of any entry in the register, makes an order for the rectification of the register;

(c) In any case and at any time with the consent of all persons interested;

(d) Where the court or the registrar is satisfied that any entry in the register has been obtained by fraud;

(e) Where two or more persons are, by mistake, registered as proprietors of the same registered estate or of the same charge;

(f) Where a mortgagee has been registered as proprietor of the land instead of as proprietor of a charge and a right of redemption is subsisting;

(g) Where a legal estate has been registered in the name of a person who if the land had not been registered would not have been the estate owner; and

(h) In any other case where, by reason of any error or omission in the register, or by reason of any entry made under a mistake, it may be deemed just to rectify the register ...

(3) The register shall not be rectified, except for the purposes of giving effect to an overriding interest or an order of the court, so as to affect the title of the proprietor who is in possession –

(a) unless the proprietor has caused or substantially contributed to the error or omission by fraud or lack of proper care; or ...

(c) unless for any other reason, in any particular case, it is considered that it would be unjust not to rectify the register against him.

Chowood Ltd v Lyall (No 2) (1930) CA

C Ltd were registered as the absolute owners of land which included two strips of woodland. Their neighbour (L) had in fact acquired title to the woodland by means of adverse possession (see 6.5) prior to registration. C sued L for trespass and she counter-claimed for rectification. At first instance it was ordered that the register be rectified. The plaintiff appealed.

Held that the register should be rectified in order to give effect to L's overriding interest under the LRA 1925 s 70(1)(f), in accordance with s 82(3).

Re Leighton's Conveyance (1937)

A daughter tricked her mother into transferring property to her. The daughter then mortgaged the property, the mortgagees having no knowledge of the fraud. The mother applied for rectification.

Held that the mother was entitled to rectification of the proprietorship register as against the daughter, but not to rectification of the charges register as against the mortgagees.

Re 139 High Street Deptford (1951)

D bought a small shop, including an annexe, under a railway arch, and he was registered as the proprietor. Unknown to D or his vendor, the annexe belonged to the British Transport Commission, who claimed rectification under s 82(3).

Held that rectification should be ordered because D had 'substantially contributed' to the mistake by lodging the conveyance which mis-described the property. D was, however, allowed to claim an indemnity (see 3.8 below).

Re Sea View Gardens (1967)

In 1934 a company conveyed a plot of land to the plaintiff's predecessor in title, but no memorandum of sale was entered on the company's deeds. In 1964 the company purported to sell the land to the defendant, who was registered as the proprietor by way of first registration. The defendant built upon the land and the plaintiff applied for rectification.

Held that the defendant had 'substantially contributed' to the mistake by lodging the conveyance, and therefore the registrar could use his dis-cretion under s 82(1) to rectify the register. However, it would not be 'just' within the meaning of s 83(2)(c) to order rectification in this case because the plaintiff, knowing that the defendant was building upon the land, stood by while the building was completed before applying for rectifica-tion of the register.

Epps v Esso Petroleum Co Ltd (1973)

J leased both a house and a garage, and he parked his car on a strip of land between the two. Twenty years later the house, together with the strip of land, was conveyed to his wife, Mrs J. The following year the owners of the garage granted a new lease to Mr J, but they mistakenly included the strip of land which they had previously conveyed to Mrs J. After Mr J's lease expired, the garage, together with the strip of land, was conveyed to B, who was registered as the first proprietor. In 1964, B transferred the garage to Esso Ltd, and in 1968 Mrs J conveyed the house to Mr and Mrs Epps. The Epps claimed rectification on the grounds that, at the time of the transfer of the garage to Esso, Mrs J was in actual occupation of the strip of land and therefore she had an overriding interest under the LRA 1925 s 70(1)(g).

Held that rectification should be refused. At the time of the transfer the vendors were in possession and the fact that Mr Jones occasionally parked his car on the strip of land did not mean that he was in actual occupation. The only other relevant factor was whether it would be unjust not to recti-fy the register (s 82(3)). Both the plaintiffs and the defendants purchased their relative plots believing the strip to be included, but the defendants were in possession. In the words of Templeman J, 'whereas the defendants bought a disputed strip, the plaintiffs bought a law suit'. It was up to the plaintiffs to make further enquiries before purchasing the property.

Freer v Unwins Ltd (1976)

F owned a sweet and tobacconist's shop, which was one of many shops in a block. He had the benefit of covenants which restricted the owners of the other shops from selling sweets or tobacco. The burden of the covenants was registered in the Land Charges Register against the names of the relevant estate owners. When title to one of the shops came to be registered, the burden of the covenant was not entered in the charges register, and U Ltd, who were vintners, leased the shop and began to sell sweets and tobacco. F sought an injunction and rectification.

Held that the register should be rectified to show the covenant. However, the rectification could not be retrospective and the covenant would still not bind U Ltd, who would not have leased the property had they been aware of the covenant at the time of the assignment. F was not even entitled to an indemnity because the cause of his loss was not the rectification of the register (see 3.8 below) but the registry's failure to note the covenant.

Argyle Building Society v Hammond (1985) CA

Mr Steed (S), the registered proprietor of freehold land, emigrated to the USA, leaving his mother, his sister (Mrs H) and his brother-in-law (H) in the property. Mr and Mrs H persuaded S to sign a power of attorney, which enabled his mother to sell the property on his behalf. They then transferred the house to themselves by way of forged deed, and were registered as the legal proprietors. Mr and Mrs H then took out a mortgage loan with the Argyle Building Society but failed to make repayments. The building society sought possession and S was permitted to become a party to the action in order to seek rectification. At first instance the judge ordered possession and ruled that he had no power to order rectification. S appealed.

Held that the court did have discretion to rectify under s 82(1)(d). A new trial was ordered (see *Norwich and Peterborough Building Society v Steed* (1993) below).

Norwich and Peterborough Building Society v Steed (1993) CA

For the facts of this case see *Argyle Building Society v Hammond* above. The Norwich and Peterborough Building Society (formerly the Argyle BS) brought an action for possession in the High Court, and S counterclaimed for rectification on the grounds that the transfer was a forgery. Expert evidence suggested that the signature on the transfer was that of S's mother and the claim of forgery was dropped in favour of a plea of *non est factum*. The plea was unsuccessful and the transfer deemed to be within the power of attorney. The transfer was therefore voidable rather than void. Knox J ordered rectification of the proprietorship register but, as the building society were innocent third parties, refused to order removal of the charge. S appealed.

Held, dismissing the appeal, that S could not plead *non est factum*. If his mother was unaware of the fact that she had been appointed attorney, or was incapable of performing her duties, that was the fault of S for appointing her without exercising due care. The transfer, being voidable rather than void, was valid at the date of the execution of the charge. In the absence of fraud or a successful plea of *non est factum* the court does not have authority to order rectification unless the grounds are among those listed in s 82(1).

3.8   Indemnity

Land Registration Act 1925 s 83:
(1) ... any person suffering loss by reason of any rectification of the register under this Act shall be entitled to be indemnified.
(2) Where an error or omission has occurred in the register, but the register is not rectified, any person suffering loss by reason of such error or omission, shall ... be entitled to be indemnified.
(3) Where any person suffers loss by reason of the loss or destruction of any document lodged at the registry for inspection or safe custody or by reason of an error in any official search, he shall be entitled to be indemnified under this Act.
(4) ... a proprietor of any registered land or charge claiming in good faith under a forged disposition shall, where the register is rectified, be deemed to have suffered loss by reason of such rectification and shall be entitled to be indemnified under this Act.
(5) No indemnity shall be payable under this Act in any of the following cases –
  (a) Where the applicant or a person from whom he derives title ... has caused or substantially contributed to the loss by fraud or lack of proper care ...

Re Chowood's Registered Land (1933)
See *Chowood v Lyall (No 2)* (above at 3.7) for the facts. C Ltd now sought to be indemnified for their loss.

Held that C Ltd took the land subject to L's overriding interest under the LRA 1925 s 70(1)(f). The rectification of the register did not place C Ltd in any worse position than they were in before, and therefore C's loss cannot have been caused by the rectification. As no loss was incurred there should be no indemnity.

Note ——————————————————————————————
The Law Commission (Third Report on Land Registration No 158) have recommended that the indemnity provisions be extended to include compensation for proprietors against whose title an overriding interest

is asserted. The indemnity should be at the discretion of the registrar and may be conditional on the overriding interest being entered on the register. It is estimated that such a reform would be inexpensive as most overriding interests should be readily discoverable by a prudent purchaser and, as such, would not entitle the proprietor to an indemnity.

Q Do you think that, if the Law Commission's proposals were implemented, an applicant in Chowood Ltd's position would be awarded an indemnity?

3.9 Overreaching and registered land

Law of Property Act 1925 s 2
(See 2.2.1.)

City of London Building Society v Flegg (1988) HL

In 1977 Mr and Mrs F purchased Bleak House with their daughter and son-in-law, Mr and Mrs Maxwell-Brown. The Fs provided £18,000 of the purchase money but the property was transferred into the names of the M-Bs only. In 1982 the M-Bs mortgaged the property, without the knowledge of the Fs, to the plaintiff building society. The plaintiffs sought possession after Mr and Mrs M-B defaulted on the mortgage repayments. The Fs claimed that they had an interest in the property by way of resulting trust because of their contributions to the purchase price. They were in actual occupation of the property at the time that the mortgage was obtained, and the mortgagees had made no enquiries of them. They therefore had an overriding interest under the LRA 1925 s 70(1)(g) and that interest bound the mortgagee. The Court of Appeal found for the Fs and the building society appealed.

Held, allowing the appeal, that Mr and Mrs F did have an interest which was capable of being an overriding interest. However, because there were two trustees for sale, any beneficial interest which the Fs might have in the property under the trust would be overreached on sale in accordance with the Law of Property Act 1925 s 27 (see 5.6.2). Lord Templeman contrasted the case with *Williams & Glyn's Bank Ltd v Boland* (above at 3.6.3) upon which the Court of Appeal had relied. In Boland there was a sole trustee, the property being transferred into Mr B's name only. 'If the wife's interest had been overreached by the mortgagee advancing capital moneys to two trustees there would have been nothing to justify the wife remaining in occupation as against the mortgagee.' As there were two trustees in this case, the Fleggs could not resist the mortgagee's claim for possession.

Note ————————————————————————————
The mechanism of overreaching provides another method by which mortgagees can protect themselves from the consequences of a 'Boland-

type' situation. If they are faced with a sole trustee they can insist upon the appointment of a second trustee before the loan is advanced. The interests of any beneficiaries under an implied trust for sale (ie potential Mrs Bolands) will then be overreached.

3.10 The doctrine of notice and registered land

Peffer v Rigg (1977)

P and R were married to two sisters. They purchased a house in order to provide a home for their mother-in-law. It was registered in R's name only, but it was agreed that they should have an equal share in the property, and that they were to share all outgoings. A formal trust deed evidenced these arrangements. P neither entered his interest on the register nor, as he was not in actual occupation, could he claim to have an overriding interest under the LRA 1925 s 70(1)(g). Mrs R moved into the house with her mother after matrimonial difficulties. Eventually R and Mrs R divorced and, as part of the divorce settlement, R conveyed the house to his ex-wife for £1. Mrs R claimed that, as P's interest had not been entered on the register, she took free from his interest under the LRA 1925 s 20(1) as a purchaser for valuable consideration. P claimed that, as Mrs R was aware of his interest and of the fraudulent nature of the transaction, she held the property on constructive trust for herself and P.

Held that Mrs R was a constructive trustee and that the register should be rectified accordingly. Graham J examined both Mrs R's argument and the LRA 1925 in great detail. He accepted that s 20(1) permits a purchaser for valuable consideration to take free of an interest which has not been entered on the register whether they have notice of it or not. However, s 3(xxxi) defines valuable consideration as including marriage but excluding nominal consideration. He found £1 to be nominal consideration and dismissed the argument that the consideration was in reality much more than £1 because it was part of a divorce settlement.

Similarly s 59(6) asserts that a purchaser need not be concerned with any matter which has not been entered on the register. Section 3(xxi), however, defines 'purchaser' as being in good faith for valuable consideration. Mrs R was certainly not a purchaser in good faith because she was quite well aware of the fraud; and she had provided only nominal consideration. She could rely upon neither s 20(1) nor s 59(6). If she could not rely upon these provisions, it is a general principle of trust law that when somebody knowingly acquires property in breach of trust he holds as constructive trustee for the original beneficiaries.

Q Was £1 nominal consideration?

Q If £1 was nominal consideration, is it possible to fault Graham J's statutory interpretation?

Q There has been much criticism of this decision because it has been seen as reintroducing the doctrine of notice into registered land (eg Kevin Gray, *Elements of Land Law* (Butterworths, 1993, 2nd edn) pp 190-3) It could be argued that P had a means of protecting his interest – ie by entering a notice, caution or restriction on the register. Do you agree with this view?

Q What did Mrs R have notice of? Was it P's interest? Or, was it the fraudulent nature of the transaction? If it was the former, the old doctrine of notice has been applied, but if it was the latter it could be argued that Graham J was merely adhering to established principles of equity by refusing to allow the LRA 1925 to be used as an instrument of fraud. See Martin Dixon, *Lecture Notes on Land Law* (Cavendish, 1994) p 39.

Williams & Glyn's Bank Ltd v Boland (1981) HL
See 3.6 for the facts. Lord Wilberforce was in no doubt about the aims of the registered land system and the role of the doctrine of notice: 'Above all, the system is designed to free the purchaser from the hazards of notice – real or constructive – which, in the case of unregistered land, involved him in enquiries, often quite elaborate, failing which he might be bound by equities ... The only kind of notice recognised is by entry on the register ... In my opinion therefore, the law as to notice ... has no application even by analogy to registered land.'

Lyus v Prowsa Developments Ltd (1982)
L exchanged contracts to purchase a house from a firm of property developers. The developers became insolvent and their bankers, as mortgagee, sold the land to PD Ltd. The bank were under no obligation to honour the contract with L but nevertheless they sold the land subject to the contract, and a term to this effect was inserted into the contract between the bank and PD Ltd. No mention was made of the contract with L on the transfer and therefore no interest was entered in the register. PD Ltd then sold the land to the second defendants subject to L's contract 'so far, if at all, as it may be enforceable against Prowsa Developments Ltd'. L sought an order for specific performance. Both PD Ltd and the second defendants claimed that the contract was void because it had not been registered.

Held that PD Ltd took the land subject to L's contract. Similarly, the second defendants, having agreed to take the land subject to L's contract, could not now claim to be free from it. The property was held by the second defendants on constructive trust for L and specific performance should be ordered accordingly. Dillon J explained that 'the fraud on the part of the defendants in the present case lies not just in relying on the legal rights conferred by an Act of Parliament, but in the first defendant reneging on a positive stipulation in favour of the plaintiffs in the bargain under which the first defendant acquired the land. That, as it seems to me, makes all the difference' (see also *Binions v Evans* (1972) at 6.1.3).

As in *Peffer v Rigg* (above) a constructive trust has been used in order to prevent a statute being used as an instrument of fraud. As Dillon J has noted, the trust is imposed not simply because the defendants had notice of L's rights (in which case it would be an application of the old doctrine of notice), but because they had promised to be bound by those rights. The defendants were bound because they had notice of the fraudulent nature of the transaction, rather than because they had notice of L's contract (see also *Barclays Bank Ltd v O'Brien* (1994) at 10.2.5).

Q Alternatively, it could be argued that L should have entered his estate contract as a notice or a caution against the property developers' title in the register. Which view do you think is correct?

Howell v Montey (1990) CA

In 1986 H obtained a judgment against M for £2,173, and a charging order nisi on M's house was granted on 3 August 1987. Later that month M contracted to sell his house to M2, who searched the register and obtained priority until 29 September 1987. The sale of the house was completed on 4 September, and H applied to have a charging order registered on 16 September 1987. M2 did not apply to register his title to the property until 9 October, by which time his period of priority had expired. The order nisi was made absolute on 16 December. M2 argued that he should take the house free from the charging order because he had no knowledge of it. H argued that M2 was bound by the charging order because his title was registered too late for him to assert priority according to the Land Registration (Official Searches) Rules 1988 r 5. Upon application by M2, the registrar removed the charging order because the sale of the house was completed before the charging order was entered on the register. The judge at first instance affirmed the registrar's decision. H appealed.

Held, dismissing the appeal, that M2 should take free from the charging order because they were innocent purchasers who had no knowledge of the order.

Note ———

This decision goes considerably further than *Peffer v Rigg* or *Lyus v Prowsa* (above) because there is no fraud involved. M2 had simply failed to deliver his transfer to the registry within the priority period. This decision appears to be a straightforward application of the old doctrine of notice. See Paul Coughlan (1990) Conv 392.

Q Charging orders are made by the court against an individual or individuals. Is it right that they should bind third parties? See 5.5.1 below.

4 Strict settlements

4.1 What is settled land?

Settled Land Act 1925 s 1:

(1) Any deed, will, agreement for a settlement or other agreement, Act of Parliament, or other instrument, or any number of instruments ... under or by virtue of which instrument or instruments any land ... stands for the time being –

(i) limited in trust for any persons by way of succession; or

(ii) limited in trust for any person in possession –

(a) for an entailed interest whether or not capable of being barred or defeated;

(b) for an estate in fee simple or for a term of years absolute subject to an executory limitation, gift, or disposition over on failure of his issue or in any other event;

(c) for a base or determinable fee or any corresponding interest in leasehold land;

(d) being an infant, for an estate in fee simple or for a term of years absolute; or

(iii) limited in trust for any person for an estate in fee simple or for a term of years absolute contingently on the happening of any event; or ...

(v) charged, whether voluntarily or in consideration of marriage or by way of family arrangement, and whether immediately or after an interval, with the payment of any rentcharge for the life of any person, or any less period, or of any capital, annual or periodical sums for the portions, advancement, maintenance, or otherwise for the benefit of any persons, with or without any term of years for securing or raising the same;

creates or is for the purposes of this Act a settlement and is in this Act referred to as a settlement, or as the settlement, as the case requires –

(7) This section does not apply to land held upon trust for sale.

Settled Land Act 1925 s 27(1):

A conveyance of a legal estate in land to an infant alone, or to two or more persons jointly, both or all of whom are infants, for his or their own benefit shall operate only as an agreement for valuable consideration to execute a settlement by means of a principal vesting deed and a trust instrument in favour of the infant or infants, and in the meantime to hold the land in trust for the infant or infants.

Law of Property Act 1925 s 19(1):
A conveyance of a legal estate in land to an infant alone or to two or more persons jointly both or all of whom are infants, shall have such operation as is provided for in the Settled Land Act 1925.

4.2   Formalities

Settled Land Act 1925 s 4(1):
Every settlement of a legal estate in land *inter vivos* shall, save as in this Act otherwise provided, be effected by two deeds, namely a vesting deed and a trust instrument and if effected in any other way shall not operate to transfer the legal estate.

4.2.1   The trust instrument (the private document)

Settled Land Act 1925 s 4(3):
The trust instrument shall –
   (a) declare the trusts affecting the settled land;
   (b) appoint or constitute trustees of the settlement;
   (c) contain the power, if any, to appoint new trustees of the settlement;
   (d) set out, either expressly or by reference, any powers intended to be conferred by the settlement in extension of those conferred by this Act;
   (e) bear any *ad valorem* stamp duty which may be payable ... in respect of the settlement.

Settled Land Act 1925 s 6:
Where a settlement is created by the will of an estate owner who dies after the commencement of this Act –
   (a) the will is for the purposes of this Act a trust instrument; and
   (b) the personal representatives of the testator shall hold the settled land on trust, if and when required to do so, to convey it to the person who, under the will, or by virtue of this Act, is the tenant for life or statutory owner, and, if more than one, as joint tenants.

4.2.2   The vesting deed (the public document)

Settled Land Act 1925 s 4(2):
By the vesting deed the land shall be conveyed to the tenant for life or statutory owner (and if more than one as joint tenants) for the legal estate the subject of the intended settlement ... Provided that, where such legal

estate is already vested in the tenant for life or statutory owner, it shall be sufficient, without any other conveyance, if the vesting deed declares that the land is vested in him for that estate.

Settled Land Act 1925 s 5:
(1) Every vesting deed for giving effect to a settlement or for conveying settled land to a tenant for life or statutory owner during the subsistence of the settlement ... shall contain the following statements and particulars, namely –

(a) A description, either specific or general, of the settled land;

(b) A statement that the settled land is vested in the person or persons to whom it is conveyed or in whom it is declared to be vested upon the trusts from time to time affecting the settled land;

(c) The names of the persons who are the trustees of the settlement;

(d) Any additional powers conferred by the trust instrument relating to the settled land which by virtue of this Act operate and are exercisable as if conferred by this Act on a tenant for life;

(e) The name of any person for the time being entitled under the trust instrument to appoint new trustees of the settlement.

4.3   The settlor

Settled Land Act 1925 s 108(2):
In the case of conflict between the provisions of a settlement and the provisions of this Act, relative to any matter in respect whereof the tenant for life or statutory owner exercises or contracts or intends to exercise any power under this Act, the provisions of this Act shall prevail; and, notwithstanding anything in the settlement, any power ... relating to the settled land thereby conferred on the trustees of the settlement or other persons exercisable for any purpose ... shall, after the commencement of this Act, be exercisable by the tenant for life or statutory owner as if it were an additional power conferred on the tenant for life within the next following section of this Act and not otherwise.

Settled Land Act 1925 s 109(1):
Nothing in this Act precludes a settlor from conferring on the tenant for life, or ... on the trustees of the settlement, any powers additional to or larger than those conferred by this Act.

Note ——————————————————————
The settlor may not restrict the powers of the tenant for life, however. See s 106 at 4.4.1.

4.4 The tenant for life

Settled Land Act 1925 s 19(1) and (2):

(1) The person of full age who is for the time being beneficially entitled under a settlement to possession of settled land for his life is for the purposes of this Act the tenant for life of that land and the tenant for life under that settlement.

(2) If in any case there are two or more persons of full age so entitled as joint tenants, they together constitute the tenant for life for the purposes of this Act.

Settled Land Act 1925 s 20:

(1) Each of the following persons being of full age shall, when his estate or interest is in possession, have the powers of a tenant for life under this Act, (namely) –

(i) A tenant in tail, including a tenant in tail after possibility of issue extinct, and a tenant in tail who is by Act of Parliament restrained from barring or defeating his estate tail, and although the reversion is in the Crown, but not including such a tenant in tail where the land in respect whereof he is so restrained was purchased with money provided by Parliament in consideration of public services;

(ii) A person entitled to land for an estate in fee simple or for a term of years absolute with or subject to ... an executory limitation, gift or disposition over on failure of his issue or in any other event;

(iii) A person entitled to a base or determinable fee ...;

(iv) A tenant for years determinable on life, not holding merely under a lease at a rent;

(v) A tenant for the life of another ...;

(vi) A tenant for his own life, or for years determinable on life, whose estate is liable to cease in any event during that life ...

Re Carne's Settled Estates (1898)

A mansion house was vested in trustees to allow P to occupy it rent free for as long as she wished, with remainders over in favour of other beneficiaries. P asked the court *inter alia* to declare whether or not she was a tenant for life under the Settled Land Act 1882.

Held that she was a tenant for life and was entitled to exercise all of the statutory powers, including the power of sale.

4.4.1 The role of the tenant for life

Settled Land Act 1925 s 106:

(1) If in a settlement, will, assurance, or other instrument executed or made before or after ... the commencement of this Act a provision is inserted –

(a) purporting or attempting, by way of direction, declaration, or otherwise, to forbid a tenant for life or statutory owner to exercise any power under this Act, or his right to require the settled land to be vested in him; or

(b) attempting, or tending, or intended, by limitation, gift, or disposition over of settled land, or by a limitation, gift or disposition of other real or any personal property, or by the imposition of any condition, or by forfeiture, or in any manner whatever, to prohibit or prevent him from exercising , or to induce him to abstain from exercising, or to put him into a position inconsistent with his exercising, any power under this Act, or his right to have the settled land vested in him;

that provision, as far as it purports, or attempts, or tends or is intended to have, or would or might have, the operation aforesaid, shall be deemed to be void.

Note ——————————————————————
The settlor may increase the powers of the tenant for life. See s 109(1) at 4.3.

Settled Land Act 1925 s 107(1):

A tenant for life or statutory owner shall, in exercising any power under this Act, have regard to the interests of all parties entitled under the settlement, and shall, in relation to the exercise thereof by him, be deemed to be in the position and to have the duties and liabilities of a trustee for those parties.

Re Acklom (1929)

A testator bequeathed his leasehold house and its contents to his sister for life. The trustees were directed to sell the house and divide the proceeds between a number of charities 'if and when she (the sister) shall not wish to reside or continue to reside there'. The testator died in 1918 and his sister lived in the house until 1925, when she went abroad. Her return was delayed due to illness and she eventually sold the property, as tenant for life, in 1927. The trustees took out a summons asking whether the sister, by ceasing to reside in the house, had forfeited her interest according to the terms of the settlement, and whether she had any interest in the proceeds of sale.

Held that the sister had not forfeited her interest and that she was entitled to the income from the proceeds. Maugham J accepted that this result conflicted with the terms of the settlement but 'there is no doubt at all that under section 106 of the Settled Land Act 1925 (above), which applies to provisions of wills made before or after the Act, a provision which limits or prevents the tenant for life from exercising his power of sale is void'.

4.4.2 Powers of the tenant for life

Some powers do not require consent or notice to be given

Settled Land Act 1925 s 42(5):
A lease at the best rent that can reasonably be obtained without fine ... may be made –
(i) Where the term does not exceed twenty-one years –
(a) Without any notice of an intention to make the lease having been given under this Act; and
(b) notwithstanding that there are no trustees of the settlement; and
(ii) Where the term does not extend beyond three years from the date of the writing, by any writing under hand only containing an agreement instead of a covenant by the lessee for payment of rent.

Note ———————————————————————————————————
The tenant for life may also accept surrender of leases and make improvements without giving notice or obtaining consent. See SLA 1925 ss 83-84.

Most powers require notice to be given to the trustees

Settled Land Act 1925 s 101(1):
Save as otherwise expressly provided by this Act, a tenant for life or statutory owner, when intending to make a sale, exchange, lease, mortgage, or charge or to grant an option –
(a) shall give notice of his intention in that behalf to each of the trustees of the settlement, by posting registered letters, containing the notice, addressed to the trustees severally, each at his usual or last known place of abode in the United Kingdom; and
(b) shall give a like notice to the solicitor for the trustees ...
every letter under this section being posted not less than one month before the making or granting by the tenant for life or statutory owner of the sale, exchange, lease, mortgage, charge, or option, or a contract of the same ... Provided that a notice under this section shall not be valid unless at the date thereof the trustee is a trust corporation, or the number of trustees is not less than two.

Note ———————————————————————————————————
For the provisions relating to the individual powers see: sale and exchange: ss 38–40; lease: ss 41–42; options: s 51; mortgage: s 71.

Some powers require the consent of the trustees

Settled Land Act 1925 s 58(1):
A tenant for life may, with the consent in writing of the trustees, of the settlement ... compromise, compound, abandon, submit to arbitration or

otherwise settle any claim, dispute, or question whatsoever relating to the settled land, or any part thereof ....

Some powers require the consent of the trustees or the court

Settled Land Act 1925 s 65:

(1) The powers of disposing of settled land conferred by this Act on a tenant for life may be exercised as respects the principal mansion house, if any, on any settled land, and the pleasure grounds and park and lands, if any, usually occupied therewith:

Provided that those powers shall not be exercised without the consent of the trustees of the settlement or an order of the court –

(a) if the settlement is a settlement made or coming into operation before the commencement of this Act and the settlement does expressly provide to the contrary; or

(b) if the settlement is a settlement made or coming into operation after the commencement of this Act and the settlement expressly provides that these powers or any of them shall not be exercised without such consent or order.

(2) Where a house is usually occupied as a farmhouse, or where the site of any house and the pleasure grounds and park and lands, if any, usually occupied therewith do not together exceed twenty-five acres in extent, the house is not to be deemed a principal mansion house within the meaning of this section, and may accordingly be disposed of in like manner as any other part of the settled land.

Note ───────────────────────────────
See also the power to cut and sell timber (s 66).

Some powers require the consent of the court

Settled Land Act 1925 s 64(1):

Any transaction affecting or concerning the settled land, or any part thereof, or any other land ... which in the opinion of the court would be for the benefit of the settled land, or any part thereof, or the persons interested under the settlement, may, under an order of the court, be effected by a tenant for life, if it is one which could have been validly effected by an absolute owner.

Note ───────────────────────────────
See also the power to sell heirlooms (s 67).

Hambro v Duke of Marlborough (1994)

In 1705 Queen Anne gave the Blenheim Estates to the Duke of Marlborough in gratitude for his victory at Blenheim. The following year the lands were settled by Act of Parliament upon successive Dukes in tail male. The Act contained an entrenching provision which forbade any of the Duke's heirs from barring the entail. The irresponsible behaviour of the current Duke's eldest son, the Marquis of Blandford, was a cause of great concern to the Duke and attracted a great deal of publicity. The Duke, in collusion with the trustees, sought to bring the settlement to an end by conveying the property to the trustees on protective trusts, thereby preventing the Marquis from becoming the next tenant in tail with all of the powers conferred by the 1925 Act. The trustees applied to the court on a preliminary issue, asking whether the court had jurisdiction under the SLA 1925 s 64 to authorise the conveyance to the trustees without the consent of the Marquis. The Marquis argued that: (i) s 64 did not apply to conveyances which resulted in the land ceasing to be settled land, because the transaction has to be for the benefit of the settled land or the beneficiaries; (ii) the section did not enable the beneficial interest of a person who was *sui juris* to be varied without his consent; and (iii) the proposed conveyance was contrary to the entrenching provision in the settlement.

Held that the court did have jurisdiction to authorise the conveyance. In answer to the claims made by the Marquis, it was held: (i) that the court had jurisdiction under s 64 notwithstanding the fact that the land would cease to be settled land provided that the transaction was for the benefit of the settled land or of the beneficiaries; (ii) that there was nothing in s 64 to suggest that it did not apply to beneficiaries who were *sui juris*, or that their consent was necessary; and (iii) that the proposed conveyance was contrary to the entrenching provision but that provision could not overrule the Settled Land Acts. The entail remained unbarrable even after the Fines and Recoveries Act 1833 because such Parliamentary settlements were exempted from that Act. However, they were not exempted from the Settled Land Act 1882 and they are expressly covered by s 20(1)(i) of the 1925 Act (see 4.4 above). The later statute thereby overrode the entrenching section of the earlier Act and conferred upon the tenant in tail all of the powers of the tenant for life under the 1925 Act.

4.5　The trustees

Settled Land Act 1925 s 30:
(1) Subject to the provisions of this Act, the following persons are trustees of a settlement for the purposes of this Act ... namely –
　(i) the persons, if any, who are for the time being under the settlement, with power of sale of the settled land ... or with power of consent to or approval of the exercise of such power of sale, or if there are no such persons; then
　(ii) the persons, if any, for the time being, who are by the settlement declared to be trustees thereof for the purposes of the Settled Land Acts 1882 to 1890, or any of them, or this Act, or if there are no such persons; then ...

(3) Where a settlement is created by will, or a settlement has arisen by the effect of an intestacy, and apart from this subsection there would be no trustees for the purposes of this Act of such settlement, then the personal representatives of the deceased shall, until other trustees are appointed, be by virtue of this Act the trustees of the settlement, but where there is a sole personal representative, not being a trust corporation, it shall be obligatory on him to appoint an additional trustee to act with him for the purposes of this Act ...

Settled Land Act 1925 s 34(1):
If at any time there are no trustees of a settlement, or where in any other case it is expedient, for the purposes of this Act, that new trustees of a settlement be appointed, the court may, if it thinks fit, on the application of the tenant for life, statutory owner, or of any other person having, under the settlement, an estate or interest in the settled land, in possession, remainder or otherwise, or, in the case of an infant, of his testamentary or other guardian or next friend, appoint fit persons to be trustees of the settlement.

4.5.1 Trustees shall execute the vesting deed

Settled Land Act 1925 s 9(2):
As soon as practicable after a settlement, or an instrument which for the purposes of this Act is deemed to be a trust instrument, takes effect as such, the trustees of the settlement may, and on the request of the tenant for life or statutory owner shall, execute a principal vesting deed, containing the proper statements and particulars, declaring that the legal estate in the settled land shall vest or is vested in the person therein named, being the tenant for life or statutory owner, and including themselves if they are the statutory owners, and such deed shall, unless the legal estate is already so vested, operate to convey or vest the legal estate in the settled land to or in the person or persons aforesaid and, if more than one, as joint tenants.

4.5.2 Trustees may have the powers of the tenant for life

Settled Land Act 1925 s 23(1):
Where under a settlement there is no tenant for life, nor, independently of this section, a person having by virtue of this Act the powers of a tenant for life then –
(a) any person of full age on whom such powers are by the settlement expressed to be conferred; and
(b) in any other case the trustees of the settlement;
shall have the powers of the tenant for life under this Act.

4.5.3   Trustees to issue a receipt for capital money

Settled Land Act 1925 ss 94(1) and 95:

94. (1) Notwithstanding anything in this Act, capital money arising under this Act shall not be paid to fewer than two persons as trustees of the settlement, unless the trustee is a trust corporation.

95. The receipt or direction in writing of or by the trustees of the settlement, or where the sole trustee is a trust corporation, of or by that trustee, or by the personal representatives of the last surviving or continuing trustee, for or relating to any money or securities, paid or transferred to or by the direction of the trustees, trustee or representatives, as the case may be, effectually discharges the payer or the transferor therefrom, and from being bound to see to the application or being answerable for any loss or misapplication thereof, and, in case of a mortgagee or other person advancing money, from being concerned to see that any money advanced by him is wanted for any purpose of this Act, or that no more than is wanted is raised.

4.5.4   Trustees to execute a deed of discharge

Settled Land Act 1925 s 17(1) and (3):

(1) Where the estate owner of any settled land holds the land free from all equitable interests and powers under a trust instrument ... the trustees of the settlement ... shall ... be bound to execute, at the cost of the trust estate, a deed declaring that they are discharged from the trust so far as regards that land ...

(3) Where a deed ... of discharge contains no statement to the contrary, a purchaser of a legal estate in the land to which the deed ... relates shall be entitled to assume that the land has ceased to be settled land, and is not subject to any trust for sale.

4.6   Dispositions of the settled land

4.6.1   Protection for the purchaser and beneficiaries

Beneficial interests to be overreached.

Law of Property Act 1925 s 2(1)(i):

(See 2.2.1.)

Settled Land Act 1925 s 18(1):

(b) if any capital money is payable in respect of a transaction, a conveyance to a purchaser of land shall only take effect under this Act if the capital money is paid to or by the direction of the trustees of the settlement or into court; and

(c) notwithstanding anything to the contrary in the vesting instrument, or the trust instrument, capital money shall not, except where the trustee is a trust corporation, be paid to or by the direction of fewer persons than two as trustees of the settlement.

The curtain principle – details of the trust do not concern the purchaser

Settled Land Act 1925 s 110(2):
A purchaser of a legal estate in settled land shall not, except as hereby expressly provided, be bound or entitled to call for the production of the trust instrument or any information concerning that instrument ... and whether or not he has notice of its contents he shall ... be bound and entitled if the last or only principal vesting instrument contains the statements and particulars required by this Act to assume that –

(a) the person in whom the land is by the said instrument vested or declared to be vested is the tenant for life or statutory owner and has all the powers of the tenant for life under this Act, including such additional or larger powers, if any, as are therein mentioned;

(b) the persons by the said instrument stated to be the trustees of the settlement, or their successors appearing to be duly appointed, are the properly constituted trustees of the settlement;

(c) the statements and particulars required by this Act and contained ... in the said instrument were correct at the date thereof ....

The paralysing section – dispositions not to take effect until a vesting instrument is made

Settled Land Act 1925 s 13:
Where a tenant for life or statutory owner has become entitled to have a principal vesting deed or a vesting assent executed in his favour, then until a vesting instrument is executed or made pursuant to this Act in respect of the settled land, any purported disposition thereof *inter vivos* by any person, other than a personal representative ... shall not take effect except in favour of a purchaser of a legal estate without notice of such tenant for life or statutory owner having become so entitled as aforesaid, but, save as aforesaid, shall operate only as a contract for valuable consideration to carry out the transaction after the requisite vesting instrument has been executed or made, and a purchaser of a legal estate shall not be concerned with such disposition unless the contract is registered as a land charge.

4.6.2 Protection for purchasers in good faith

Settled Land Act 1925 s 110(1):
On a sale, exchange, lease mortgage, charge, or other disposition, a purchaser dealing in good faith with a tenant for life or statutory owner shall, as against all parties entitled under the settlement, be conclusively taken to have given the best price, consideration, or rent, as the case may require,

that could reasonably be obtained by the tenant for life or statutory owner, and to have complied with the requisitions of this Act.

Settled Land Act 1925 s 112(2):
Where any provision in this Act refers to sale, purchase, exchange, mortgaging, charging, leasing, or other disposition or dealing, or to any power, consent, payment, receipt, deed, assurance, contract, expenses, act, or transaction, it shall (unless the contrary appears) be construed as extending only to sales, purchases, exchanges, mortgages, charges, leases, dispositions, dealings, powers, consents, payments, receipts, deeds, assurances, contracts, expenses, acts, and transactions under this Act.

Q Does this section mean that s 110(1) is only applicable to transactions which are 'under the Act' and that the section does not apply to dispositions by the tenant for life which are beyond his powers under the Act? See J Hill (1991) 107 LQR 603–604.

4.6.3 Protection for the beneficiaries – unauthorised dispositions shall be void

Settled Land Act 1925 s 18(1):
Where land is the subject of a vesting instrument and the trustees of the settlement have not been discharged under this Act, then –
  (a) any disposition by the tenant for life or statutory owner of the land, other than a disposition authorised by this Act or any other statute, or made in pursuance of any additional or larger powers mentioned in the vesting instrument, shall be void, except for the purpose of conveying or creating such equitable interests as he has power, in right of his equitable interests and powers under the trust instrument, to convey or create.

Mogridge v Clapp (1892) CA
H believed himself to be the absolute owner of land, but he was in fact only a tenant for life. He granted a building lease for 99 years to M, who made no investigation of H's title but believed him to be the absolute owner. C contracted to purchase the property from M but refused to complete the purchase after discovering that H was only a tenant for life. M sought specific performance of the contract, claiming firstly that H himself was not even aware that he was a tenant for life, and secondly that notice could not be given in accordance with the terms of the Settled Land Act 1882 to the trustees because none had been appointed. C argued that the lease was invalid because it did not comply with the Act, and, whether the lease was void or not, M's title was so questionable that it should not be forced upon a purchaser.

Held that the lease was valid and that the plaintiff was entitled to specific performance. The plaintiff, having dealt in good faith with tenant for life was protected by s 45(3) of the 1882 Act (now s 110(1) of the 1925 Act above).

Weston v Henshaw (1950)

In 1921 a father sold land absolutely to his son, who sold it back to his father in 1927. The father, by his will, then settled the land upon his wife for life, then to his son for his life, and then to his grandson upon attaining the age of 25. The father died in 1931, followed by his wife in 1940, whereupon the land was vested in the son by way of vesting assent. The son then mortgaged the property, showing the mortgagee only the deeds prior to the 1927 conveyance, and appearing therefore to be the absolute owner in fee simple. After the son died, the grandson brought an action for a declaration that the mortgage was void as against him.

Held that the mortgage was void as against the grandson. Danckwerts J thought that, although the mortgagee was a *bona fide* purchaser and had no way of discovering that the son was only a tenant for life, s 18 applies whether the purchaser is in good faith or not.

Q Does this decision conflict with *Mogridge v Clapp*? The latter case was not considered in *Weston v Henshaw*.

Re Morgan's Lease (1972)

M, a tenant for life, granted to the plaintiffs a 10-year lease in 1950. In 1960, upon expiry of the term, he purported to grant another lease for seven years, together with an option to renew the lease for a further seven years. The plaintiffs at all times believed M to be the absolute owner. M died in 1962, and the defendants had a vesting assent executed in their favour. In 1967 the plaintiffs gave notice that they wished to exercise the option to renew the lease, but the defendant landlords refused to comply with their request on the grounds that the purported lease and option were void because they were not made in accordance with the Settled Land Act 1925. The plaintiffs claimed to have a valid option and sought specific performance.

Held that the plaintiffs, having dealt with the tenant for life in good faith, could rely upon s 110(1) and specific performance was granted. After considering *Mogridge v Clapp*, Ungoed Thomas J stated that 'my conclusion is that s 110 applies whether or not the purchaser knows that the other party to the transaction is a tenant for life'.

Q Which of the two cases above (*Weston* or *Morgan*) is to be preferred?

Q Is a similar situation to *Weston v Henshaw* likely to occur in registered land?

Q Might it be possible to reconcile the two cases on the grounds that in *Weston* the tenant for life acted fraudulently and totally *ultra vires*, whereas in *Re Morgan's Lease* the tenant for life merely granted a seven-year lease (which he would have had the power to do) and granted an option (which he would have had the power to do after giving notice to the trustees)? See Kevin Gray, *Elements of Land Law* (Butterworths, 1993, 2nd edn) pp 633-4; also s 112(2), above.

Bevan v Johnston (1990) CA

A house was left by will to R for life with remainders to certain named beneficiaries. In 1975 R orally granted a weekly tenancy of part of the house to J, but a vesting assent was not granted in R's favour until 1978. J remained in occupation until 1986, when R died. When J offered rent to B, R's executor, he refused to accept it. Rent was, however, accepted from J by the trustees of the trust for sale which arose on R's death. B sought possession. In the Court of Appeal, J argued that, as the grant of the tenancy was not by deed it did not comply with the SLA s 42, and it was therefore void in accordance with s 18. When the trustees accepted rent from J, however, a tenancy was created, and B had no rights to call for possession.

Held that B was entitled to possession.

> **Note**
>
> The reason for this decision appears to be that the trustees could not have granted a valid tenancy because they did not hold the legal estate at the time of the purported grant. However, J's argument concerning s 18 was accepted. The reasoning of *Weston v Henshaw* appears to have been followed, rather than that of *Re Morgan's Lease*. Neither case was referred to in the judgments and the issue of s 110 was not raised.

Q Was s 18 applied because the purported grant of the tenancy was seen as being not 'under the Act' and therefore beyond the powers of the tenant for life? If that is the case, it explains why s 110 was not even considered.

Q Was the purported grant of the tenancy *ultra vires*, or should it be seen as 'under the Act' in substance if not in form? See the case note by J Hill (1991) 107 LQR 601.

4.7 Unintentional strict settlements

Bannister v Bannister (1948) CA

D agreed to sell her cottage to her brother-in-law, P. P gave an oral undertaking that D would be allowed to live in the cottage rent-free for as long as she wished. The cottage was conveyed to P for about one half of its true market value and was occupied by both P and D. P then allowed tenants into occupation and attempted to evict D, claiming that she was a mere tenant at will (see 7.6.1).

Held that, because of the agreement between the parties, D held the house on constructive trust for himself and P, and, following Re *Carne's Settled Estates* (above at 4.4), D had a life interest in the property. That made her a tenant for life under the Settled Land Act 1925 because, according to s 1(1) of the Act (see 4.1), any interest which is limited in trust for any person by way of succession or is limited in trust for any person in possession subject to a contingency creates a strict settlement. The only exception is land expressed to be held upon trust for sale (s 1(7)).

Q This decision gave D all the statutory powers of a tenant for life, including that of sale. Was that the intention of the parties?

Binions v Evans (1972) CA

(See 6.1.3.)

Ungurian v Lesnoff (1989)

L gave up her flat and an academic career in Poland in order to come to England to live with U. He purchased a house in London in his sole name and moved into it with L, one of his sons, and two of L's sons from a previous marriage. L and her sons made considerable improvements to the house, but made no contributions to the purchase price. The couple parted after four years, U leaving L in the house. U sought to recover possession.

Held that U held the house on constructive trust for himself and L, and that L's interest under the trust was a life interest. Vinelott J followed *Bannister v Bannister* and *Binions v Evans* (above) in ruling that the life interest made her a statutory life tenant under the Settled Land Act 1925.

Q Should Mrs L have been given a power of sale over the house?

Q Could Mrs L not have been a beneficiary under a constructive trust for sale, in which case she would not necessarily have a power of sale? See Lord Denning MR's judgment in *Binions v Evans* at 6.1.3.

Costello v Costello (1995) CA

Mr and Mrs C had been tenants of a council house for nearly 40 years. In 1986 they exercised their right to buy the property, the purchase money (£18,500) being provided by their son, C. Mr and Mrs C executed a deed stating that they held the property in trust for C absolutely and that they would transfer the property to him when required to do so. In return, C promised to allow Mr and Mrs C to occupy the house rent-free for the rest of their lives. Mr C died in 1989, and, when relations between C and his mother became strained, C sought to have the property transferred into his sole name, although he stressed that he did not wish to evict his mother. Mrs C claimed to be a tenant for life under the Settled Land Act 1925. At first instance the judge ruled that she was a contractual licensee. Mrs C appealed.

Held, allowing the appeal, that Mrs C was a tenant for life, and therefore the legal estate did not have to be vested in C until after her death. The Court of Appeal accepted that this conclusion led to consequences which were unforeseen at the time of the execution of the deed, but the provisions of the Settled Land Act overrode the terms of the settlement.

Note ───────────────────────────────

Had there been no deed, Mrs C would probably have been protected. Mr and Mrs C would have held the legal estate as joint tenants for themselves and C, who would have had an interest by way of resulting trust. Mr and Mrs C would probably have had a beneficial interest, their right-to-buy discount counting as a contribution to the purchase (see *Springette v Defoe* (1992) at 6.1.2).

Q Were other options available to the court which would prevent Mrs C being given a power of sale over the house? Consider a life interest under an implied trust for sale, sale to be subject to the consent of C (see 5.2.1); or alternatively, an estoppel licence (see 6.2).

5   Trusts for sale

5.1   Definition of a trust for sale

Law of Property Act 1925 s 205(1)(xxix):
'Trust for sale' in relation to land, means an immediate binding trust for sale, whether or not exercisable at the request or with the consent of any person, and with or without a power at discretion to postpone sale; 'trustees for sale' mean the persons (including a personal representative) holding land on trust for sale, and 'power to postpone sale' means power to postpone in the exercise of a discretion.

Note —————————————————————————————————
For the meaning of 'immediate' and 'binding' see Kevin Gray, *Elements of Land Law* (Butterworths, 1993, 2nd edn) pp 524-5.

5.2   Formation of a trust for sale

5.2.1   Express trusts for sale may be of successive or concurrent interests

Note —————————————————————————————————
Although the method of formation is different, both express trusts and statutory trusts for sale operate in accordance with the Law of Property Act 1925. Unlike the settlor of a strict settlement, it is possible for the settlor of an express trust for sale to restrict the power of sale which he gives to the trustees in the trust instrument. The conveyance of the legal estate to the trustees is sufficient to form the vesting deed.

The settlor may require that consents be obtained before sale

Law of Property Act 1925 s 26(1):
If the consent of more than two persons is by the disposition made requisite to the execution of a trust for sale of land, then, in favour of a purchaser, the consent of any two such persons to the execution of trust or to the exercise of any statutory or other powers vested in the trustees for sale shall be deemed sufficient.

5.2.2 The statutory trusts – whenever there are concurrent interests

Note ───────────────────────────────────────

The conveyance of the legal estate to two or more persons is sufficient to constitute the trust.

Law of Property Act 1925 s 35:
For the purposes of this Act land held upon the 'statutory trusts' shall be held upon the trusts and subject to the provisions following, namely, upon trust to sell the same and to stand possessed of the net proceeds of sale, after payment of costs, and of the net rents and profits until sale after payment of rates, taxes, costs of insurance, repairs, and other outgoings, upon such trusts, and subject to such powers and provisions, as may be requisite for giving effect to the rights of persons (including an incumbrancer of a former undivided share or whose incumbrance is not secured by a legal mortgage) interested in the land and the right of a person who, if the land had not been made subject to a trust for sale by virtue of this Act, would have been entitled to an entailed interest in an undivided share in the land, shall be deemed to be a right to a corresponding entailed interest in the net proceeds of sale attributable to that share ...

Conveyances of legal estates to infants jointly with persons of full age

Law of Property Act 1925 s 1(6):
A legal estate is not capable of subsisting or being created in an undivided share in land or being held by an infant.

Law of Property Act 1925 s 19(2):
A conveyance of a legal estate in land to an infant, jointly with one or more persons of full age, shall operate to vest the legal estate in the other person or persons on the statutory trusts, but not so as to sever any joint tenancy in the net proceeds of sale or in the rents and profits until sale, or affect the right of a tenant for life or statutory owner to have settled land vested in him.

Note ───────────────────────────────────────

A statutory trust for sale will also result from intestacy. See Administration of Estates Act 1925 s 33.

5.3 The legal estate

5.3.1 The legal estate to be held by a maximum of four trustees

Trustee Act 1925 s 34(2):
In the case of settlements and dispositions on trust for sale of land made or coming into operation after the commencement of this Act –

(a) the number of trustees thereof shall not in any case exceed four, and where more than four persons are named as such trustees, the four first named (who are able and willing to act) shall alone be the trustees, and the other persons named shall not be trustees unless appointed on the occurrence of a vacancy;

(b) the number of the trustees shall not be increased beyond four.

5.3.2   Appointment of trustees

Note ——————————————————————————————————————
No formalities are required for a statutory trust for sale other than vesting the legal estate in more than one person.

Law of Property Act s 24(1):
The persons having power to appoint new trustees of a conveyance of land on trust for sale shall be bound to appoint the same persons (if any) who are for the time being trustees of the settlement of the proceeds of sale, but a purchaser shall not be concerned to see whether the proper persons are appointed to be trustees of the conveyance of the land.

Trustee Act 1925 s 41(1):
The court may, whenever it is expedient to appoint a new trustee or new trustees, and it is found inexpedient difficult or impractical to do so without the assistance of the court, make an order appointing a new trustee or new trustees either in substitution for or in addition to any existing trustee or trustees, or although there is no existing trustee.

5.3.3   Two or more trustees must hold the legal estates as joint tenants (ie with a right of survivorship)

Law of Property Act 1925 s 1(6):
A legal estate is not capable of subsisting or being created in an undivided share in land or being held by an infant.

Law of Property Act 1925 s 34:
(1) An undivided share in land shall not be capable of being created except as provided by the Settled Land Act 1925 or as hereinafter mentioned.
(2) Where, after the commencement of this Act, land is expressed to be conveyed to any persons in undivided shares and those persons are of full age, the conveyance shall ... operate as if the land had been expressed to be conveyed to the grantees, or, if there are more than four grantees, to the first four named in the conveyance, as joint tenants upon the statutory trusts hereinafter mentioned ....

5.3.4 The legal joint tenancy may not be severed

Law of Property Act 1925 s 36(2):
No severance of a joint tenancy of a legal estate, so as to create a tenancy in common in land shall be permissible, whether by operation of law or otherwise, but this subsection does not affect the right of a joint tenant to release his interest to the other joint tenants, or the right to sever a joint tenancy in an equitable interest whether or not the legal estate is vested in the joint tenants (see 5.4.3 for the text which follows).

5.3.5 Powers of the trustees

Law of Property Act 1925 s 28(1):
Trustees for sale shall, in relation to land or to manorial incidents and to the proceeds of sale, have all the powers of a tenant for life and the trustees of a settlement under the Settled Land Act 1925, including in relation to the land the powers of management conferred by that Act during a minority ....

Power to postpone sale

Law of Property Act 1925 s 25:
(1) A power to postpone sale shall, in the case of every trust for sale of land, be implied unless a contrary intention appears.
(2) Where there is a power to postpone the sale, then (subject to any express direction to the contrary in the instrument, if any, creating the trust for sale) the trustees for sale shall not be liable in any way for postponing the sale, in the exercise of their discretion, for any indefinite period; nor shall a purchaser of a legal estate be concerned in any case with any directions respecting the postponement of sale.

Re Rooke (1953)
A testator directed his trustees to sell his farm 'as soon as possible after my death', and that the proceeds should form part of his residuary estate. The residue was to be enjoyed by his widow for her life and then, after her death, it was to be distributed among the testator's brother and sisters. The trustees allowed the widow to remain in the farm after the death of the testator, and the brother and sisters, who were entitled in remainder, objected.

Held that the trustees had no power to postpone sale. The statutory power to postpone sale in s 25 did not apply because the testator had shown a contrary intention.

5.4 The beneficial interests

5.4.1 Equity follows the law – in the absence of evidence to the contrary an equitable joint tenancy will be presumed

Characteristics of a joint tenancy – the four unities

AG Securities v Vaughan (1990) HL

For the facts of this case see 7.7. It had to be decided whether the four occupants of a large flat were joint tenants or mere licensees. As Lord Oliver stated, all four of the unities must be present in order for there to be a joint tenancy. If one of the unities is absent there can only be a tenancy in common. The four unities are:

(i) unity of possession – each co-owner must be equally entitled to possession of the whole land. This is required even for a tenancy in common;

(ii) unity of interest – all co-owners must have the same interest in the land. It must be the same in duration, and extent;

(iii) unity of time – the interests of each co-owner must have vested at the same time;

(iv) unity of title – each co-owner must claim title under the same document.

5.4.2 Creation of a tenancy in common

When any of the four unities is missing

When words of severance have been used

> Note ─────────────────────────────
> Examples of words of severance include: 'equally'; 'in equal shares'; 'to be divided between'; 'between'; 'amongst'; and 'in equal moieties'.

Commercial partners are presumed to be tenants in common

Lake v Craddock (1732)

Five partners bought some waterlogged land, intending to drain it for profit.

Held that it was a tenancy in common because the right of survivorship is incompatible with a commercial undertaking, and because the parties had contributed in unequal shares.

Mortgagees are presumed to be tenants in common as between themselves

(See *Petty v Styward* (1631))

Purchasers who contribute in unequal shares are presumed to be tenants in common

Bull v Bull (1955) CA

The plaintiff and his mother contributed in unequal shares to the purchase price of a house. Legal title to the house was conveyed to the plaintiff alone. The mother claimed that her contribution was not intended as a gift and that she was therefore entitled to an interest by way of resulting trust in proportion to her contributions. The mother and daughter-in-law quarrelled and the son sought to evict his mother. The judge at first instance dismissed the action and the son appealed.

Held that the mother was a tenant in common and 'all tenancies in common are equitable only and take effect behind a trust for sale ... until a sale takes place these equitable tenants in common have the same rights to enjoy the land as legal tenants used to have ... neither of them is entitled to evict the other ...' (*per* Denning LJ). The son, as a sole trustee, could not give a valid receipt in order to overreach his mother's interest. However, as Denning LJ observed, if he appointed another trustee he could sell the property, thereby overreaching his mother's interest, which would then be in the proceeds of sale.

Business tenants are presumed to be tenants in common

Malayan Credit Ltd v Jack Chia–MPH Ltd (1986) PC

MC and JC leased some office space. They paid rent separately; MC paid 38% of the rent and JC paid 62%. The parties had a dispute and MC sought either sale of the lease or division of the property. MC argued that, as words of severance had not been used, and as there was no presumption of a tenancy in common, the offices were held as a joint tenancy. The proceeds of sale should, they argued, be divided equally between the tenants, or, if the office space was divided, it should be split equally. The Singapore Court of Appeal found for MC, and JC appealed.

Held, allowing the appeal, that they were tenants in common, and that the property should be divided in unequal shares. Lord Brightman stated that:

> there are other circumstances in which equity may infer that the beneficial interest is intended to be held by the grantees as tenants in common. In the opinion of their Lordships, one such case is where the grantees hold the premises for their several individual business purposes.

5.4.3 An equitable joint tenancy may be severed

(See the Law of Property Act s 36(2) at 5.3.4.)

Severance by written notice

Law of Property Act s 36(2):

(See 5.3.4 for preceding paragraph.)
Provided that, where a legal estate (not being settled land) is vested in joint tenants beneficially, and any tenant desires to sever the joint tenancy in equity, he shall give to the other joint tenants a notice in writing of such desire or do such other acts or things as would, in the case of personal estate, have been effectual to sever the tenancy in equity, and thereupon under the trust for sale affecting the land, the net proceeds of sale, and the net rents and profits until sale, shall be held upon the trusts which would have been requisite for giving effect to the beneficial interests if there had been an actual severance.

> Note
> The written notice must be served *inter vivos* and comply with the requirements of the LPA 1925 s 196. Notice cannot be given by will.

Law of Property Act 1925 s 196(4):

Any notice required or authorised by this Act to be served shall also be sufficiently served, if it is sent by post in a registered letter addressed to the lessee, lessor, mortgagee, mortgagor, or other person to be served, by name, at the aforesaid place of abode or business office, or counting-house, and if that letter is not returned through the post office undelivered; and that service shall be deemed to be made at the time at which the registered letter would in the ordinary course be delivered.

Re Draper's Conveyance (1969)

A husband and wife held their house as joint tenants. Upon their divorce the wife obtained an order under the Married Women's Property Act 1882 which called for the house to be sold and the proceeds distributed according to the shares of the spouses. The husband died before the house was sold, and the wife claimed to be entitled to the house absolutely by survivorship.

Held that the wife held the legal estate for herself and her husband's estate in equal shares because the service of the summons was sufficient to sever the joint tenancy.

Re 88 Berkeley Road, London, NW9 (1971)

P and G were joint tenants of a house. G decided to sever the joint tenancy and her solicitors sent notice by recorded delivery to P. P was not at home when the letter arrived and G herself signed for the letter. When G died P claimed to be entitled to the entire beneficial interest by the right of survivorship. The joint tenancy, she claimed, had not been severed because she had never received the letter.

Held that the joint tenancy had been severed. Whether P had received the letter or not, notice of severance had been given in accordance with the LPA 1925 s 36(2) and s 196(4).

Harris v Goddard (1983) CA

Mr and Mrs H were joint tenants of the matrimonial home. When their marriage broke down Mrs H petitioned for divorce, requesting that the court make an order for transfer or settlement of the matrimonial home. Mr H died before the hearing and the house was sold. Mr H's executors claimed that the service of the divorce petition was sufficient to effect a severance of the joint tenancy and that one half of the proceeds of sale should go to his estate.

Held that there was no severance and that Mrs H was entitled to the proceeds by survivorship. The divorce petition did not sever the joint tenancy because it did not demonstrate an intention to sever immediately; it merely invited the court to consider severance at some time in the future.

Severance by a joint tenant acting upon his own share

Note ───

This is the first of the methods of severance listed by Page-Wood V-C in *Williams v Hensman* (1861). Any form of *inter vivos* alienation will suffice, eg a joint tenant who mortgages his share will automatically effect a severance (he has no 'share' to mortgage if he does not). See *First National Securities Ltd v Hegerty* (1985) CA.

Severance by mutual agreement

Burgess v Rawnsley (1975) CA

H, aged 63, and Mrs R, 60, met at a scripture rally in Trafalgar Square and became good friends. H had the opportunity of purchasing the house in which he had been a tenant for many years, and Mrs R agreed to purchase the property with him as joint tenants. H retained the bottom flat and Mrs R was to have occupied the top flat, but she never moved in. She then came to an oral agreement with H to sell her share to him for £750, but she later refused to sell. H then died and the court was asked to decide whether the joint tenancy had been severed, or whether Mrs R was absolutely entitled by survivorship.

Held that the oral agreement was sufficient to sever the joint tenancy and that H's share should go to his estate. Lord Denning MR stated that, 'I think there was evidence that Mr Honick and Mrs Rawnsley did come to an agreement that he would buy her share for £750. That agreement was not in writing and it was not specifically enforceable. Yet it was sufficient to effect a severance.'

Note ───

This is the second of the *Williams v Hensman* methods of severance.

Severance by mutual conduct

Burgess v Rawnsley (1975) CA

Lord Denning MR was of the opinion that 'even if there was not any firm agreement but only a course of dealing, it clearly evinced an intention by both parties that the property should henceforth be held in common and not jointly'. His view was not shared by the majority of the Court of Appeal, however (Sir John Pennycuik and Browne LJ), who felt that the facts in this case did not warrant an inference of severance by mutual conduct.

Note ──

This is the last of the *Williams v Hensman* methods of severance.

Q Is it possible to sever a joint tenancy by mutual conduct by performing actions which would not have severed it by one of the other methods? (See eg, *Hunter v Babbage* (1995).)

Severance by the bankruptcy of one joint tenant

Re Palmer (1994) CA

P and his wife were joint tenants of a property. P died and the claims against his estate were so great that his executor presented a petition for an insolvency administration order. A trustee of the estate was appointed and he sought a declaration that he was entitled to a one-half share in the property. At first instance the judge found for the trustee, because the insolvency order was deemed to take effect at the date of death for the purposes of s 421 of the Insolvency Act 1986; and it is usually presumed that a judicial act was made on the first moment of the day when it was done. The joint tenancy had been severed before P's death and therefore the trustee was entitled to P's share in the property. Mrs P appealed.

Held, allowing the appeal, that by the time the insolvency administration order was granted the property had already passed to Mrs P by right of survivorship. Section 421 of the Insolvency Act 1986 referred to 'the estate of a deceased person', and it could not apply to property which would not otherwise have formed part of the estate. It was further stated *per curiam* that the presumption that a judicial act is deemed to take place on the first moment of the day when it is done should not be applied when, in so doing, the court is presuming something which it knows to be untrue.

Re Dennis (1995) CA

D and his wife were joint tenants of two properties. On 21 September D committed an act of bankruptcy by failing to comply with a bankruptcy notice, and on 20 December 1982 a petition to declare D bankrupt was presented. Mrs D died on 23 February 1983, leaving her entire estate to her children. Mr D was not adjudicated bankrupt until 11 November 1983, and the trustee sought a declaration that he was solely entitled to both properties. The question was whether severance had occurred before the death of Mrs D. If the date of severance was the date of the order the whole estate passed to D by survivorship and therefore vested in his trustee in bankruptcy. The trustee could then use the proceeds of sale to satisfy creditors. If, on the other hand, the date of severance was the date on which the bankruptcy occurred, the estate was already severed by the time Mrs D died, and the proceeds from the sale of the property would be divided in equal shares between the trustee and Mrs D's estate. At first instance it was decided that the date of severance was the date of the order, and that both properties vested solely in the trustee. Mrs D's personal representatives appealed, claiming that severance had taken place before Mrs D's death. They claimed that, according to the Bankruptcy Act 1914 s 37, severance occurred at the time of D's original act of bankruptcy.

Held, allowing the appeal, that the date of severance was 21 September, the date of D's original act of bankruptcy. As the trustee could rely upon the doctrine of relation back to found a claim when the debtor died in the interim, it followed that the personal representatives of a deceased joint tenant could also rely upon the doctrine to defeat the trustees claim to property by survivorship.

Severance by merger of interest

This occurs when one joint tenant acquires the share of another, thereby destroying the unity of interest between the parties. For examples of this form of severance, see Kevin Gray, *Elements of Land Law* (Butterworths, 1993, 2nd edn) p 510.

Severance as a result of unlawful killing

Note ───

It is a rule of public policy that a person is not allowed to benefit from unlawful killing. Any benefit to which the killer would have been entitled under the deceased's will or intestacy is forfeited (eg, see *In the Estate of Crippen* (1911)). Similarly, if the parties have been joint tenants the joint tenancy is severed and the killer is not allowed to take the share of the deceased by survivorship. The forfeiture rule may, in certain circumstances, be modified by the court if the offender is guilty of manslaughter, but not if he is guilty of murder.

Forfeiture Act 1982 ss 2(1) and (4):
Where a court determines that the forfeiture rule has precluded a person
... who has unlawfully killed another from acquiring any interest in property mentioned in subsection (4) below, the court may make an order
under this section modifying the effect of that rule.
(4) ...
(b) any beneficial interest in property which (apart from the forfeiture
rule) the offender would have acquired in consequence of the death of
the deceased, being property which, before the death, was held on trust
for any person.

Re K (1986) CA
Mr and Mrs K were joint tenants of the matrimonial home. By his will Mr
K bequeathed to Mrs K a legacy of £1,000, and a life interest in his residuary estate. Because Mrs K killed her husband, according to the rule of forfeiture she should not have been able to take any benefit under the will,
and the joint tenancy should have been severed, her husband's share going
to his estate rather than to Mrs K by survivorship. As Mrs K was convicted only of manslaughter she sought relief from forfeiture under the
Forfeiture Act 1982.

Held that, considering the conduct of both Mr and Mrs K, and the financial positions of both Mrs K and any other persons likely to be entitled
under the will or on intestacy, Mrs K should be relieved from forfeiture.

Severance by operation of law
Occasionally an order of the court will effectively sever a joint tenancy. For
example, an order made under the Inheritance (Provision for Family and
Dependants) Act 1975.

5.4.4   Calculation of shares ...

Nielson-Jones v Fedden (1975)
Mr and Mrs T were joint tenants of the matrimonial home. The marriage
broke down and the parties separated, intending to divorce. They decided
to redistribute the matrimonial property themselves and they signed a
home-made document giving Mr T 'entire discretion' to sell the matrimonial home and to use the proceeds to purchase another property. Mr T
found a purchaser but unfortunately he died before completion of the sale.
Mrs T (who later became Mrs N-J) appointed a co-trustee and sold the
property. She claimed to be solely entitled to the proceeds of sale, but Mr
T's personal representatives claimed that the home-made document either
assigned all of his wife's interest in the house to Mr T, or that it was sufficient to effect a severance.

Held that Mrs N-J was solely entitled to the proceeds. No agreement had
been reached regarding severance, the signed document being merely

authority for Mr T to sell the property on behalf of his wife and himself. Walton J declared *obiter* that when severance occurs 'the person severing will take 1/nth of the property beneficially, where 'n' is the original number of the joint tenants.'

Note ————————————————————————————————————
More accurately, 'n' should be the number of original joint tenants who are still surviving.

... when there is no express declaration

Bernard v Josephs (1982) CA

Miss B and J were engaged to be married and they arranged to purchase a house with the aid of a 100% local authority mortgage. B contributed £200 to the initial expenses, and J contributed £650. J then spent £200 on redecoration and repairs. B paid for the food and housekeeping and J paid the mortgage. The property was conveyed into their joint names without any express declaration as to the beneficial interests. After 18 months the parties split up and B sought a declaration that she was entitled to one half of the proceeds of sale. At first instance the judge awarded J credit for his initial contributions, but found that the property was held in equal shares. J appealed.

Held that when there was no express declaration of trust the presumption that the property should be held in equal shares does not always apply. The court should look at the contributions and all of the circumstances of the case (*per* Lord Denning MR and Kerr LJ) or at the intention of the parties, having regard to their contributions (*per* Griffiths LJ). In this case the intention was that the house should be the matrimonial home; it was therefore held in equal shares.

Q Would it have made any difference had J made a substantial contribution towards the purchase price? See 6.1.

...when there is an express declaration

Goodman v Gallant (1986) CA

Mr and Mrs G were joint tenants of the matrimonial home. When the marriage broke down M came to live with Mrs G in the house and they purchased Mr G's share. The conveyance to M and Mrs G stated that the property was held 'upon trusts to sell ... as joint tenants'. When Mrs G and M parted, Mrs G gave M written notice of severance, claiming that she had a three-quarter interest in the property. M claimed to have a half share because he was a joint tenant until written notice was served upon him.

Held that the statement of beneficial interest in the conveyance was conclusive. The property was held as a joint tenancy until that joint tenancy was severed. Upon severance the property was severed in equal shares, and M was entitled to a half share.

Calculation of shares on divorce

Matrimonial Causes Act 1973 s 24(1):

On granting a decree of divorce ... or at any time thereafter ... the court may make any one or more of the following orders, that is to say –

(a) an order that a party to the marriage shall transfer to the other party ... such property as may be so specified, being property to which the first-mentioned party is entitled ...;

(b) an order that a settlement of such property as may be so specified, being property to which a party to the marriage is so entitled, be made to the satisfaction of the court for the benefit of the other party to the marriage and of the children of the family or either or any of them ....

Note ———
Problems regarding the calculation of shares usually occur when co-owners are not married to each other. Problems can also occur when marriage partners dispute the ownership of property during the marriage (see Matrimonial Proceedings and Property Act 1970 s 37 at 6.1.3). When the parties are divorcing, however, the divorce court is able to use its considerable discretion under the Matrimonial Causes Act 1973 (see above) in order to arrive at a solution. See also resulting and constructive trusts at 6.1.

5.5 The doctrine of conversion

Are interests under a trust for sale interests in the land or merely interests in the proceeds of sale?

Irani Finance Ltd v Singh (1971) CA

The first and second defendants held land as joint tenants. The land was subject to a mortgage which they assigned to the third defendant. IF Ltd was owed money by the first and second defendants and they obtained a charging order under s 35 of the Administration of Justice Act 1956. It was argued for the defendants that an order could not be made under the 1956 Act unless it was against land or an interest in land, and that an interest under a trust for sale was merely an interest in the proceeds of sale.

Held that the defendants had only an interest in the proceeds of sale of land and not an interest in the land itself. Cross LJ said:

'The whole purpose of the trust for sale is to make sure, by shifting the equitable interests away from the land and into the proceeds of sale, that a purchaser of the land takes free from the equitable interests. To hold these to be equitable interests in the land itself would be to frustrate this purpose.'

Note ———
Is it satisfactory that an interest under a trust for sale should be an interest in land for some purposes but not for others?

Elias v Mitchell (1972)

Miss E and M were business partners. They owned a house, of which M was the sole registered proprietor, subject to an agreement that he held the property on trust for the partners in equal shares. In 1970 M transferred the property to D, the second defendant. Miss E lodged a caution against dealings at the land registry before D had registered the transfer, and D claimed that, as E's interest was in personalty rather than in the land, she should not have been able to enter a caution.

Held that, although an undivided share in land was excluded from the definition of land in s 3(viii) of the LRA 1925, it was included in the definition of minor interests under s 3(xv)(a), and therefore a caution could be lodged in respect of Miss E's undivided share.

Cedar Holdings Ltd v Green (1981) CA

Mr and Mrs G held the matrimonial home in joint names. After they divorced, Mr G and another woman, who pretended to be Mrs G, mortgaged the property to the plaintiffs. When they discovered the fraud, the plaintiffs sought a declaration that the entire beneficial interest was charged in their favour. Mrs G claimed that the house was not subject to any charge.

Held that the beneficial interests were not land but merely interests in the proceeds of sale, and therefore the house was not charged.

Williams & Glyn's Bank v Boland (1981) HL

For the facts of this case, see 3.6. Lord Wilberforce declared that Mrs B's interest under an implied trust for sale was an interest in the land for the purposes of the LRA 1925 s 70(1)(g). He said: 'to describe the interests of spouses in a house jointly bought to be lived in as a matrimonial home as merely an interest in proceeds of sale, or rents and profits until sale is just a little unreal'. *Cedar Holdings v Green* (above) was thought to be wrongly decided.

Note —————————————————————————

Since this decision, the importance of the doctrine of conversion has declined, at least in the context of the matrimonial home. It has not declined altogether, however – see *Harman v Glencross* (1985) *per* Ewbank J.

———————————————————————————————

Q Does the doctrine of conversion serve any useful purpose which is not adequately served by overreaching? See Law Commission Report No 181; Kevin Gray, Elements of Land Law (Butterworths, 1993, 2nd edn) pp 541-6; E H Burn, *Cheshire and Burn's Modern Law of Real Property* (Butterworths, 1994, 15th edn) pp 235-8.

5.5.1 Charging orders and conversion

Note ───────────────────────────────────────
After the decision in *Irani Finance Ltd v Singh* (above) the status of charging orders was in doubt. The 1979 Act (below) sought to clarify the position.

Charging Orders Act 1979 s 2:

(1) ... a charge may be imposed by a charging order only on –

(a) any interest held by the debtor beneficially –

...

(ii) under any trust; or

(b) any interest held by a person as trustee of a trust ... if the interest is in such an asset or is an interest under another trust; and –

(i) the judgment or order ... was made against that person as trustee of the trust; or

(ii) the whole beneficial interest under the trust is held by the debtor unencumbered and for his own benefit; or

(iii) in a case where there are two or more debtors, all of whom are liable to the creditor for the same debt, they together hold the whole beneficial interest under the trust unencumbered and for their own benefit.

Perry v Phoenix Assurance plc (1988)

Mr and Mrs R owned land jointly. P obtained a judgment against them both and applied for a charging order, which was entered in error against Mr R's name only. Mr and Mrs R then applied for a mortgage with PA, who searched the Land Charges Register and discovered only the charge against Mr R. PA accordingly granted the mortgage and the Rs defaulted. PA sold the property as mortgagee and there were insufficient funds to meet the liabilities. P claimed that he should be paid in priority to PA.

Held that the charging order was not registrable against an undivided share in the land, and that P was not entitled to be paid in priority to PA.

Clark v Chief Land Registrar (1994) CA

For the facts of this case, see 3.5.2. The plaintiffs obtained a charging order against two judgment debtors. The judgment debtors held the entire beneficial interest between them and a caution was lodged at the Land Registry in accordance with s 2(1)(b)(ii) of the Charging Orders Act 1979. The caution was held to be valid and the plaintiffs were held to be entitled to an indemnity when the defendant failed to give them notice of a subsequent dealing in the land.

Note ───────────────────────────────────────
The difference between Perry and Clark is that, in the earlier case, only one of the co-owners had a charging order entered against them and

therefore, applying the doctrine of conversion, the charging order was against the proceeds of sale rather than against the land; it could not bind the other party. In Clark, however, both co-owners were subject to the charging order and the order could be registered against the entire legal estate.

5.6 Protection for the beneficiaries and the purchaser

5.6.1 Overreaching and the trust for sale

Law of Property Act 1925 s 2:
(See 2.2.1.)

5.6.2 The curtain principle

Law of Property Act 1925 s 27:
(1) A purchaser of a legal estate from trustees for sale shall not be concerned with the trusts affecting the proceeds of sale of land subject to a trust for sale ... or affecting the rents and profits of the land until sale, whether or not those trusts are declared by the same instrument by which the trust for sale is created.
(2) Notwithstanding anything to the contrary in the instrument (if any) creating a trust for sale of land or in the settlement of the net proceeds, the proceeds of sale or other capital money shall not be paid to or applied by the direction of fewer than two persons as trustees for sale, except where the trustee is a trust corporation, but this subsection does not affect the right of a sole personal representative as such to give valid receipts for, or direct the application of, proceeds of sale or other capital money, nor, except where capital money arises on the transaction, render it necessary to have more than one trustee.

5.7 Sale of the trust property

Law of Property Act 1925 s 26(1) and (3):
(1) (See 5.2.1) [A settlor may require that consent be obtained before sale.]
(3) Trustees for sale shall so far as practicable consult the persons of full age for the time being beneficially interested in possession in the rents and profits of the land until sale, and shall, so far as consistent with the general interest of the trust, give effect to the wishes of such persons, or, in the case of dispute, of the majority (according to the value of their combined interests) of such persons, but a purchaser shall not be concerned to see that the provisions of this subsection have been complied with.
In the case of a trust for sale, not being a trust for sale created by or in pursuance of the powers conferred by this or any other Act, this subsection

shall not apply unless the contrary intention appears in the disposition creating the trust.

Note ───
In other words, s 26(1) applies to an express trust for sale and s 26(3) applies to a statutory trust for sale. For the limitations of the consultation procedure under s 26(3), see Kevin Gray, *Elements of Land Law* (Butterworths, 1993, 2nd edn) p 595.
───

Law of Property Act 1925 s 30(1):

If the trustees for sale refuse to sell or to exercise any of the powers conferred by either of the last two sections (ie powers of management and delegation), or any requisite consent cannot be obtained, any person interested may apply to the court for a vesting or other order for giving effect to the proposed transaction or for an order directing the trustees for sale to give effect thereto, and the court may make such order as it thinks fit.

Re Buchanan-Wollaston's Conveyance (1939) CA

A, B, C and D owned four separate properties with sea views. In order to maintain the views, they purchased as joint tenants a strip of land fronting the sea. They also entered into a deed of covenant by which they undertook not to part or deal with the co-owned land except by majority vote. B sold his individual property and wished to withdraw his investment from the co-owned strip. The other parties refused to sell, and B applied for sale under s 30.

Held that sale should not be ordered. Although the primary purpose of a trust for sale was sale of the trust property, and sale will usually be ordered in the event of a dispute, there can be a secondary (or collateral) purpose. In this case there was a secondary purpose, that of maintaining sea views, and that purpose was expressed in the deed. While that purpose was still subsisting, sale should not be ordered. In addition, B had entered into a deed of covenant and he 'could not ... ask the court to act in a way inconsistent with his own contractual obligations' (*per* Sir Wilfred Greene MR).

Re Mayo (1943)

A testator devised his house to his wife for life and then to his son and daughter in equal shares. After the widow's death the property was held on trust for sale by the son, the daughter and another as trustee, for the benefit of the son and daughter in equal shares. The son wanted the property to be sold, but the other two trustees wished to postpone the power of sale. The son applied under s 30.

Held that sale should be ordered. The primary purpose of the trust was sale and, in the absence of *mala fides* on the part of the son, 'a trust for sale will prevail, unless all three trustees agree in exercising the power to postpone ...' (*per* Simonds J).

Jones v Challenger (1961) CA

In 1956 Mr and Mrs C purchased a leasehold house. There was only 10 years left to run on the lease. Mrs C left her husband in 1957 and he divorced her on the grounds of adultery. He stayed on in the house and his ex-wife (who by now had become Mrs J), wishing to realise her interest in the property, applied for sale under s 30. At first instance the judge thought that it would not be reasonable to turn Mr C out of the house. Mrs J appealed.

Held that sale should be ordered, though Mr C should be given the opportunity of purchasing his ex-wife's share at an independent valuation. Mrs J had a share in the house and, as a lease is a wasting asset, she required that the house be sold as soon as possible. There had been a collateral purpose, that of providing a matrimonial home, but, as that purpose was no longer subsisting, the primary purpose of sale must prevail.

Re Evers's Trust (1980) CA

M and W lived together but were not married. In 1976 they had a child and two of W's children from a former marriage also began to live with them. In 1978 they purchased a cottage together for £13,950. W contributed £2,400 and M contributed just over £1,000 plus expenses. The balance was raised by way of a mortgage and the property was conveyed to M and W as joint tenants. In 1979 M left W and the children in the cottage and applied for an order for sale under s 30. At first instance the judge ruled that there should be no sale until the child of M and W was 16 or until further order. Leave was given for either party to re-apply if there was a change in circumstances. M appealed.

Held, dismissing the appeal, that, as the cottage was bought as a family home, there was a collateral purpose and that purpose was still subsisting. M had left the property but W still lived there with the children of the family and therefore sale should be postponed.

Note ————————————————————————————————

This case is important because the parties were not married. Upon the dissolution of a marriage the divorce court has wide discretion to redistribute property on divorce under the Matrimonial Causes Act 1973. The decision in *Re Evers's Trust* is similar to the Mesher and Harvey orders which are used by the divorce court. (*Mesher v Mesher* (1980) – sale postponed until the youngest child reaches 17 or 18; and *Harvey v Harvey* (1982) – sale postponed until the child reaches a certain age or the custodial parent dies, remarries, or moves house etc.)

Abbey National Plc v Moss (1994) CA

In 1971 Mr and Mrs M purchased a house as joint tenants. Mr M died in 1981 and Mrs M became the sole owner by survivorship. The house was occupied by Mrs M, her daughter and son-in-law (Mr and Mrs L), and their children. Mrs L persuaded her mother to transfer the property into the joint names of herself and her mother, the stated purpose being to simplify the transfer of the property on Mrs M's death. Mrs M agreed on the condition that the property would never be sold in her lifetime. In 1986 Mrs L applied to the plaintiffs for a mortgage loan on the property. She obtained the loan in joint names by forging her mother's signature. In 1988 she evicted her mother and commenced proceedings under s 30 in order to effect a sale of the house. Mrs L eventually allowed her mother back into the house and she then left the country with her family. No further mortgage repayments were made. The plaintiffs commenced possession proceedings and sought sale of the property under s 30. The judge at first instance found for the plaintiffs because the mortgage was held to be effective against the daughter's beneficial interest, and sale was ordered. Mrs M appealed.

Held, allowing the appeal, that when the property was transferred to the mother and daughter it was with the intention that the house would provide a home for Mrs M for the rest of her life. That collateral purpose was still subsisting and therefore sale should be postponed until after Mrs M died. The judge at first instance had relied upon Re *Citro* (1990) (see below at 5.7.1), on the basis that the circumstances were similar to bankruptcy. Peter Gibson LJ agreed that similar rules should apply, but he was able to distinguish the latter case. Re *Citro*, he asserted, only applied when the collateral purpose was to provide a matrimonial home; when that was the case the collateral purpose would not defeat the trustee in bankruptcy. However, when the collateral purpose is a purpose other than that of providing a matrimonial home, Re *Citro* did not apply, and the s 30 application had to be considered on its merits. The court 'may make such order as it thinks fit' (LPA 1925 s 30), and, considering the method by which Mrs L acquired an interest in the property, 'to order a sale seems to me not to be right and proper but to be totally inequitable' (*per* Peter Gibson LJ).

5.7.1 Section 30 and the trustee in bankruptcy

Insolvency Act 1986 s 336:
(3) Where a person and his spouse or former spouse are trustees for sale of a dwelling house and that person is adjudged bankrupt, any application by the trustee of the bankrupt's estate for any order under section 30 of the Law of Property Act 1925 ... shall be made to the court having jurisdiction in relation to the bankruptcy.
(4) On such application as is mentioned in subsection (2) or (3) the court shall make such order under section 1 of the (Matrimonial Homes) Act of 1983 or section 30 of the Act of 1925 as it thinks just and reasonable having regard to –

(a) the interests of the bankrupt's creditors;

(b) the conduct of the spouse or former spouse, so far as contributing to the bankruptcy;

(c) the needs and financial resources of the spouse or former spouse;

(d) the needs of any children; and

(e) all the circumstances of the case other than the needs of the bankrupt.

(5) Where such an application is made after the end of the period of one year beginning with the first vesting ... of the bankrupt's estate in a trustee, the court shall assume, unless the circumstances of the case are exceptional, that the interests of the bankrupt's creditors outweigh all other considerations.

Note

The section only applies to spouses and ex-spouses. Other co-owners will be subject to the rules as applied in the cases below, which were heard before the provisions of the Insolvency Act 1986 came into force.

Re Bailey (1977)

Mr and Mrs B divorced in 1974 and Mr B became bankrupt in 1975. His trustee in bankruptcy sought sale of the former matrimonial home under s 30. Mrs B asked the court to exercise its discretion to postpone sale for two years in order that her son could stay in the property long enough for him to complete his studies for his 'A' Level examinations.

Held that there should be no postponement of sale. Walton J stated that 'a person must discharge his liabilities before there is any room for being generous. One's debts must be paid, and paid promptly ...'. Megarry V-C said that the son's circumstances would have been important in a normal matrimonial property case, but in a bankruptcy case, when the commercial claims of the creditors have to be considered, the son's circumstances are 'only incidentally to be taken into consideration'.

Re Holliday (1981) CA

Mr and Mrs H purchased the matrimonial home in joint names in 1970. In 1974 H left Mrs H and their three children and went to live with another woman. Mrs H obtained a divorce in 1975 and intended to seek a property adjustment order under s 24 of the Matrimonial Causes Act 1973. Before she could obtain such an order, however, H declared himself bankrupt, and his trustee in bankruptcy sought sale of the property under s 30 of the LPA 1925. Mrs H claimed that H's bankruptcy order was an abuse of process because its purpose was merely to frustrate her property adjustment order. At first instance the judge ordered an immediate sale. Mrs H appealed.

Held that the property should be sold in order to satisfy H's creditors, but that the sale should be postponed until the second child of the marriage was 17. This postponement of sale amounted to five years from the date of the hearing, and almost ten years from the date of the bankruptcy order.

Note
This case is unusual because sale was postponed for such a long period. The circumstances of the case were unique. Mr H declared himself bankrupt even though his liabilities amounted only to about £6,000, compared to his share in the house, which amounted to about £14,000. The postponement would not cause great hardship to his creditors. Mrs H, on the other hand, would have been made homeless with her young family, having no chance of buying another house in the same area.

Q To what extent do you think that Mr H's questionable motives for declaring himself bankrupt influenced this decision? See Walton J's comments in *Re Lowrie* below.

Re Lowrie (1981)
Mr L was adjudicated bankrupt in 1979. He remained in the matrimonial home with his wife. The trustee applied for sale of the home under s 30, and the county court ordered sale to be postponed for 30 months. The trustee appealed

Held that the property should be sold as soon as possible. Walton J passed comment upon Re *Holliday*: 'The petition in bankruptcy had been presented by the husband himself as a tactical move, and quite clearly as a tactical move, to avoid a transfer of property order in favour of his wife, or ex-wife, at a time when no creditors were pressing and he was in a position in the course of a year or two out of a very good income to discharge whatever debts he had. He had gone off leaving the wife in the matrimonial home, which was the subject matter of the application, with the responsibility for all the children on her own. One can scarcely ... imagine a more exceptional set of facts, and the court gave effect to those exceptional facts.' As the facts in this case were not exceptional there was no need to grant a lengthy postponement of sale.

Re Mott (1987)
Queenie Mott was 70 and had lived in a house for over 40 years with each of her late husbands. Her son had purchased the freehold of the house from the local authority but was in financial difficulties, his creditors being the Inland Revenue and the DHSS (now DSS). The creditors applied to have him declared bankrupt and he disappeared, leaving his mother in the house. The trustee in bankruptcy applied for sale of the house under s 30, and Mrs M sought postponement of sale until after her death. She was in poor health and her doctor was of the opinion that her health would deteriorate if she was forced to move.

Held that sale should be postponed until after Mrs M's death. Hoffmann J decided that, if sale was ordered, the hardship likely to be suffered by Mrs M would far outweigh the legal and moral claims of the creditors.

Note ———————
Another very unusual case. Mrs M's age and the fact that postponement of sale would not cause hardship to the creditors appear to have been the deciding factors.

Re Citro (1991) CA
The two Citro brothers, C and D, ran a panel-beating and car-spraying business. They were declared bankrupt and the trustee applied for sale of their homes under s 30. D was separated from his wife, who lived in the family home with the three children of the marriage. C lived at home with his wife and their three children. The brothers' debts exceeded the value of their interests in the houses. Hoffmann J postponed sale until the youngest child of each family became 16. In D's case that would mean postponement until 1994, and in C's case it would mean postponement until 1995. The trustee appealed.

Held that the period of postponement should be reduced to six months. Nourse LJ reviewed the previous authorities, deciding that Re *Holliday* was an exceptional case. He then applied those authorities to the present case: 'Did Hoffmann J correctly apply [the law] to the facts which were before him? I respectfully think that he did not. First ... the personal circumstances of the two wives and children, although distressing, are not by themselves exceptional ... Thirdly ... he did not ask himself the critical question whether a further postponement would cause hardship to the creditors.' He concluded by referring to s 336 of the Insolvency Act 1986, which would apply to similar situations in the future but was not directly applicable in this case. If the Act applied, he stated, the interests of the bankrupt's creditors would outweigh all other considerations unless the circumstances are exceptional. As the circumstances were not exceptional, the court had no alternative but to allow the trustee's appeal.

5.8 Termination of a trust for sale
A trust for sale will come to an end when:
● The land is sold. Of course if the land is sold to more than one person it will be subject to another trust for sale;
● One beneficiary obtains the entire beneficial interest. This can be achieved either by purchasing the shares of the other beneficiaries, or, if the land is held as a joint tenancy, by survivorship;
● Partition of the land. The land is physically divided – each beneficiary obtains his own title deeds (unregistered land) or land certificate (registered land).

6 Informal acquisition of rights and interests

6.1 Resulting, implied or constructive trusts

6.1.1 They may be created without formalities

Law of Property Act 1925 s 53(2):
(See 1.5.2.)

There is no clear distinction between resulting and constructive trusts

Gissing v Gissing (1971) HL
For the facts of this case, see 6.1.2 below. 'A resulting, implied or constructive trust – and it is unnecessary for present purposes to distinguish between these three classes of trust – is created by a transaction between the trustee and the *cestui que trust* in connection with the acquisition by the trustee of a legal estate in the land, whenever the trustee has so conducted himself that it would be inequitable to allow him to deny to the *cestui que trust* a beneficial interest in the land acquired' (*per* Lord Diplock).

Hussey v Palmer (1972) CA
For the facts of this case, see 6.1.3 below. 'Although the plaintiff alleged that there was a resulting trust, I should have thought that the trust in this case, if there was one, was more in the nature of a constructive trust: but this is more a matter of words than anything else. The two run together. By whatever name it is described, it is a trust imposed by law whenever justice and good conscience require it' (*per* Lord Denning MR).

6.1.2 Resulting trusts

Presumption of resulting trust – contributions towards the acquisition of the realty

Bull v Bull (1955) CA
See 5.4.2 for the facts of this case. Mrs Bull was able to claim an interest in the property because of her contributions to the purchase price. Such an interest has to take effect under a trust for sale and, as the parties contributed in unequal shares, a tenancy in common was presumed.

BRIEFCASE on Land Law

Gissing v Gissing (1971) HL

Mr and Mrs G married in 1935. They purchased a house in 1951 for £2,695, most of which was raised by way of a mortgage. The house was conveyed into the sole name of Mr G, who also paid all the mortgage instalments. Mrs G paid £220 for furnishings and the laying of a lawn. She also paid most of the housekeeping costs for both Mr G and their son. In 1961 Mr G left to live with another woman, but he continued to pay the mortgage instalments, and, according to Mrs G, he assured her that the house was hers. Mrs G obtained a divorce on the grounds of her husband's adultery and she applied to the court for a declaration regarding her beneficial interest in the house. At first instance, Buckley J held that Mr G was the sole beneficial owner, but his decision was reversed by the Court of Appeal. Mr G appealed.

Held, allowing the appeal, that Mrs G had made no contributions towards the acquisition of the house, and therefore it could not be inferred that she was to have a beneficial interest in the property. Lord Diplock stated that if the wife had contributed towards the purchase it would be possible for the court to infer a common intention on the part of the parties that she was to have a beneficial interest. The contribution is not sufficient to give rise to an interest in itself, but it raises the presumption, which may be rebutted by evidence to the contrary, of an intention to benefit. Lord Diplock also stated that:

> Even where there has been no initial contribution by the wife to the cash deposit and legal charges but she makes a regular and substantial direct contribution to the mortgage instalments it may be reasonable to infer a common intention of the spouses from the outset that she should share in the beneficial interest or to infer a fresh agreement reached after the original conveyance that she should acquire a share.

Note ———

Similar cases are now dealt with by the divorce court, who may take into account factors other than contributions to the realty (see the Matrimonial Causes Act 1973 s 25). However, the presumption of resulting trust is still important when the partners are not married, when there is a dispute about the ownership of property during marriage, or on death or bankruptcy.

Springette v Defoe (1992) CA

S and D lived together as man and wife in a council flat and then in a council house. Because S had been a council tenant for 11 years, the council offered her a discount of 41% if she wished to exercise her right to buy the house. S and D decided to purchase the house between them. S contributed £2,500 in cash and D contributed £280. The rest of the purchase price was raised by way of a mortgage, which was in joint names and they contributed equally towards the repayments. When the relationship broke down, D left the house, claiming a half-share by way of constructive trust. At first instance it was held that the property was held as a joint tenancy in law and, as there was nothing to indicate to the contrary, severance should be in equal shares. S appealed.

Held that the property should be held on constructive trust in proportion to the contributions. S therefore should receive 75% (50% for contributions and her right-to-buy discount, and 25% for one-half of the amount raised by mortgage). D was entitled to 25%, which represented one-half of the contribution raised by way of mortgage.

Note ——
This was the first case to award a former tenant an interest by way of resulting or constructive trust because of their right-to-buy discount. The court was of the opinion that the trust was a constructive trust. Is it not more likely to be a resulting trust? See Helen Norman (1992) Conv 347. Does it matter whether it is resulting or constructive?

Huntingford v Hobbs (1992) CA

Mrs Hobbs, who was separated from her husband, lived in the former matrimonial home. She met H, who gave up his rented caravan in order to move in with her. On divorce, Mr Hobbs transferred the house to his wife who became the sole beneficial owner. Mrs H then agreed to purchase a house with H, using the proceeds of her house and raising the balance by way of a mortgage. The mortgage was in joint names, although the intention was that H should make the repayments. H paid the mortgage instalments and also paid for a conservatory to be built. Just over two years later H left Mrs Hobbs and married somebody else. He sought sale of the property under s 30 of the Law of Property Act 1925. The judge at first instance awarded H only £3,500, representing the cost of the conservatory plus the amount of the mortgage already repaid. H appealed, claiming that he was a joint tenant and that he was therefore entitled to one-half of the proceeds of sale. He sought to rely upon the transfer (Land Registry Form 19(JP)) which stated that the survivor of the transferees could give a valid receipt for purchase money. The survivor could not give a valid receipt if the property was held as a tenancy in common, and therefore the intention must have been that the property was to be held as a joint tenancy.

Held that the statement with regards to a valid receipt was not sufficient to be a declaration of trust and that the property should be held on resulting trust in proportions according to the contributions. Slade LJ stated:

'I would infer that if at the time of the purchase the point had been specifically put to the two parties and they had been asked in what proportions they would intend the property should be held, they would most probably have replied that it should be held in proportions corresponding with Mrs Hobbs' cash contribution and the money raised on the mortgage.'

Rebutting the presumption of resulting trust

Note ───
Contributions by themselves merely raise the presumption of resulting trust. The presumption may be rebutted if it can be established that the contribution was a gift or a loan.
───

Pettitt v Pettitt (1970) HL

For the facts of this case, see 6.1.3 below. Lord Diplock considered the possibility of applying the presumption of advancement. He considered that it would be:

> an abuse of legal technique ... to apply to transactions between the post-war generation of married couples 'presumptions' which are based upon inferences of fact which an earlier generation of judges drew as to the most likely intentions of earlier generations of spouses belonging to the propertied classes of a different social era.

Note ───
For the current status of the presumption of advancement, see Kevin Gray, *Elements of Land Law* (Butterworths, 1993, 2nd edn) pp 407–13.
───

Re *Sharpe* (1980)

S wanted to purchase a shop and maisonette for £17,000. He borrowed £12,000 from his aunt, Mrs J, in order to finance his purchase. In return for the loan, S promised to allow Mrs J, who was to give up her home, to stay in the maisonette for as long as she wished. Mrs J also spent over £2,000 on decorations and fittings and paid off some of S's debts. When S was declared bankrupt the trustee in bankruptcy sought to sell the property and entered into a contract to sell it for £17,000. Mrs J claimed to have an interest in the property by virtue of her contributions.

Held that Mrs J's contribution was merely a loan and therefore she could not claim an interest in the property by way of resulting trust. Browne-Wilkinson J found that she had a right, 'whether it be called a contractual licence or an equitable licence or an interest under a constructive trust', to remain in the property until repayment of the loan.

6.1.3 Constructive trusts

Common intention

Pettitt v Pettitt (1970) HL

For nine years Mr and Mrs P lived in a house which Mrs P had inherited. They then purchased another house with the proceeds from the sale of the first house. They lived for about four years in the second house before Mrs P left Mr P, eventually obtaining a divorce. Mr P sought a declaration under s 17 of the Married Women's Property Act 1882 that he was entitled to a share in the house. He had carried out a number of improvements which, he claimed, added approximately £1,000 to the value of the house. At first instance Mr P was awarded £300, a decision which was affirmed by the Court of Appeal. Mrs P appealed.

Held, allowing the appeal, that there was no agreement between the parties that Mr P should acquire an interest in the property, and that on the facts it was not possible to infer a common intention that Mr P was to benefit. Section 17 of the Married Women's Property Act 1882 did not give the court discretion to vary existing property rights between the parties.

Note
As a result of this case, Parliament enacted s 37 of the Matrimonial Proceedings and Property Act 1970 (see below). This was followed three years later by the Matrimonial Causes Act (see 5.4.4).

Matrimonial Proceedings and Property Act 1970 s 37:
It is hereby declared that where a husband or wife contributes in money or money's worth to the improvement of real or personal property in which or in the proceeds of sale of which either or both of them has or have a beneficial interest, the husband or wife so contributing shall, if the contribution is of a substantial nature and subject to any agreement between them to the contrary express or implied, be treated as having then acquired by virtue of his or her contribution a share or an enlarged share, as the case may be, in that beneficial interest of such an extent as may have been then agreed or, in default of such agreement, as may seem in all the circumstances just to any court before which the question of the existence or extent of the beneficial interest of the husband or wife arises (whether in proceedings between them or in other proceedings).

Thomas v Fuller-Brown (1988) CA
T went to live with Mrs F-B in her house. He designed and built a two-storey extension, constructed a through-lounge, did some electrical and plumbing work, replastered and redecorated the house, landscaped the garden, laid a driveway, carried out chimney and roof repairs, constructed a hall and rebuilt a kitchen. When the relationship ended he claimed an interest in the house.

Held that, as there had never been any express intention that he was to have an interest, and as there was nothing to suggest that there had ever been such an intention, he had no interest in the property whatsoever. As Slade LJ stated, 'under English law the mere fact that A expends money or labour on B's property does not by itself entitle A to an interest in the property. In the absence of an express agreement or common intention to be inferred from all the circumstances or any question of estoppel, A will normally have no claim whatever on the property in such circumstances. The decision in *Pettitt v Pettitt* makes this clear ...'.

*In the absence of evidence of an express agreement, the party assert-
ing an interest must have made a substantial contribution to the realty
in order that a common intention may be inferred*

Hussey v Palmer (1972) CA

H sold her house and went to live with her daughter and son-in-law, P. P
arranged to have an extension built for the occupation of H, and H paid
£607 for the building work. After several months H left the property
because of domestic discord and she sought to recover her £607. She
claimed an interest by way of constructive trust. At first instance the judge
held that the £607 was a loan and that there was no case for a resulting
trust. Mrs H appealed.

Held that Mrs H had an interest in the property. Lord Denning MR was
of the opinion that Mrs H had an interest by way of resulting or constructive trust. There was no express agreement but she had made a significant
contribution to the realty. This contribution evidenced the common intention and meant that Mrs H had relied to her detriment on the agreement.
For P to go back on the agreement would be inequitable and a constructive
trust should be implied.

Burns v Burns (1984) CA

In 1961 Mr and Mrs B began to live together. They never married but they
cohabited for 17 years and had two children. A house was purchased in
1963 in the sole name of Mr B, who paid all the mortgage instalments. In
1980 Mrs B left Mr B and claimed an interest in the property by virtue of
her contributions to the household over the previous 17 years. She had
brought up their two children and paid for their clothing, performed all
the domestic duties in the house, contributed to household expenses, purchased fittings and a washing machine, and redecorated the interior of the
house. At first instance it was held that Mrs B had no interest in the house.
Mrs B appealed.

Held, that, as her contributions were not referable to the realty, Mrs B
had no interest in the house. There was no evidence of an express agreement and Mrs B did not contribute to the purchase price. May LJ asserted
that had Mrs B made regular mortgage repayments, or even used her
money for household expenses so that Mr B could more easily pay the
mortgage, she might have had an interest in the house. As there was no
evidence of such an agreement, Mrs B, though she might have worked as
hard as Mr B in maintaining the family etc, could not claim to have any
interest at all in the house.

Q Would Mrs B have been in a better situation had she been married to Mr
B?

Ivin v Blake (1995) CA

B and I were brother and sister, both of whom had helped their parents to run various public houses. There was also another child of the marriage. When the father died it was agreed that a house should be purchased for the mother. All three children were to live with the mother, and the house was large enough to take in lodgers. The house was purchased in the sole name of B, who was *prima facie* solely responsible for the mortgage repayments. In fact, the mother paid both the initial deposit and the mortgage instalments until the mortgage was finally redeemed. B married and left home shortly after the purchase, but returned 14 years later. I, at first alone and then with her husband, continued to live at home with her mother and continued to help her, as she had done for many years. The mother died in 1985, and she appointed B as her executor, devising and bequeathing the whole of her real and personal estate to her three children in equal shares. The mother left a letter saying that she wanted the sale of the house to be deferred until I and her husband had found somewhere else to live. B gave I and her husband notice to quit the property. I sought a declaration that B held the house merely as a constructive trustee, and B counterclaimed, seeking a declaration that he was the sole beneficial owner. At first instance the judge found for B on the basis that it had been agreed that the house was to belong to him when his mother died. I appealed.

Held that there was no evidence of any agreement that I was to have a beneficial interest in the house, and any contributions made by her were not directly referable to the realty. Therefore her contributions were not sufficient to raise a presumption of resulting or constructive trust. However, the mother held the entire beneficial interest in the house by way of resulting or constructive trust (she paid all of the purchase money), and B held the property on trust for her. As the mother held the entire beneficial interest in the property, the house should pass under terms of her will to her three children in equal shares as beneficial tenants in common.

When there is evidence of an express agreement the detriment needs to be referable to the agreement, but not necessarily directly to the realty

Eves v Eves (1975) CA

Mr and Mrs E were not married. They lived together for four and a half years and they had two children. Mr E bought a house in his sole name, assuring Mrs E that it would have been purchased in joint names had she been 21 years old. Mrs E did a great deal of work redecorating the property, using a 14lb sledgehammer to break up a patio and dumping the rubble in a skip. Mr E then left Mrs E, and she claimed a share of the house. At first instance the judge was unable to find a common intention. Mrs E appealed.

Held that Mrs E was entitled to a one-quarter share in the property. Lord Denning MR found that the parties had expressly agreed that Mrs E would have had a legal interest if she had been 21 years old at the time of the acquisition of the property. Mrs E's subsequent conduct showed that she relied to her detriment on that agreement, or common intention. It would be a fraud on the agreement if Mr E took the property absolutely. In this case, however, no order was made for the sale of the property.

Note

It appears rather strange to refer to common intention in cases such as this, especially as Mr E probably never intended Mrs E to have an interest in the house. However, a common intention was perceived, albeit wrongly, by Mrs E.

Grant v Edwards (1986) CA

E purchased a house in joint names with his brother. The latter was included in order to obtain a mortgage, but he never lived in the property nor did he make any contributions towards the purchase. Mrs G was told by E that her name had to be kept off the title deeds because it would prejudice her forthcoming divorce proceedings. Mrs G claimed an interest by virtue of her considerable contributions to household expenditure, housekeeping, and bringing up the children of the 11-year relationship.

Held that Mrs G was entitled to a half share in the property. Browne-Wilkinson V-C found that Linda Grant had acted to her detriment on the express agreement that she was to have a share in the property. Her contributions were not referable to the realty but they were referable to the common agreement. There was 'a sufficient link between the detriment suffered by the claimant and the common intention'. Without Mrs G's contributions, E would not have been able to keep up the mortgage repayments, and therefore her indirect contributions were 'essentially linked to the mortgage instalments'.

Q Why did Linda Grant's claim succeed but that of Valerie Burns fail?

Lloyds Bank plc v Rosset (1991) HL

See 3.6.3 for a more recent House of Lords ruling on the detriment required in order to give rise to a resulting or constructive trust.

Hammond v Mitchell (1991)

Miss M, a Bunny Girl, went to live with H, a second-hand car dealer, in his flat. She gave up work when she became pregnant with the first of their two children. They began a series of joint business ventures that were initially very successful, their total assets amounting to almost £450,000. H purchased two bungalows, one in Essex and the other in Spain. Both the properties were conveyed into his sole name, but Miss M asserted that he had told her that 'when we are married it (ie the Essex bungalow) will be half yours anyway'. H claimed that the property had to be conveyed into his sole name because of tax problems and because of his divorce proceedings. The relationship ended and Miss M sought a declaration under s 30 of the LPA 1925 that she was entitled to a half share in both properties. *Held* that Miss M was entitled to a share of the Essex bungalow, but not of the Spanish bungalow. Waite J found that there had been an express agreement regarding the Essex bungalow, and that Miss M's willingness to support H's speculative ventures and her assistance in running the business constituted sufficient detrimental reliance to support her claims for an interest by way of constructive trust. There was no express agreement regarding the Spanish bungalow, however, and, as Lord Bridge stated in *Lloyds Bank plc v Rosset*, it is doubtful in such circumstances whether anything less than a contribution to the purchase price will be sufficient to support claims of a constructive trust. Waite J examined the facts and decided that Miss M's conduct 'fell a long way short' of justifying such an inference.

Equitable fraud

Note ───────────────────────────────────
There is always some degree of equitable fraud present when a constructive trust is implied (see Kevin Gray, *Elements of Land Law* (Butterworths, 1993, 2nd edn) pp 435-6). One party is usually seeking to go back on an original agreement or common intention. A constructive trust may also be implied against somebody other than a party to the original agreement when they have assisted in perpetrating the fraud (eg see *Peffer v Rigg* at 3.10) or when the they have agreed to honour the original agreement (eg see *Lyus v Prowsa Developments Ltd* also at 3.10).

Binions v Evans (1972) CA

Mrs E's husband had been employed for many years by the Tredegar Estate, which provided him with a cottage rent-free. After he died, the trustees of the estate entered into an agreement with the 79-year-old Mrs E that, if she kept her cottage in good repair and did not sublet it, she could live there rent-free for the remainder of her life as a tenant at will (see 7.6.1). Two years later the trustees sold the cottage to B expressly subject to Mrs E's tenancy agreement. The trustees accepted a lower price for the cottage because of Mrs E's occupation. Six months later B gave Mrs E notice to quit as a mere tenant at will. Mrs E contested B's claim for possession.

Held that possession should be denied. The Court of Appeal were unanimous in finding that Mrs E had a life interest in the property, but they differed as to the nature of that interest. The majority (Megaw and Stephenson LJJ) followed *Bannister v Bannister* (1948) and found Mrs E to be a tenant for life under the Settled Land Act 1925 (see above at 4.7). Lord Denning, however, decided that Mrs E was a contractual licensee (see below at 6.3.3) by virtue of her agreement with the Tredegar Estate. That contract may not have been capable of binding third parties, but 'suppose that the defendant did not have an equitable interest at the outset, nevertheless it is quite plain that she obtained one afterwards when the Tredegar Estate sold the cottage. They stipulated with the plaintiffs that they were to take the house 'subject to' the defendant's rights under the agreement. They supplied the plaintiffs with a copy of the contract: and the plaintiffs paid less because of her right to stay there. In these circumstances, this court will impose a constructive trust for her benefit ...'.

Q Do you prefer Lord Denning's conclusion or that adopted by Megaw and Stephenson LJJ? Consider whether Mrs E should have been given all the powers of a tenant for life under the SLA 1925.

Tinsley v Milligan (1994) HL
T and M jointly purchased a house which they ran as a lodging house. The house was registered in T's sole name in order that M could make fraudulent Social Security claims. When T and M quarrelled, T moved out and she brought an action asserting ownership of the property and seeking possession. M claimed that the house was held on resulting trust in equal shares, but T asserted that M could not claim beneficial ownership under a trust because of her fraudulent purpose. T claimed either that the maxim *ex turpi causa oritur non actio* should apply, or alternatively that equity should refuse to recognise the trust because 'he who comes to equity must come with clean hands'. T failed at first instance and the Court of Appeal refused to allow her appeal because she had collaborated in the illegality. She appealed to the House of Lords.

Held that M had an interest by way of resulting trust because of her contribution to the purchase of the property. She was able to assert her rights because she did not need to rely upon her own illegality in order to raise the presumption of resulting trust.

6.1.4 Rights acquired under resulting or constructive trusts may bind purchasers even though they have been created informally ...

... if they are not overreachable, and ...
(See 2.2.1; and *City of London Building Society v Flegg* (1988) at 3.9.)

... if the land is unregistered, the purchaser has notice, actual or constructive, of those rights; or ...
(See *Kingsnorth Finance Co Ltd v Tizard* (1986) at 2.2.3.)

... if the land is registered land, those rights are coupled with actual occupation and the purchaser either makes no enquiries of the possessor of those rights, or the rights are disclosed after such enquiry has been made.
(See the Land Registration Act 1925 s 70 (1) (g) at 3.6 and the cases in 3.6.3.)

6.2   Proprietary estoppel

Ramsden v Dyson (1866) HL

A yearly tenant believed that his landlord would grant him a new lease for 60 years, and he erected a building on the demised premises. The landlord refused to grant a 60-year lease and the tenant claimed to be entitled to the grant in equity.

Held that the tenant was yearly tenant. Lord Cranworth stated that if A builds on land belonging to B believing it to be his own, and if B is aware of the mistake but does not attempt to disillusion A, B will be prevented from asserting his legal title to the land. If B was allowed to assert his legal title he would be unjustly enriched at A's expense. In this case, however, the tenant did not build in the belief that he had an absolute right to the grant, and the landlord did not know that he was building under that mistaken belief. The tenant therefore 'cannot insist on refusing to give up the estate at the end of his term. It was his own folly to build'.

Willmott v Barber (1880) CA

W was the assignee of a lease and B was the lessor. The lease prohibited assignment of the lease without B's consent, but neither W nor B were aware of this. When B discovered that he had power to refuse consent he did so, and W sought to estop B from asserting his legal rights because he had allowed the lease to be assigned without informing W of his mistake.

Held in the Chancery Division that B should not be estopped from asserting his legal right because he was unaware of the fact that he had a power of consent at the time when the assignment was granted. Fry J identified five elements (known as the *Willmott v Barber* probanda) which must be present before the court will resort to estoppel. The five elements are: (i) the claimant must have made a mistake regarding his legal rights; (ii) the claimant must have expended some money or done some act on the strength of this belief; (iii) the owner of the land must know of his own right which is inconsistent with that claimed by the claimant; (iv) the owner must know of the claimant's mistaken belief; (v) the owner must have encouraged the claimant in his expenditure of money or performance of acts either directly or by abstaining from asserting his legal right. Only if these five elements are present will the degree of fraud be sufficient to estop the owner from asserting his legal right. The decision was upheld in the Court of Appeal.

Note ———

The *Willmott v Barber* probanda provided guidelines for the application of proprietary estoppel for the next 100 years. In recent years their importance has declined, but see *Matharu v Matharu* (1994) below.

Inwards v Baker (1965) CA

Young Mr Baker (B2) wanted to build a bungalow on a plot of land. Unfortunately, the plot of land was too expensive, and his father (B1) suggested that he build a larger bungalow on his (the father's) land. B1 and B2 each paid for half of the bungalow, which was mostly built by B2. B2 moved into the bungalow believing that he would be allowed to live there for as long as he wished. B1 died and the property vested in trustees for the benefit of somebody other than B2. The trustees claimed that B2 was a mere licensee and sought possession, which was granted at first instance. B2 appealed.

Held, allowing the appeal, that B2 should be allowed to remain in the property for life. Lord Denning MR found that B2 had a licence coupled with an equity which arose by way of estoppel. B2 had relied to his detriment on the assurance given by B1, who had been aware of his son's reliance. This interest would bind the trustees because 'I think that any purchaser who took with notice would clearly be bound by the equity.' (See also *Ives v High* at 2.2.3.)

Crabb v Arun District Council (1976) CA

Mr A owned a five and a half acre plot of land. His executors sold three and a half acres to the defendant council and two acres to the plaintiff, Mr C. Under the terms of the conveyances the council was to fence the boundary between their land and that retained by Mr C, and they were to leave an entrance at point A in order to provide access to Mr C's land. Mr C decided to divide his plot into two, plots A and B. Plot A was the front plot and had access to the road via point A, but plot B had no access other than via plot A. Mr C sought a further point of access and the council agreed to leave a gap in the fence at point B. The council fenced the boundary, leaving gaps at points A and B, and Mr C sold plot A without reserving any rights of access over it for plot B, which he retained. The council then shut up the access at point B, leaving plot B landlocked. Mr C protested and the council offered to provide an access at point B for £3,000. Mr C sought a declaration and an injunction, claiming that the council were estopped from denying his right of access and right of way. At first instance it was decided that the council could not be estopped because they did not know of Mr C's plans to sell plot A without reserving rights of access for himself. Mr C appealed.

Held that Mr C was entitled to rights of access and way without payment to the council. Scarman LJ relied upon the *Willmott v Barber* probanda and declared that the council were estopped from asserting their legal rights. Lord Denning adopted a more modern approach based upon detrimental reliance, and cited cases of promissory as well as proprietary estoppel. He stated that:

the judge also said that ... the defendants must have known that the plaintiff was selling the front portion without reserving a right of access for the back portion. I do not think this was necessary. The defendants knew that the plaintiff intended to sell the two properties separately and that he would need an access at point B ... Seeing that they knew of his intention – and they did nothing to disabuse him but rather confirmed it by erecting gates at point B – it was their conduct which led him to act as he did: and this raises an equity in his favour against them.

Pascoe v Turner (1979) CA

P bought a house for himself and Miss T to live in. He alone paid for the house and its contents, and the property was conveyed into his sole name. Eight years later P left Miss T for another woman but told Miss T that the house and everything in it were hers. He said that the transfer was in the hands of his solicitors. Miss T stayed on in the house, for which she purchased a gas fire and a cooker, installed a new sink, fitted carpets and bought curtains. A few years later, P and Miss T quarrelled and he gave her two months' notice to determine the 'licence'. At first instance the judge found both the house and its contents to have been gifts. P appealed.

Held that the contents of the house were gifts. The house could not be a gift because of the formality requirements of ss 52–54 of the Law of Property Act 1925 (see 1.5 above). Miss T was therefore a mere licensee, who could not, thought Cumming-Bruce LJ, claim a constructive trust because there was no common intention. However, P did make a promise to Miss T, and as a result of that promise she expended money on the property. P stood by and allowed her to act to her detriment, and he should therefore be estopped from asserting his legal rights to the property. In deciding the remedy, the court was aware that it should grant the minimum equity to do justice to the claimant. However, in this case a licence to occupy the property for life would give Miss T no protection against a purchaser without notice, and, considering the age of Miss T, and P's determination to evict her if at all possible, it was decided that P should convey the fee simple to her.

Greasley v Cooke (1980) CA

C, aged 16, went to work as a maid for Mr G in his house in 1938. She cohabited with one of G's sons from 1948 until the son died in 1975. C received wages for her duties only until G died in 1948, after which she continued to look after the house and the family, which included a mentally ill daughter. She was led to believe by the family that she could regard the property as her home for the rest of her life and she never asked for payment. After the son's death, C was given notice to quit. She refused to leave the house and possession proceedings were initiated by the family. C counterclaimed, seeking a declaration that she was entitled to occupy the property for the rest of her life because the family were estopped from asserting their legal rights. At first instance the family withdrew the claim, but, on the counterclaim the judge ruled that the burden was on C to prove that she had acted to her detriment on the promise made to her by the family. She had not discharged that burden: she could have chosen to remain in the property without payment in order to be with G's son, her lover, rather than because she relied on the promise. As C was unable to discharge the burden of proof, possession should be ordered. C appealed.

Held that once C had shown that she had relied upon the promise, there was a presumption that she acted to her detriment. The burden was on the family to prove otherwise. They did not appear at the hearing and therefore they could not discharge the burden. Lord Denning MR stated that the expenditure of money was not necessary in order for a claimant to have acted to their detriment. C's conduct in this case constituted sufficient detriment , and she should be allowed to remain in the house rent free for as long as she wished.

Taylor's Fashions Ltd v Liverpool Victoria Trustees Co Ltd (1982)

O Ltd owned the freehold of two shops, Nos 21 and 22, in a block. In 1948 they granted a lease of No 22 for 28 years to M, together with an option to renew for a further 14 years if M installed a lift. The option was not registered as a class C (iv) land charge. In 1949 the freehold reversion was sold to the defendants, who had notice of the option but were not aware at the time that it was void for want of registration. In 1958 M assigned their lease to the plaintiffs, T Ltd, who installed a lift. The defendants were aware of and acquiesced in the installation of the lift.

O Ltd, the original owners of the freeholds, became the tenants of No 21, subject to a break clause which entitled the defendants to determine the lease if T Ltd did not exercise their option. They also took a lease from the defendants of No 20, which also contained a break clause enabling the defendants to determine the lease should T Ltd not exercise the option on No 22. In 1976 T Ltd purported to exercise the option on No 22 and the defendants claimed that it was void for want of registration. As the option was void it could not be exercised, and the defendants, attempting to enforce the break clauses in the leases of Nos 20 and 21, sought possession of all three shops.

Held that the option was void because it had not been registered. T Ltd were not entitled to renew the lease on No 22 but the defendants were estopped from asserting their legal rights against O Ltd. Oliver J declined to apply the *Willmott v Barber* probanda, believing them to be relevant only to cases of unilateral mistake. He preferred to apply 'a very much broader approach which is directed at ascertaining whether ... it would be unconscionable for a party to be permitted to deny that which, knowingly or unknowingly, he has allowed another to assume to his detriment ...'. The fact that the defendants were not aware that the option was void when T Ltd installed the lift was only one of the factors to be taken into consideration: it did not mean that the defendants could not be estopped from asserting their legal rights. However, the defendants did not encourage

T Ltd in the belief that the option was valid, and T Ltd had not proved that the lift had been installed in the belief that it was valid. With regard to the break clauses on Nos 20 and 21 however, the defendants had represented to O that the option was valid and had encouraged O to incur expenditure in the belief that it was valid. The defendants should be estopped from exercising the break clauses.

Note

The approach adopted by Oliver J appears to have been followed in most modern cases, despite the fact that it was only a decision of the High Court. But see *Matharu v Matharu* (below) for a recent application of the *Willmott v Barber* probanda.

Baker v Baker (1993) CA

Mr B was a secure tenant of a council flat in Finchley. His son and daughter-in-law (the Bs) lived in Bath. It was agreed that B should provide the deposit for a house in Torquay in which all the Bs were to live. In return for providing the deposit, Mr B was to be allowed to reside rent-free in the house for as long as he wished. Mr B provided £33,950 and the balance (a similar amount) was provided by a mortgage on the property. Legal title to the house was to be held by the Bs alone. Mr B moved into the house but, because of domestic discord, left the house shortly afterwards. He claimed a beneficial interest in the house by way of resulting trust, or, alternatively, that an estoppel had been created in his favour. He had relied to his detriment on a promise that he was to be allowed to live in the property for as long as he wished. At first instance the judge ruled that Mr B had no proprietary interest but that he did have a right by virtue of an estoppel, and he awarded him £33,950. The Bs appealed.

Held that the presumption of resulting trust had been rebutted by the contrary intention that Mr B was only to have a right to live in the property for as long as he wished. There was no intention that he should have a share in the property. There was, however, an estoppel in Bs favour, but the award of £33,950, being the amount which would have been due to him by virtue of a resulting trust, was too much. The proper award should have been 'the minimum equity to do justice' and the case was remitted for assessment of the amount due to Mr B.

Matharu v Matharu (1994) CA

M1 owned two properties. He lived with his wife, his son (M2) his son's wife (Mrs M2), and their three children in one of the properties. M2 went to live with his mistress and Mrs M2 initiated divorce proceedings. Eventually M2 returned and the M2s moved into the other house owned by M1. Mrs M2 believed at all times that the house belonged to M2. M2 paid for extensive improvements to the house and paid M1's mortgage instalments when they became due. He also constructed a through-lounge and a kitchen/diner; installed central heating; replaced an old staircase; refurbished the cellar; removed two chimney breasts; replaced all the doors; and replaced the bathroom. In 1988 the M2's marriage broke down and Mrs M2 obtained an injunction excluding M2 from the house. M2 died in 1991 but Mrs M2 remained in the house with her three daughters. After the building society had informed her that M2 was not the legal proprietor of the house, Mrs M2 installed a modern kitchen in the property. The M1s then sold their house and went to live in Canada, but they returned in 1992. They sought possession of the house occupied by Mrs M2 and her three daughters. Mrs M2 claimed that she had assumed that the house was owned by M2, and that she had been encouraged in that belief by M1. At first instance it was held that Mrs M2 had no proprietary interest in the property but that she had an interest by way of proprietary estoppel. M1 appealed.

Held that Mrs M2 did not have a proprietary right in the property, but she had a right by way of proprietary estoppel. She was to be allowed to remain in the house for as long as she wished. Roch LJ used the *Willmott v Barber* probanda in order to assess whether M1 could be estopped from asserting his legal rights. He found that Mrs M2 had made a mistake as to her legal rights; she expended money in the faith of that mistaken belief; M1 knew of his legal right, which was inconsistent with M2's belief; M1 knew of Mrs M2's mistaken belief; and he encouraged Mrs M2 in her expenditure. He should therefore be estopped from asserting his legal rights.

Q Did Mrs Matharu expend money in reliance on her mistaken belief?

6.2.1   The remedy granted may extend from a licence to the entire fee simple
(See the cases above in 6.1.)

6.2.2   Estoppel and third parties

Note ————————————————————————————————

See Simon Baughen (1994) 14 Legal Studies 147. It appears that under certain circumstances both the benefit and the burden of the equity acquired under proprietary estoppel can pass to third parties. In unregistered land it appears that the equity may bind anybody who has notice of the right (see *Ives v High* at 2.2.3). Its status in registered land is more questionable. It has been suggested that the right may be protected as an overriding interest under s 70(1)(g) of the LRA 1925. It would certainly be difficult to enter it as a minor interest as it is uncertain whether the right exists until it is granted by the court. See Martin Dixon, *Lecture*

Notes on Land Law (Cavendish, 1994) p 212. For a detailed discussion of the nature of the equity, see Kevin Gray, *Elements of Land Law* (Butterworths, 1993, 2nd edn) pp 356-68.

Q Is estoppel a right or a remedy?

Q Is there any difference between a common intention constructive trust and proprietary estoppel? See the debate between David Hayton (1990) Conv. 370 and (1993) 109 LQR 485 and Patricia Ferguson (1993) 109 LQR 114.

Q Has estoppel replaced the doctrine of part performance since the coming into force of s 2 of the Law of Property (Miscellaneous Provisions) Act 1989? See Christine Davis (1993) 13 OJLS 99.

6.3   Licences

6.3.1   Bare licences

Wood v Leadbitter (1845)

W bought a ticket for one guinea entitling him to enter the grandstand at Doncaster racecourse. Because of W's conduct on a previous occasion, L, an employee of the steward of the course, ordered him to leave. W refused and was ejected by L, who used no more force than was necessary in the circumstances. W brought an action for assault and false imprisonment.

Held that W was a mere licensee, and, as such, once his licence was revoked he became a trespasser who could be ejected provided that the degree of force used was not excessive. Alderson B stated that 'a licence by A to hunt in his park, whether given by deed or by parol, is revocable; it merely renders the act of hunting lawful, which, without the licence, would have been unlawful'.

Note ———————————————————————

The modern view would be that W was a contractual licensee. Had W taken action on the contract however, his damages would have been nominal.

6.3.2   Licences coupled with an interest

Wood v Leadbitter (1845)

See above for the facts. Alderson B went on to assert that 'if the licence be ... a licence not only to hunt, but also to take away the deer when killed to his own use this is in truth a grant of the deer, with a licence annexed to come onto the land: and supposing the grant of the deer to be good, then the licence would be irrevocable by the party who had given it; he would be estopped from defeating his own grant, or act in the nature of a grant'.

James Jones & Sons Ltd v Earl of Tankerville (1909)

J entered into a contract for the sale of timber growing on T's land. By the contract J was to enter the land, cut the timber, saw it, and remove it. J erected a sawmill and began to remove the timber. T then repudiated the contract and ejected J and his men from the land. J sought damages and an injunction restraining T from preventing the execution of the contract. T claimed that such an injunction would be equivalent to an order of specific performance and should be refused, and that the permission to enter the land was a mere licence. They argued that the remedy should be restricted to damages.

Held that the injunction should be granted, and that J should be able to enter the land. Parker J stated that 'a licence to enter a man's property is *prima facie* revocable, but is irrevocable even at law if coupled with or granted in aid of a legal interest conferred on the purchaser, and the interest so conferred may be a purely chattel interest or an interest in realty'.

Note ───
When a profit *à prendre* is granted a licence may be implied. For example, if A grants B a profit to cut timber or peat from his land he must, provided that the grant is valid, also impliedly be giving him a licence to come onto his land in order to exercise the profit. Such a licence will be irrevocable throughout the period of the grant.

6.3.3 Contractual licences

Winter Garden Theatre (London) Ltd v Millennium Productions Ltd (1948) HL

W granted M a licence to use the Winter Garden Theatre for productions of plays, ballets etc for six months, together with an option to renew for a further six months. Thereafter M was to have a licence terminable by them on giving one month's notice. No provision was made for termination by W. More than three years after the initial agreement, W gave M one month's notice of termination. M sought a declaration that the licence was not revocable, or, if it was, that reasonable notice had to be given.

Held that reasonable notice had to be given in order to terminate the licence. However, M had failed to show that the notice given was unreasonable, and the notice was valid and effectual.

Chandler v Kerley (1978) CA

In 1972 Mr and Mrs K purchased a house for £11,000, raising £5,800 by way of mortgage. Mr K paid all the mortgage instalments. In 1974 the marriage broke down and Mr K moved out of the house, leaving Mrs K and their two children in the house. Mr K continued to pay the mortgage instalments. Mrs K then met C, who became her lover. In 1975 Mr K stopped paying the building society because he could not afford it, and it was decided to put the property up for sale because the building society was threatening to foreclose. Unfortunately, a buyer could not be found and the property was eventually sold to C for £10,000, nearly £5,000 below the original asking price. After the building society had been repaid Mr K took £1,800 of the proceeds and Mrs K took only £1,000, on the understanding that she was to be allowed to remain in the property for as long as she wished. The relationship between C and Mrs K came to an end within six weeks of C's purchase of the house, and Mrs K was given one month's notice of termination of her licence in April 1976. Mrs K claimed that she was either a tenant for life under the Settled Land Act (see above at 4.7) or a beneficiary under a constructive trust who was entitled to remain in the property for as long as she wished (see *Binions v Evans* at 6.1.3 above). At first instance the judge found there to be a constructive trust. C appealed.

Held, that Mrs K had a contractual licence terminable on reasonable notice, and that in the circumstances 12 months was reasonable notice. In the absence of an express promise, the plaintiff should not be saddled with the burden of housing another man's wife and children.

Contractual licences and third parties

King v David Allen & Sons, Billposting Ltd (1916) HL

K came to an agreement with DA that the latter should have exclusive rights to fix posters and advertisements on to the walls of a cinema which was to be built on K's property. In return for the right, DA were to pay £12 per annum for four years. K then leased the cinema to C, the lease containing no mention of the agreement with DA. C refused to allow DA to advertise on the walls of the cinema and DA brought an action for breach of the agreement.

Held that the agreement was merely a personal obligation; it was not an interest in the land. Therefore DA could claim damages in contract against K for breach of the agreement, but they could not enforce the agreement against C, who were not privy to the contract.

Errington v Errington and Woods (1952) CA

A father purchased a house in his own name for his son and daughter-in-law to live in. The purchase price was £750, £250 of which was provided by the father himself and £500 was raised by way of mortgage. He told the daughter-in-law that the £250 was a gift, but that the son and daughter-in-law had to pay the mortgage instalments. He promised to transfer the house into the names of his son and daughter-in-law when the mortgage had been repaid. The son went into occupation with his wife and they paid the mortgage instalments as they became due. The father died nine years later, before the mortgage had been repaid, and he left the property by will to his wife. The son then left his wife and went to live with his mother, but the daughter-in-law continued to make the mortgage repayments. The mother brought an action seeking possession against the daughter-in-law and her sister, who was also living in the property.

Held that the son and his wife were contractual licensees and that they could not be evicted as long as they continued to make the mortgage repayments. Denning LJ decided that the father's promise was a unilateral contract which could not be revoked once the son and daughter-in-law had begun to rely upon the promise and make the mortgage repayments. Once the mortgage had been repaid the couple would be entitled to have the property transferred to them in accordance with the agreement. 'They have acted upon the promise and neither the father nor his widow ... can eject them in disregard of it.'

Note

This decision was revolutionary in that the widow, a third party, was deemed to be bound by a contract to which she was not a party. The contractual licence in this case became effectively an interest in the land.

Q Denning LJ spoke of detrimental reliance on the promise. Would it be possible to infer an estoppel licence from these facts?

Q Would it be possible to infer a licence coupled with a constructive trust, as in *Binions v Evans* (see above at 6.1.3)? Was there any common intention? Did the widow take the property expressly subject to the agreement?

Ashburn Anstalt v Arnold & Co (1989) CA

C Ltd held the freehold of a shop which was leased to Mr Arnold, who sublet the property to Arnold & Co. Both the head lease and the sublease were assigned to M Ltd, subject to an agreement that Arnold & Co would be allowed to remain in the property rent-free until it received notice that M Ltd were ready to demolish and redevelop the property, whereupon Arnold & Co would be granted a lease of a shop on the redeveloped site.

M Ltd then assigned the benefit of these leases to C Ltd, thereby merging the leasehold with the freehold interest. C Ltd then sold the property to the Legal & General Assurance Society, who in turn sold it to the plaintiff, AA, subject to the agreement between Arnold & Co and M Ltd. AA sought possession on the grounds that the agreement was a contractual licence which did not bind them because they were not a party to the contract. A & Co claimed either to have a lease, which was binding by virtue of being an overriding interest under s 70(1)(g) of the Land Registration Act 1925; or, alternatively, following *Binions v Evans* (see above at 6.1.3), that AA took the freehold subject to the agreement and therefore a constructive trust should be implied. The judge at first instance found for A & Co. AA appealed.

Held that the agreement created a lease which was binding upon AA because of s 70(1)(g). Fox LJ was of the opinion that, had the agreement been only a contractual licence, AA would not have been bound by it. A contractual licence cannot, on its own, bind parties who are not privy to the contract. It is not an interest in the land and cannot be an overriding interest. A constructive trust should not be imposed automatically because AA took the property 'subject to' the agreement; the court must be satisfied that it would be unconscionable for the estate owner to assert his rights. There was no evidence that AA paid a lower price because of the agreement, and the obligation was not clearly expressed in the conveyance.

6.3.4 Estoppel licences
(See 6.2.)

6.4 Spousal rights of occupation

National Provincial Bank v Ainsworth (1965) HL
A was the registered proprietor of a house in which he lived with his wife and four children. He left his wife and mortgaged the house to the plaintiff bank, without telling them that he no longer lived in it. He later charged all his business property to the bank in order to raise more money. When the bank learned that A had left his wife and that Mrs A had initiated divorce proceedings they called in the debt. Mr A defaulted and the bank sought possession against Mrs A, who claimed to have an overriding interest by virtue of her deserted wife's equity coupled with actual occupation. The bank had made no enquiries of her, and therefore they were bound by her interest under the Land Registration Act 1925 s 70(1)(g). At first instance, Cross J decided that Mrs A's right was no more than a personal right which was enforceable against Mr A only. The Court of Appeal, however, upheld Mrs A's appeal and found that she had an overriding interest. The bank appealed.

Held that Mrs A had a personal right only. It was not an interest in the land and could not bind third parties.

> Note
> Following this decision, the Matrimonial Homes Act 1967 (now MHA 1983 below) was enacted. It enabled spouses to protect their right of occupation against third parties. Protection of the interest does not give an interest in the land, however, the usual effect of registration being to suspend dealings in the land pending a divorce settlement.

Matrimonial Homes Act 1983:
1. ...(1) Where one spouse is entitled to occupy a dwelling house by virtue of a beneficial estate or interest or contract or by virtue of any enactment giving him or her the right to remain in occupation, and the other spouse

is not so entitled, then, subject to the provisions of this Act, the spouse not so entitled shall have the following rights ...

(a) if in occupation, a right not to be evicted or excluded from the dwelling house or any part thereof by the other spouse except with the leave of the court given by an order under this section;

(b) if not in occupation, a right with leave of the court so given to enter into and occupy the dwelling house.

(2) So long as one spouse has rights of occupation, either spouse may apply to the court for an order –

(a) declaring, enforcing, restricting or terminating those rights; or

(b) prohibiting, suspending or restricting the exercise by either spouse of the right to occupy the dwelling house; or

(c) requiring either spouse to permit the exercise by the other of that right.

(3) On an application for an order under this section, the court may make such order as it thinks just and reasonable having regard to the conduct of the spouses in relation to each other and otherwise, to their respective needs and financial resources, to the needs of any children and to all the circumstances of the case ...

2. ... (4) Notwithstanding that a spouse's rights of occupation are a charge on an estate or interest in the dwelling house, those rights shall be brought to an end by –

(a) the death of the other spouse; or

(b) the termination ... of the marriage, unless in the event of a matrimonial dispute or estrangement the court sees fit to direct otherwise by an order made under section 1 above during the subsistence of the marriage ...

(8) Where the title to the legal estate by virtue of which a spouse is entitled to occupy a dwelling house ... is registered under the Land Registration Act 1925 or any enactment replaced by that Act –

(a) registration of a land charge affecting the dwelling house by virtue of this Act shall be effected by registering a notice under that Act; and

(b) a spouse's right of occupation shall not be an overriding interest within the meaning of that Act affecting the dwelling house notwithstanding that the spouse is in actual occupation of the dwelling house.

Note

1 See 2.2.2 for entry of a class F land charge in the Land Charges Register in unregistered land.

2 The Matrimonial Homes Act charge is an exception to the rule that the land or charge certificate must be produced in order to enter a notice on the register.

Wroth v Tyler (1974)

Mr T wished to move house upon his retirement, and he agreed to sell his bungalow to W. The day after he exchanged contracts Mrs T entered a Matrimonial Homes Act charge on the property without telling her husband, who learned of the charge via his mortgagee building society a few weeks later. Mrs T refused to remove her charge and W sought damages and/or specific performance with vacant possession.

Held that W was entitled to damages. Megarry J decided that he could not award specific performance with vacant possession (however see *Kaur v Gill* (1988)) without ordering Mr T to sue his wife. An order for specific performance subject to the rights of Mrs T would split up the Ts, and make W the legal proprietor of a house in which Mrs T was entitled to live.

Note ———————————————————

Because Mr T was unable to pay the damages awarded to W, he was declared bankrupt. His trustee in bankruptcy was able to remove Mrs T in order to sell the property with vacant possession.

6.5 Adverse possession

Land Registration Act 1925 s 75:

(1) The Limitation Acts shall apply to registered land in the same manner and to the same extent as those Acts apply to land not registered, except that where, if the land were not registered, the estate of the person registered as the proprietor would be extinguished, such estate shall not be extinguished but shall be deemed to be held by the proprietor for the time being in trust for the person who, by virtue of the said Acts, has acquired title against any proprietor ...

(2) Any person claiming to have acquired a title under the Limitation Acts to a registered estate in the land may apply to be registered as proprietor thereof.

(3) The registrar shall, on being satisfied as to the applicant's title, enter the applicant as proprietor either with absolute, good leasehold, qualified or possessory title, as the case may require ...

Note ———————————————————

The most appropriate title will often be possessory title, which may be upgraded to title absolute if the registrar is satisfied that there will be no adverse claims (see 3.4.3 and 3.4.4).

Limitation Act 1980 s 15(1):

No action shall be brought by any person to recover any land after the expiration of twelve years from the date on which the right of action accrued to him or, if it first accrued to some person through whom he claims, to that person.

Note

The 12-year limitation period is increased to 30 years in certain circumstances – eg when the action to recover land is brought by the Crown.

6.5.1 The principles of adverse possession

Powell v McFarlane (1977)

P claimed title to land by adverse possession because he had for many years grazed his cow on the land, cut the hay, repaired the fences and cut the brambles.

Held that on the facts he had not acquired title to the land by way of adverse possession. Slade J stated that the court will always presume that the person with the paper title is in possession of the land unless the person claiming the contrary can produce 'clear and affirmative evidence'. That evidence must show factual possession of the land, demonstrating 'a sufficient degree of exclusive physical control', and the intention to possess, or *animus possidendi*. He defined *animus possidendi* as 'the intention, in one's own name and on one's own behalf, to exclude the world at large, including the owner with the paper title if he be not himself the possessor, so far as is reasonably practicable and so far as the process of law will allow'.

6.5.2 The *animus possidendi*

Littledale v Liverpool College (1900)

D owned two fields. There was a hedged strip of land between the two fields which had also been conveyed to D. P had a right of way over the strip of land in order to get to his own field. More than 12 years before the action commenced P erected gates at both ends of the strip. He locked the gates and retained all keys. He claimed title to the land by way of adverse possession and sought to prevent D from trespassing on the strip. The action was dismissed at first instance and P appealed.

Held, dismissing the appeal, that the act of erecting and locking the gates was in its nature equivocal, and could have been done merely to protect his land from members of the public. There was no evidence that the gates had been erected in order to exclude D. Lindley MR stated that the adverse possessor must have 'the intention of excluding the owner as well as other people'.

Buckinghamshire County Council v Moran (1990) CA

In 1955 BCC purchased a plot of land which they intended to use for future road development. The plot was enclosed on three sides, but was open on the boundary with a house owned by X. X incorporated the plot into his garden, mowed the grass, planted flowers and trimmed the hedges. In 1971 M purchased the house 'with all such rights estate title and interests as the vendors may have in or over' the plot. M continued to use the plot as a garden, and he fitted a new lock on the gate. In 1975 BCC wrote to M asking him why he was exercising rights over the plot, to which M replied, in a 'without prejudice' letter, that he was keeping the land until the road was built. BCC did not claim possession until 1985. At first instance Hoffmann J found that the plot belonged to M by adverse possession. BCC appealed, claiming that M did not intend to own the land, but merely intended to keep it until the road was built. He therefore did not have the required *animus possidendi.*

Held that M had acquired title by adverse possession. Slade LJ considered *Littledale v Liverpool College* (above) and *Leigh v Jack* (below) and concluded 'that the court should be slow to make a finding of adverse possession in a case such as the present'. However, BCC's appeal should be dismissed because 'what is required for this purpose is not an intention to own or even an intention to acquire ownership but an intention to possess – that is to say, an intention for the time being to possess the land to the exclusion of all other persons, including the owner with the paper title'.

6.5.3 The intention of the paper owner

Leigh v Jack (1879) CA

L sold two plots of land to J. The plots were bounded by land upon which L proposed to build a road. For a period of over 20 years (which was then the limitation period), J had used the site of the proposed road to store factory materials. L had at some time within that 20-year period repaired a gate at one end of the proposed road. Mrs L, the plaintiff and tenant for life of L's property, sought to recover possession. J claimed title by adverse possession.

Held that Mrs L was entitled to recover possession of the land. Bramwell LJ found that, as L had no intention to use the land during the period in question, but merely intended 'to devote it at some future time to public purposes', J's actions were not inconsistent with L's rights.

Q Do you think that this decision should have been followed in Moran? Both Slade and Nourse LJJ felt able to distinguish the cases, because the plot had been totally enclosed in the later case. As Nourse LJ noted, if *Leigh v Jack* is followed rigidly, any owner may resist claims of adverse possession by claiming to have plans to develop the land at some time in the future.

6.5.4 Successive squatters

Mount Carmel Investments Ltd v Peter Thurlow Ltd (1988) CA

MC became the registered proprietor of mews property in 1962. The property was left empty and, in 1970, R forced entry into a garage in order to use it to store vintage cars. In 1971 R took possession of the rest of the premises. He purported to grant a lease of the property to K Ltd, a company of which he was a director. In 1974 K Ltd allowed PT into exclusive occupation of the property. When R's forgery was discovered he left the country, and all entries relating to the lease were removed from the register. MC eventually purchased R's rights in the property for £1. In 1981 MC demanded possession and, when PT refused to vacate the property, they brought proceedings in 1983. At first instance the judge dismissed the claim for possession but awarded damages for the period between 1981, when possession had been demanded, and October 1982, when he considered MC's title to have been extinguished by adverse possession. MC appealed, and PT cross-appealed, claiming that MC were not entitled to damages.

Held, dismissing the appeal and allowing the cross-appeal, that the letter demanding possession in 1981 was insufficient to terminate PT's possession. MC would either have to re-enter the property or bring proceedings within the limitation period to do that. Time began to run the moment that R took possession in 1970 and continued with PT's possession. Once MC's title had been extinguished they could not then claim rent or damages in trespass for the period of adverse possession.

6.5.5 The squatter must not acknowledge the paper owner's title

Edginton v Clark (1964) CA
E occupied a vacant bombed site from 1947 until 1961, when C entered the site as weekly tenants of the freeholders and dispossessed him. E brought an action for trespass, claiming to have acquired title to the site by adverse possession. C produced two letters offering to purchase the site which E had written to the freeholder in 1954. At first instance the judge decided that the letters were an acknowledgement of the freeholders' title and E had not occupied the land for 12 years before or after the acknowledgement. E appealed.

Held, dismissing the appeal, that when an intending purchaser offers to purchase land he is not acknowledging that the vendor has good title to that land. However, he is acknowledging that the vendor's title is better than his own, and that is all that is required to defeat a claim of adverse possession.

Note ———
On the theory behind adverse possession and relativity of title see Kevin Gray, *Elements of Land Law* (Butterworths, 1993, 2nd edn) pp 286-311.

Colchester Borough Council v Smith (1992) CA
T had occupied land owned by CBC for more than 12 years. He claimed title to the land by adverse possession. The council denied the claim, but

offered him a tenancy of the land. T accepted the tenancy, which included a clause stating that T had no title to or interest in the land other than the tenancy. T failed to pay the rent agreed and the council re-entered the land, where they discovered a group of travellers claiming to be T's licensees. The council sought a declaration that it was the freehold owner of the land and that T had no interest in it other than under the tenancy agreement. T claimed that he had already acquired title to the land by the time the purported tenancy agreement was granted. At first instance Ferris J found that, because of the tenancy agreement, T was estopped from asserting a claim by way of adverse possession. T appealed.

Held, dismissing the appeal, that even though T's title would, under normal circumstances be indefeasible and CBC's title could not be revived, T had taken legal advice and entered into a *bona fide* agreement with the council. He should be estopped from litigating the antecedent dispute.

6.5.6 Adverse possession and leasehold property

Fairweather v St Marylebone Property Co Ltd (1963) HL

X was the freehold owner of two adjoining properties, Nos 311 and 315. He built a shed across the boundary between the two properties. Three-quarters of the shed was situated in the garden of No 315, and the rest, including the entrance, was in the garden of No 311. In 1893 both properties were let by separate leases for 99 years. M became the sublessee of No 311; he treated the shed as his own, making minor repairs etc, and it was accepted that he had acquired title to the shed by adverse possession in 1932. In 1951, M sublet No 311 and the shed for 21 years, and the sublease was eventually assigned to F in 1960. M acquired the freehold to No 311 in 1958, and SMPCL acquired the freehold to No 315 subject to the 99-year lease the following year. The lessees of No 315 surrendered their lease to SMPCL shortly afterwards, and SMPCL sought possession of No 315, including the land occupied by the shed. F claimed that SMPCL were not entitled to possession until the 99-year lease had expired.

Held that SMPCL were entitled to possession. M had acquired title by adverse possession against the tenant of No 315. That would entitle M to remain in possession for the remainder of the tenant's leasehold term. However, as the lease had been surrendered, the leasehold title merged with the freehold and the freeholder was entitled to immediate possession.

Q There has been much criticism of this decision because, although the landlord's reversion is not affected by title acquired by adverse possession against his tenant, in this case the landlord was surely claiming possession through the tenant's 99-year lease. Do you think that the freeholder should have been entitled to possession of the land occupied by the shed?

Spectrum Investment Co v Holmes (1981)

In 1902, a 99-year lease was granted by the owner of a house. The lease was registered and was transferred to D in 1944, subject to an oral monthly sub-tenancy which had been created in 1939. The subtenant offered rent to D's solicitors but the rent was not accepted, and the subtenant remained in occupation, without paying rent, from 1944 until she died in 1951. Her daughter, H, continued to reside in the property without paying rent. S Ltd acquired the freehold in 1957, and in 1968 H applied to the Land Registry to be registered as the proprietor of the leasehold interest with possessory title (see 3.4.3). The Registry notified D of H's application, but received no response. They accordingly closed D's title and opened a new title in H's favour. In 1975 D purported to surrender the remainder of her interest to S Ltd, who sought to regain possession, or alternatively to have the register rectified in favour of D.

Held that D's title had been closed at the Land Registry and she was no longer the registered proprietor of the leasehold interest. The surrender was therefore void because she had no leasehold term to surrender. Rectification was available neither to S Ltd nor to D because the Registrar had acted in accordance with his mandatory duty under the LRA 1925 s 75 (see above at 6.5). S Ltd were not entitled to possession until the end of the leasehold term.

Q Does this decision mean that the surrender will be valid if the land is unregistered but invalid if it is registered? Browne-Wilkinson J did not deal with the question directly in *Spectrum v Holmes*.

6.5.7 Adverse possession and registered land

Land Registration Act 1925 s 75:
(See 6.5.)
The adverse possessor may register his title at the Land Registry by way of first registration. The original title will be extinguished.

Land Registration Act 1925 s 70(1)(f):
(See 3.6.)
The adverse possessor's rights are protected as an overriding interest before registration. Until the adverse possessor's title is registered the paper owner holds the estate on trust for the adverse possessor (LRA 1925 s 75(1) above at 6.5).

Land Registration Act ss 82–83:
Disputes regarding adverse possession may cause claims to be made for rectification of the register (see 3.7, especially *Chowood v Lyall (No 2)* (1930) and *Spectrum v Holmes* (1981), above at 6.5.6). Similarly, claims may be made for an indemnity (see 3.8 and Re *Chowood's Registered Land* (1933)).

Q Do we still need adverse possession? See Martin Dockray (1985) Conv 272.

7 Leases

7.1 Definition of a lease

Law of Property Act 1925 s 1(1)(b):
(See 1.4.1.)
A lease, or tenancy, or term of years absolute, is the second legal estate.

Law of Property Act 1925 s 205 (1) (xxvii):
'Term of years absolute' means a term of years (taking effect either in possession or in reversion whether or not at a rent) ... either certain or liable to determination by notice, re-entry, operation of law, or by a provision for cesser on redemption, or in any other event (other than the dropping of a life, or the determination of a determinable life interest) ... and in this definition the expression 'term of years' includes a term for less than a year, or for a year or years and a fraction of a year or from year to year ....

7.2 Creation of leases

7.2.1 Legal leases

Legal leases for more than three years must be created by deed

Law of Property Act 1925 s 52(1):
(See 1.5.1.)

Legal leases for three years or less may be created by parol

Law of Property Act 1925 s 54(2):
Nothing in the foregoing provisions of this Part of this Act shall affect the creation by parol of leases taking effect in possession for a term not exceeding three years (whether or not the lessee is given power to extend the term) at the best rent which can reasonably be obtained without taking a fine.

Legal assignments must be by deed

Crago v Julien (1992) CA
Mr J had been the weekly tenant of a flat since 1966. When Mr and Mrs J divorced in 1982 he gave a written undertaking to do everything necessary

to transfer the tenancy to Mrs J, who stayed in the flat. In 1987 Mrs J asked the managing agents to change the name on the rent book to her own. They refused and advised the landlord, Mrs C, to serve notice to quit and seek possession. Mrs J refused to leave the flat, arguing that, as the lease could be created by parol, it had been validly assigned. Mrs C claimed that Mr J was the tenant, and, as he was no longer living in the flat, he could not claim protection under the Rent Act 1977. The purported assignment of the lease to Mrs J was invalid because it did not comply with the formality requirements of the Law of Property Act 1925 s 52.

Held that the assignment was not valid. The exemption in s 54(2) applied to the creation of leases for three years or less, not to assignments of those leases.

7.2.2 Equitable leases

Note ──

The term 'equitable lease' is in one sense a misnomer. It is not a lease at all, but merely a contract for a lease. For most purposes the contract will be as good as the lease itself because equity may grant specific performance of the contract.

Walsh v Lonsdale (1882) CA

L agreed in writing to grant W a lease of a mill for seven years, the rent to be payable in advance if demanded. No deed was executed. W went into possession and paid rent quarterly in arrears for three years. When W failed to pay, L demanded one year's rent in advance. W did not pay and L distrained (ie seized goods in satisfaction of the debt). W brought an action for illegal distress and specific performance of the agreement. L claimed that the agreement for the lease created an equitable lease under the terms of the agreement and that he had a right to distrain under that agreement. W claimed that, as he had paid rent by reference to the year and that rent had been accepted, he was a legal yearly tenant, and that the rent did not have to be paid in advance.

Held that the landlord was entitled to distrain. Sir George Jessel MR thought that there were two possible tenancies, the legal yearly tenancy and the equitable tenancy under the agreement. He decided that 'there is only one court and equity rules prevail in it. The tenant holds under an agreement for a lease. He holds, therefore, under the same terms in equity as if the lease had been granted'.

Note ──

Thus the rule in *Walsh v Lonsdale*, by which a contract to convey a legal lease, easement or mortgage effectively creates an equitable lease, easement or mortgage. The rule is dependent upon specific performance of the contract, however.

Contracts created before 27 September 1989 should be evidenced in writing or by some act of part performance.

Law of Property Act 1925 s 40:
(See 1.5.3.)

Contracts created after 26 September 1989 should be in writing, incorporating all the terms expressly agreed, and signed by each party to the contract.

Law of Property (Miscellaneous Provisions) Act 1989 s 2:
(See 1.5.3.)

Tenancies by estoppel

Church of England Building Society v Piskor (1954) CA
P contracted to buy a leasehold house and was allowed into possession before completion. Two months later he purported to grant a weekly subtenancy to A. He completed the assignment of the lease to himself shortly afterwards, obtaining a mortgage at the same time from the plaintiff building society. A further sublet the property to X, who was entitled to the protection of the Rent Acts. When P defaulted on the mortgage the building society sought possession, claiming that the purported grant by P to A created an estoppel which was binding upon P only. He could not grant a valid tenancy because he did not own the legal estate at the time of the purported grant, and by the time he obtained the legal estate it was already mortgaged to the plaintiffs, who would not be bound by A's (and therefore X's) tenancy. The defendants claimed that the estoppel was 'fed' by the conveyance of the legal estate to P and that it was therefore binding upon the plaintiffs.

Held that there was a *scintilla temporis* between completion and charge during which the estoppel could be fed, and that the plaintiffs should not be entitled to possession.

Note ───────────────────────────────
This case was considered to be wrongly decided in *Abbey National Building Society v Cann* (1991) HL (see 3.6.3), when it was declared that there is no *scintilla temporis* between completion and charge.

7.3   Protection of leases

7.3.1   Legal leases

Note ───────────────────────────────
As legal leases are rights *in rem* they do not require protection in unregistered land.

Legal leases for a term in excess of 21 years are registrable as titles in their own right

Land Registration Act 1925 s 2(1):
(See 3.4.)

Legal leases for 21 years or less are overriding interests

Land Registration Act 1925 s 70(1)(k):
(See 3.6.)

7.3.2   Equitable leases

Equitable leases of unregistered land may be registered as estate contracts (Class C (iv) Land Charge)

Land Charges Act 1972 s 2(4):
(See 2.2.2.)

Equitable leases of registered land are minor interests and should be protected by notice or caution on the register. If not so protected and the lessee is in actual occupation the lease may be an overriding interest.

Land Registration Act 1925 ss 3 and 70(1)(g):
(See 3.5 and 3.6.)

7.4   Statutory protection for periodic tenants

Landlord and Tenant Act 1954, Part II:

> Note
> Commercial tenants receive some protection under this Act. Landlords may only terminate a tenancy in accordance with the Act and a tenant may apply to the court if the landlord refuses to grant a renewal of the tenancy without adequate grounds.

Protection from Eviction Act 1977 s 5(1):
... no notice by a landlord or a tenant to quit any premises let ... as a dwelling shall be valid unless –
(a) it is in writing and contains such information as may be prescribed; and

(b) it is given not less than 4 weeks before the date on which it is to take effect.

Note ⎯⎯⎯⎯⎯⎯⎯⎯⎯⎯⎯⎯⎯⎯⎯⎯⎯⎯⎯⎯
Similar rules apply to licences (s 5 (1A)). This modifies the common law rules which state that the notice required is one full term, or six months in the case of a yearly tenancy. If the property concerned is a dwelling, even weekly tenants must be given four weeks' notice.

Rent Act 1977:

Note ⎯⎯⎯⎯⎯⎯⎯⎯⎯⎯⎯⎯⎯⎯⎯⎯⎯⎯⎯⎯
Most private-sector residential tenancies created before 15 January 1989 gained protection from the Rent Acts. If a landlord terminated the contractual tenancy by serving notice to quit, the tenant became a statutory tenant and could only be evicted by order of the court. The landlord had to establish one of the statutory grounds. Rents were also regulated by the Rent Acts, which did not apply to licences. The lease/licence distinction was therefore of crucial importance to landlords who wished to regain possession of their property.

Housing Act 1985:

Note ⎯⎯⎯⎯⎯⎯⎯⎯⎯⎯⎯⎯⎯⎯⎯⎯⎯⎯⎯⎯
This Act applies to public-sector tenancies and licences. It provides secure tenants with security of tenure on similar terms to that provided by the Rent Acts.

Agricultural Holdings Act 1986:

Note ⎯⎯⎯⎯⎯⎯⎯⎯⎯⎯⎯⎯⎯⎯⎯⎯⎯⎯⎯⎯
Limited statutory rights of security of tenure are conferred by this Act on agricultural tenants. The tenant may *inter alia* acquire a right to renew his lease.

Housing Act 1988:

Note ⎯⎯⎯⎯⎯⎯⎯⎯⎯⎯⎯⎯⎯⎯⎯⎯⎯⎯⎯⎯
Most private sector residential tenancies created after 14 January 1989 are subject to this Act. The assured tenant under this Act has rights similar to those conferred by the Rent Acts, but rents are not regulated. Landlords may now grant an assured shorthold tenancy (s 20(1)) provided that the tenancy is for a term of six months or longer and they serve notice on tenants in the prescribed form at the start of the tenancy. The landlord is entitled to possession at the end of the term of the

assured shorthold tenancy. Because landlords are now able to grant assured shorthold tenancies, the lease/licence distinction has become less important than it was under the Rent Acts.

7.5 Essential characteristics of a lease

Street v Mountford (1985) HL

For the facts, see 7.7 below. Lord Templeman stated that to 'constitute a tenancy the occupier must be granted exclusive possession for a fixed or periodic term certain in consideration of a premium or periodic payments'.

Note ───

There are three elements: exclusive possession; for a term certain; and at a rent or premium.

Prudential Assurance Co Ltd v London Residuary Body (1992) HL

For the facts, see 7.5.2 below. Lord Templeman defined 'demise for years' as 'a contract for the exclusive possession and profit of land for some determinate period'.

Q Why was rent necessary in *Street v Mountford* but not in the above case? See 7.5.3.

7.5.1 Exclusive possession ...

Addiscombe Garden Estates Ltd v Crabbe (1958) CA

C, the owner of tennis courts and a club house, granted to A a 'licence' to use the premises for two years in consideration of monthly payments. After the two years had expired A claimed the right to renew the tenancy under the Landlord and Tenant Act 1954. C claimed that the agreement was a 'licence' agreement and that there was no mention of the words landlord or tenant.

Held that the agreement created a tenancy. Jenkins LJ stated that 'the whole of the document must be looked at'. The agreement contained covenants, and exclusive possession was granted for a certain term. It was therefore a lease.

Note ───

Denial of the element of exclusive possession became the chief method by which landlords sought to evade the provisions of the Rent Act 1977. See the lease/licence distinction below at 7.7.

7.5.2 ... for a term certain ...

Lace v Chantler (1944) CA

Premises were subleased 'furnished for duration' at a weekly rent. The landlord served a valid notice to quit the weekly letting, but the tenant claimed to have a tenancy for the duration of the war.

Held that a tenancy for the duration of the war could not be created.

Note _____

A tenancy for an uncertain term was created in *Ashburn Anstalt v Arnold* (1989) (above at 6.3.3) but the case has been overruled on this point.

Prudential Assurance Co Ltd v London Residuary Body (1992) HL

The Greater London Council (GLC) acquired land which it intended to use for widening Walworth Road. In the meantime, the Council allowed the previous owner of the land to remain in occupation at an annual rent until the land was needed for redevelopment. The council later decided not to widen the road. When the GLC was dissolved its property passed to the LRB, and the original owner sold his 'lease' to P Ltd. The LRB served notice to quit on P Ltd and sold the land. P Ltd claimed to have a tenancy which could not be determined until the road was required for widening.

Held that the purported lease was void because its duration was uncertain. However P Ltd held on a yearly tenancy because they had paid rent and it had been accepted on that basis. Lord Templeman distinguished between an uncertain term and a right to determine the lease on the happening of a specified event:

A lease can be made for five years subject to the tenant's right to determine if the war ends before the expiry of five years. A lease can be made from year to year subject to a fetter on the right of the landlord to determine the lease before the expiry of five years unless the war ends. Both leases are valid because they create a determinable certain term of five years.

Law of Property Act 1922 s 145 and Schedule 15 para 5:

5. A grant ... of a term, subterm, or other leasehold interest with a covenant or obligation for perpetual renewal ... shall ... take effect as a demise for a term of two thousand years or in the case of a subdemise for a term less in duration by one day than the term out of which it is derived ....

Law of Property Act 1925 s 149(3):

A term, at a rent or granted in consideration of a fine, limited after the commencement of this Act to take effect more than twenty-one years from the date of the instrument purporting to create it, shall be void, and any contract made after such commencement to create such a term shall likewise be void ....

Law of Property Act 1925 s 149(6):
Any lease or underlease at a rent, or in consideration of a fine, for life or lives or for any term of years determinable with the life or lives, or marriage of the lessee, or any contract therefor ... shall take effect as a lease, underlease or contract therefor, for a term of ninety years determinable after the death or marriage (as the case may be) of the original lessee ....

7.5.3 ... at a rent or premium

Law of Property Act 1925 s 205(1)(xxvii):
(See 7.1.)
'Term of years' is defined as 'whether or not at a rent'.

Ashburn Anstalt v Arnold (1989) CA
See 6.3.3. A lease was created which did not involve the payment of rent or a premium.

> Note ─────────────────────────────────
> Rent is however necessary in order that residential tenants may claim protection under the Rent Act 1977 or the Housing Act 1988. For this reason it was important in *Street v Mountford* (see below at 7.7), but not in *Ashburn* or *Prudential Assurance* (above at 7.5.2).

Bostock v Bryant (1990) CA
Mr J lived with the Bryant family in a house that he owned. Mr J lived in one room and he paid the rates. The Bryants paid the gas and electricity bills. When Mr J died his executor sought to terminate the Bryants' occupation by notice. The Bryants claimed to have a tenancy which was protected under the Rent Acts.
Held that the payment of the bills did not constitute rent, which should be a quantified money payment rather than a fluctuating sum.

> Note ─────────────────────────────────
> Rent may be paid goods or services, but it must have a certain monetary value.

7.6 Categories of people who may not be tenants even if they have exclusive possession

7.6.1 Tenants at will

Javad v Aqil (1991) CA
A needed somewhere to store the stock for his leather goods business, and he entered into negotiations for a lease with J. J allowed A to go into possession of premises on payment of £2,500, being one quarter's rent in

advance, although the terms of the lease had not been fully agreed. A paid two further quarters' rent whilst negotiations continued. The parties were unable to agree the terms of the lease and J gave A two weeks' notice to quit. A refused to leave, claiming to be a periodic tenant by virtue of having offered rent ,which was accepted by J. Such a tenancy would be subject to the Landlord and Tenant Act 1954. J sought possession, which was granted at first instance. A appealed.

Held that A was a mere tenant at will. A tenancy at will is determinable by either party without notice. J was therefore entitled to possession. As Nicholls LJ stated: 'Entry into possession while negotiations proceed is one of the classic circumstances in which a tenancy at will may exist.'

Q Does this decision take into account the nature of a business tenancy? If A had retained exclusive possession for 10 years, paying rent quarterly, would he still have been a tenant at will? See Stuart Bridge (1991) 50 CLJ 232.

7.6.2 Tenants at sufferance

Wheeler v Mercer (1957) HL
Mrs M was the quarterly tenant of business premises. After the term of her tenancy ended she remained in occupation without paying rent while negotiations for a further tenancy agreement proceeded.

Held that Mrs M was neither a licensee nor a tenant at sufferance, but a tenant at will because she was in possession with the consent of the landlord. The tenant at sufferance, on the other hand, holds over at the end of the leasehold term 'without either the agreement or disagreement of the landlord' (*per* Viscount Simonds). Both classes of occupier may be evicted at will, however, and W was entitled to possession.

7.6.3 Service occupiers

Facchini v Bryson (1952) CA
An employer let his assistant into exclusive occupation of a house, at a weekly rent. The assistant did not occupy the house for the better performance of his duties, but the agreement stated that 'nothing in this agreement shall be construed to create a tenancy between the employer and the assistant'. The employer sought to terminate the licence, and the assistant claimed to have a tenancy.

Held that it was a 'service tenancy', and the employer could only obtain possession in accordance with the Rent Restriction Acts. Denning LJ declared that:

> in all cases where an occupier has been held to be a licensee there has been something in the circumstances, such as a family arrangement, an act of friendship or generosity, or such like to negative any intention to create a tenancy

[these have become known as the *Facchini v Bryson* categories] ... the occupation has all the features of a secure tenancy, and the parties cannot by the mere words of the contract turn it into something else. Their relationship is determined by the law and not by the label which they choose to put on it.

Norris v Checksfield (1991) CA

C occupied a bungalow belonging to N, his employer, under a licence agreement which stated that his licence would terminate when his employment ended. A weekly deduction of £5 per week was made from his wages in order to pay for his occupation. It was a condition of his occupation that he would drive coaches for his employer and apply for a PSV licence. When N found out that C was a disqualified driver, he dismissed C and sought possession of the bungalow. C claimed that he had exclusive possession for a term at a rent and that he was therefore a tenant.

Held that if the employee is genuinely allowed into occupation of premises by his employer for the better performance of his duties he is a service occupier and therefore a licensee.

7.6.4 The '*Facchini v Bryson* categories' – occupation based upon acts of charity, generosity or friendship

Marcroft Wagons Ltd v Smith (1951) CA

A was the tenant, with Rent Act protection, of a house from 1901 until his death in 1938. His widow and daughter continued to live in the house after his death, until Mrs A died in 1950. After Mrs A died, the daughter, S, requested that her name be put on the rent book and that the tenancy be transferred to her. B, the agents for the landlord, refused, on the grounds that the landlord, M Ltd, required the property for one of their employees. B then accepted two weeks' rent from S, saying that he did not wish to disturb her. S remained in possession, paying rent, for about six months. S claimed to have a tenancy on the grounds that she had exclusive possession and weekly rent had been offered and accepted.

Held that no tenancy had been created. Sir Raymond Evershed MR thought that the landlord had shown 'ordinary human instincts of kindliness and courtesy', and he said: 'I should be extremely sorry if anything which fell from this court were to have the result that a landlord could never grant to a person in the position of the defendant any kind of indulgence, particularly in circumstances ... when the defendant had just lost her mother.'

Heslop v Burns (1974) CA

Mrs B worked for T in his office. They became friends and T purchased a house for Mr and Mrs B to live in. They subsequently moved to two other houses owned by T, who used to visit daily for meals. T paid the rates and maintained the premises. He told Mrs B that the property would be hers after his death. T issued a rent book and, although no rent was paid, included the 'rent' in his tax returns. T died in 1970 and his executors sought possession of the house. Mrs B argued that she entered the house as a tenant at will and had acquired title by way of adverse possession. The judge at first instance accepted Mrs B's contention and the executors appealed.

Held that there was never any intention to create the legal relationship of landlord and tenant. Therefore Mrs B entered the property as a licensee rather than as a tenant at will. The licence could be revoked by the executors.

Westminster City Council v Clarke (1992) HL

C occupied a self-contained bed-sitting-room in a hostel for single homeless men. He signed a licence agreement to occupy the room, and the agreement contained clauses stating that he could be required to move to another room without notice and that he could be required to share a room. The resident warden had a key to the room. WCC sought to terminate his licence because of C's unacceptable conduct. C accepted that he had only a licence but claimed that his licence was secure under the Housing Act 1985 because he had exclusive occupation of his room. The trial judge ordered possession but C appealed. The Court of Appeal expressed reservations but, following *Family Housing Association v Jones* (1990), felt bound to give judgment for C. WCC appealed.

Held, allowing the appeal, that C was akin to a lodger and should not be given security of tenure. Lord Templeman considered that a tenancy or a licence with exclusive occupation was inconsistent with the council's statutory duty under the Housing Acts and therefore 'Mr Clarke has never enjoyed that exclusive possession which he claims'.

7.6.5 Provision of services

Otter v Norman (1989) HL

O let a room to N. O provided a continental breakfast in a communal dining room. When O sought to evict N, N claimed that he had a protected tenancy under the Rent Act 1977. It was accepted that the provision of services by a landlord would preclude a tenancy, and that tenancies which included 'board' were excluded from Rent Act protection. However, in this case it was argued that the board provided was *de minimis*. Both the judge at first instance and the Court of Appeal found for the landlord. The tenant appealed.

Held that any amount of board that was not *de minimis* was sufficient to exclude a tenancy from statutory protection. In this case, the provision of a continental breakfast, together with the crockery and cutlery with which to consume it, was not *de minimis*.

People who have a resident landlord but share common parts of a house are exempted or partially exempted from the protection of the Rent Acts or Housing Acts. Such people were termed 'lodgers' by Lord Templeman in *Street v Mountford* (at 7.7 below).

7.7   The lease/licence distinction

Somma v Hazelhurst and Savelli (1978) CA
H and Miss S signed separate but identical licence agreements with the owner of a house. They shared a double bed-sitting-room and each was severally liable for their own rent. The licence agreement stated that the licensor was not willing to grant exclusive possession of any part of the rooms and that the use of the rooms was to be 'in common with the licensor and such other licensees as the licensor may permit to use the said rooms'.

Held that H and S were licensees. Cumming-Bruce LJ could 'see no reason why an ordinary landlord ... should not be able to grant a licence to occupy an ordinary house'. The agreement was clearly stated to be a licence, and a licence was what the parties intended to create. The landlord clearly had no intention of exercising his right to share occupation of the bed-sitting-room with the couple, but Cumming-Bruce LJ could not see 'any reason why their common intentions should be categorised as bogus or unreal or as sham merely on the ground that the court disapproves of the bargain'.

Note
This approach of looking at the expressed intention of the parties was a marked contrast to the approach of Denning LJ in *Facchini v Bryson* at 7.6.3.

Street v Mountford (1985) HL
Mrs M rented a single furnished room from S at a weekly rent. The 'licence' agreement gave S the right to enter the room for any reasonable purpose and concluded with the words 'I understand that a licence in the above form does not and is not intended to give me a tenancy protected under the Rent Acts'. Mrs M made an application to have a fair rent registered under the Rent Act 1977 and S, relying upon *Somma v Hazelhurst* (above), sought a declaration that Mrs M was only a licensee. The recorder at first instance found for Mrs M, but his decision was reversed by the Court of Appeal. Mrs M appealed.

Held that Mrs M was a tenant. Lord Templeman, disapproved of the decision in Somma, and thought that the court should 'be astute to detect and frustrate sham devices and artificial transactions whose only object is to disguise the grant of a tenancy and to evade the Rent Acts'. If a landlord grants exclusive possession for a term at a rent s/he has granted a lease, regardless of the label the parties give to the agreement:

If the agreement satisfies all the requirements of a tenancy, then the agreement produced a tenancy and the parties cannot alter the effect of the agreement by insisting that they created only a licence. The manufacture of a five-pronged implement for manual digging results in a fork even if the manufacturer, unfamiliar with the English language, insists that he intended to make and has made a spade.

Hadjiloucas v Crean (1988) CA

Two single ladies, C and B, signed two separate agreements to rent a two-bedroomed flat with bathroom and kitchen. Both agreements stated that the licensee was to share with one other person and, if one lady terminated her agreement, the owner could require the other to share the flat with a stranger. Both ladies were individually responsible for the whole rent of the flat. A few months later, B left the flat and arranged, without consulting C, for R to take her place. R remained in the flat for six months before leaving. C had a fair rent assessed by the rent officer and the landlord sought possession. The judge at first instance found that the agreement created a licence because exclusive possession had not been granted. C appealed.

Held that if the ladies applied for and obtained exclusive occupation, they had a joint tenancy which remained protected until one of the agreements was terminated. Purchas LJ suspected that the reservation by the owner to require the 'licensee' to share with a stranger might have been, at the time of the grant, a clause by which neither party intended to be bound, and that it was really a smoke-screen to cover the real intentions of the parties. A retrial was ordered in order that all of the facts might be investigated.

Hilton v Plustitle (1988) CA

H owned a number of high-quality flats which he let only to companies in order to avoid problems with the Rent Acts. Miss R saw H's advertisement for company flats and offered to rent one of them. H refused, but gave her the name of his accountant, who could help her to form a company. Miss R took legal advice and decided to buy a company, which she called Plustitle. H and Miss R had a dispute regarding the rent, and H sought possession. Miss R claimed that the letting to a company was a sham and that she was therefore a tenant. At first instance the judge ordered possession and Miss R appealed.

Held that the agreement created a company let. Croom-Johnson LJ found that Miss R had taken legal advice and went into the agreement knowing the full implications of a company let. 'Unlike *Street v Mountford* the transaction did represent the true position. The company obtained a protected tenancy with the benefits attached to that but neither it nor Miss

Rose obtained a statutory tenancy when the protected tenancy came to an end.' The transaction 'was deliberately intended to avoid, but not to evade, the Rent Acts'.

Note ——————
Even if a company let is a tenancy, it will not be subject to Rent Act or Housing Act protection. It will be subject to the Landlord and Tenant Act 1954.

Stribling v Wickham (1989) CA

S was the freehold owner of a flat, which he let to three occupiers, one of whom was W. Each occupant signed a separate licence agreement in identical terms and each paid their own share of the monthly rent. They each occupied a bedroom and shared a living room, kitchen and bathroom. At the end of licence period the three licensees refused to leave and S sought possession. At first instance it was found that the respondents had a tenancy which was protected under the Rent Act 1977. S appealed.

Held that the occupiers were licensees. Parker LJ, applying *AG Securities v Vaughan* (below – *Vaughan* was heard before *Stribling* but reported later), found that there could not be joint tenancy of the property. 'Each licensee had a specific obligation to pay the amount reserved by his own agreement only. In my judgment, there is no process of "legal alchemy" by which the agreements can be placed into the mould of a tenancy.' He stated that in order to determine whether a lease or a licence has been created it is necessary to look at the nature and extent of the accommodation provided; the relationship between the sharers; the intended and actual mode of occupation; and the course of negotiations.

Mikeover Ltd v Brady (1989) CA

B and Miss G occupied M Ltd's flat. They signed two separate but identical licence agreements. They both paid £86.66 per month. Miss G moved out of the property after two years, but B remained in occupation, paying £86.66 per month. He fell into arrears and M Ltd sought, and at first instance obtained, possession. B appealed, claiming that the two agreements together created a joint tenancy and that he was protected by the Rent Act 1977.

Held that B was a licensee. Slade LJ considered that the four unities (see 5.4.1) were not present. Had a joint tenancy been granted, B would have been responsible for paying Miss G's share when she left. He considered that

> unity of interest imports the existence of joint rights and joint obligations. We therefore conclude that the provisions for payment contained in these two agreements (which were genuinely intended to impose and did impose on each party an obligation to pay no more than the sums reserved to the plaintiffs by his or her separate agreement) were incapable in law of creating a joint tenancy,

because the monetary obligations of the two parties were not joint obligations and there was accordingly no complete unity of interest ... Every case where the question of lease or licence arises must depend upon its own facts.

Antoniades v Villiers (1990) HL

A let an attic flat, which consisted of a bed-sitting-room, a kitchen, and a bathroom, to V and Miss B. They shared a double bed and 'at all material times were living together as man and wife' (per Lord Oliver). V signed a licence agreement, and Miss B signed a separate but identical agreement on the same day. Under the agreements, each assumed individual responsibility for one half of the total rent. The agreement contained a clause which allowed the licensor, or any persons nominated by him, to use the rooms along with the licensees, and another which stated that the flat was for single people. If V married any occupant of the flat his 'licence' was terminated. The Court of Appeal found that V and Miss B were licensees. They appealed.

Held, allowing the appeal, that V and Miss B were tenants. Lord Templeman applied the test he had used in *Street v Mountford* (see above). He looked at what had been created in reality, considering the surrounding circumstances and the relationship between the occupiers. It appeared that exclusive possession for a term at a rent had been granted, notwithstanding any terms to the contrary in the agreement: 'The parties cannot contract out of the Rent Acts.' Lord Oliver observed that:

the premises are not suitable for occupation by more than one couple, save on a very temporary basis ... There is an air of total unreality about these documents read as separate individual licences in the light of the circumstances that the appellants were together seeking a flat as a quasi-matrimonial home ... The unreality is enhanced by the reservation of the right of eviction without court order, which cannot seriously have been thought to be effective, and by the accompanying agreement not to get married ....

The terms were, applying the test used by Purchas LJ in *Hadjiloucas* (see above), sham provisions which had been inserted in order to evade the Rent Acts.

Note

This decision appears to conflict with the principle of *Mikeover v Brady*, which was in fact heard after (but reported before) *Antoniades*. According to *Mikeover*, it would appear that, as V and Miss B were liable only for their own share of the rent, they should have been licensees. However, in *Mikeover*, B was genuinely responsible for his own share, and he had been allowed to remain in the flat paying the same amount of rent as he had paid before Miss G left. In *Antoniades* the issue was addressed by Lord Oliver, who considered that he could not presume a licence based upon the expressed liability for rent because such presumptions 'rest upon the assumption that the licences are not sham documents, which is the very question in issue'.

AG Securities v Vaughan (1990) HL

AG Securities owned a block of flats. Flat No 25 consisted of six rooms plus a bathroom and a kitchen. Four of the rooms were bedrooms and the other two were furnished as a lounge and a sitting room. AG let the flat to four individuals who each had one bedroom, but shared the other rooms. The individual occupants each entered into separate 'licence' agreements in the same form, and each agreement contained a clause stating that exclusive possession had not been granted. Each occupier was responsible for his/her own rent, and, when one individual vacated the flat AG advertised the vacancy and installed another occupant. The occupants therefore all came to the flat at different times and paid differing rents. The Court of Appeal (Sir George Waller dissenting) found the occupiers to be tenants. AG appealed.

Held, allowing the appeal, that the agreements created four separate licences. Lord Oliver stated that 'the facts in this appeal are startlingly different from those in the case of Antoniades'. He stated that, in order for a joint tenancy to exist, the four unities (see 5.4.1) must be present. In this case, the four tenants came to the flat at different times, and had paid differing rents under totally separate agreements. 'Each person is individually liable for the amount which he has agreed, which may differ in practice from the amounts paid by all or one of the others ... For my part I agree with the dissenting judgment of Sir George Waller in finding no unity of interest, no unity of title, certainly no unity of time and, as I think, no unity of possession.'

Aslan v Murphy (No 1) (1990) CA

A owned a small basement room which he let to M. The agreement stated that A would retain the keys to the room, and that he had an absolute right of entry at all times. The agreement further claimed that A did not grant exclusive possession of any part of the room, and that M had no rights of occupation at all between the hours of 10.30 and 12 noon each day. A sought to evict M and obtained an order for possession. M appealed.

Held, allowing the appeal, that a tenancy had been created. Lord Donaldson noted that the judge at first instance had decided the case before the House of Lords' decision in *Antoniades* (above). The judge accordingly erred in taking the agreement at face value, rather than looking to the substance of the agreement. He should have asked whether

the provisions for sharing the room and those depriving the defendant of the right to occupy it for 90 minutes out of each 24 hours were part of the true bargain between the parties or were pretences. Both provisions were wholly unrealistic and were clearly pretences ... It is not a requirement that the occupier shall have exclusive possession of the keys. What matters is what underlies the provisions as to the keys.

7.8   Leasehold covenants

7.8.1   Contractual liability of the original tenant throughout the term of the lease

City of London Corporation v Fell (1993) HL
In 1976 Wilde Sapte & Co (WS) leased premises from the CLC for a term of 10 years. The lease contained a number of covenants, one of which was to pay rent. In 1979 WS assigned the lease to G Ltd. When the term of the lease had expired on 24 March 1986 G Ltd remained in occupation under the provisions of Part II of the Landlord and Tenant Act 1954. G Ltd went into liquidation and surrendered the lease to the landlords, owing rent amounting to £33,460.64 in respect of the period between 24 March 1986 and 22 January 1987. The landlords sought to recover the rent from WS on the grounds that they were liable on the covenant for the whole term of the lease. The judge at first instance found in favour of WS and the Court of Appeal dismissed the appeal. The landlords appealed.

Held that WS were not liable for G Ltd's failure to pay rent. Lord Templeman found that

> Wilde Sapte are not contractually bound to pay the landlords any rent for the period after 24 March 1986 because Wilde Sapte only contracted to pay rent until that date.' From that date, when the lease terminated, G Ltd held as tenants under the Landlord and Tenant Act 1954 and not under the lease. There were no provisions in the 1954 Act under which WS could be made liable, otherwise the effect would be 'to compel Wilde Sapte to pay £33,460.64 which Wilde Sapte never covenanted to pay in respect of an estate in land which Wilde Sapte never enjoyed.

Note ——————
The original tenant, if liable on the covenant, may be able to recover from the present lessee under the rule in *Moule v Garrett* (1872) or from the person to whom he directly assigned the lease under the Law of Property Act 1925 s 77.

Note ——————
The Landlord and Tenants (Covenants) Act 1995 abolishes privity of contract for leases granted after 1 January 1996. A tenant will no longer be liable on covenants after he has assigned the lease.

Privity of estate

Spencer's Case (1583)
Spencer and his wife leased land to S. He covenanted on behalf of himself,

his executors and administrators that he, his executors, administrators, or assigns would build a brick wall on the land. S assigned the lease to J, who assigned it to C. The question arose as to whether C was liable on the covenant to build.

Held that C was not liable on the covenant. C was not liable because the wall was a thing *in posse* (not yet in existence) and the covenant was not expressed to have been made on behalf of S's assigns. (the difference between things *in posse* and things *in esse* is no longer important – LPA 1925 s 79(1), below). More important are the rules which were stated regarding the running of leasehold covenants. It was stated that the covenants would pass on assignment provided that they touched and concerned the land and that privity of estate existed between the landlord and the assignee.

Law of Property Act 1925 s 78 (1):

A covenant relating to any land of the covenantee shall be deemed to be made with the covenantee and his successors in title and the persons deriving title under him or them, and shall have effect as if such successors and other persons were expressed ... For the purposes of this subsection in connexion with covenants restrictive of the user of land 'successors in title' shall be deemed to include the owners and occupiers for the time being of the land of the covenantee intended to be benefited.

Law of Property Act 1925 s 79(1) and (2):

(1) A covenant relating to any land of a covenantor or capable of being bound by him, shall, unless a contrary intention is expressed, be deemed to be made by the covenantor on behalf of himself his successors in title and the persons deriving title under him or them, and, subject as aforesaid, shall have effect as if such successors and other persons were expressed ... (2) For the purpose of this section in connection with covenants restrictive of the user of land 'successors in title' shall be deemed to include the owners and occupiers for the time being of such land.

The covenant must 'touch and concern' the land

P & A Swift Investments v Combined English Stores Group (1989) HL

An assignee covenanted to pay rent, and the covenant was guaranteed by a surety. Obviously the tenant was liable on the covenant because the covenant to pay rent touched and concerned the land, but the question was whether the surety could similarly be held liable.

Held that the surety was liable on the covenant. Lord Templeman considered that 'a surety for a tenant is a quasi-tenant who volunteers to be a substitute or twelfth man for the tenant's team and is subject to the same rules and regulations as the player he replaces. A covenant which runs with the reversion against the tenant runs with the reversion against the surety'. Lord Oliver formulated rules which, though not exhaustive, provide a 'satisfactory working test' for determining whether a covenant touches and concerns the land:

(1) the covenant benefits only the reversioner for time being, and if separated from the reversion ceases to be of benefit to the covenantee; (2) the covenant affects the nature, quality, mode of user, or value of the land of the reversioner; (3) the covenant is not expressed to be personal (that is to say neither being given only to a specific reversioner nor in respect of the obligations only of a specific tenant); (4) the fact that a covenant is to pay a sum of money will not prevent it from touching and concerning the land so long as the three foregoing conditions are satisfied and the covenant is connected with something to be done on, or in relation to the land.

7.8.2 The benefit of the landlord's covenants

Law of Property Act 1925 s 141(1):
Rent reserved by a lease, and the benefit of every covenant or provision therein contained, having reference to the subject-matter thereof, and on the lessee's part to be observed or performed, and every condition therein contained, shall be annexed and incident to and shall go with the reversionary estate in the land, or any part thereof, immediately expectant on the term granted by the lease, notwithstanding severance of that reversionary estate, and without prejudice to any liability affecting a covenantor or his estate.

Note
The benefits of all covenants which touch and concern the land (ie those 'having reference to the subject matter' of the lease) are transferred to the assignee of the reversion. Privity of estate is not necessary, though this will usually be required in order to transfer the burden to the assignee of the lease.

7.8.3 The burden of the landlord's covenants

Law of Property Act 1925 s 142(1):
The obligation under a condition or of a covenant entered into by a lessor with reference to the subject matter of the lease shall, if and as far as the lessor has power to bind the reversionary estate immediately expectant on the term granted by the lease, be annexed and incident to and shall go with that reversionary estate, and may be taken advantage of and enforced by the person in whom the term is from time to time vested by conveyance, devolution in law, or otherwise; and, if and as far as the lessor has power to bind the person from time to time entitled to that reversionary estate, the obligation aforesaid may be taken advantage of and enforced against any person so entitled.

Note ───
The burden of all covenants which touch and concern the land will be transferred to the assignee of the reversion. Privity of estate is not necessary, though the assignee of the lease will usually need to prove privity in order to transfer the benefit of the covenant to himself.

───

7.8.4 Equitable leases and assignments

Purchase v Lichfield Brewery Co (1915)
P purported to grant a 15-year lease to L. The purported grant was not under seal and therefore it did not create a legal estate. The grant took effect in equity as a specifically enforceable agreement for a lease. The agreement included a provision that L should not assign the lease without the consent of the landlord. L assigned his interest by way of mortgage to LBC, who never went into possession. When L failed to pay the rent, P sued LBC for it.

Held that LBC were not liable for the rent. Lush J stated that 'it is impossible that specific performance of a contract can be decreed against a person with whom there is neither privity of contract nor privity of estate.'

Note ───
Although an equitable lease does not create a legal estate, the benefit of covenants may be expressly assigned. Also, it may be possible to run the burden of restrictive covenants under the rule in *Tulk v Moxhay* (1848) (see 9.3.2).

───

7.8.5 Subtenants

Tulk v Moxhay (1848)
See 9.3.2. There will obviously be no privity of estate between the original landlord and subtenants. Restrictive covenants may be enforced provided that the burden runs under the rule in *Tulk v Moxhay*. This will only apply to negative covenants, however.

7.8.6 Landlord's remedies for breach of covenant

Forfeiture – provided that the lease contains a right of re-entry

Common Law Procedure Act 1852 ss 210 and 212:
210. In all cases between landlord and tenant, as often as it shall happen that one half year's rent shall be in arrear, and the landlord or lessor has a right by law to re-enter for the non-payment thereof, such landlord or lessor shall and may, without any formal demand or re-entry, serve a writ in ejectment for the recovery of the demised premises ... if it shall be made

appear to the court where the said action is depending ... that half a year's rent was due before the said writ was served, and that no sufficient distress was to be found on the demised premises ... then and in every such case the lessor shall recover judgment and execution, in the same manner as if the rent in arrear had been legally demanded, and re-entry made ...
212. If the tenant or his assignee do or shall, at any time before the trial ... pay or tender to the lessor or landlord ... or pay into the court ... all the rent and arrears, together with the costs, then ... all further proceedings on the said ejectment shall cease and be discontinued ...

Law of Property Act 1925 s 146:
(1) A right of re-entry or forfeiture under any proviso or stipulation in a lease for a breach of any covenant or condition in the lease shall not be enforceable ... unless and until the lessor serves on the lessee a notice –
  (a) specifying the particular breach complained of; and
  (b) if the breach is capable of remedy, requiring the lessee to remedy the breach; and
  (c) in any case, requiring the lessee to make compensation in money for the breach;
and the lessee fails, within reasonable time thereafter, to remedy the breach, if it is capable of remedy, and to make reasonable compensation in money, to the satisfaction of the lessor, for the breach.
(2) Where a lessor is proceeding, by action or otherwise, to enforce such a right of re-entry or forfeiture, the lessee may ... apply to the court for relief; and the court may grant or refuse relief, as the court, having regard to the proceedings and conduct of the parties under the foregoing provisions of this section, and to all the other circumstances, thinks fit; and in case of relief may grant it on such terms, if any, as to costs, expenses, damages, compensation, penalty, or otherwise including the granting of an injunction to restrain any like breach in the future, as the court ... thinks fit ...
(4) Where a lessor is proceeding by action or otherwise to enforce a right of re-entry or forfeiture under any covenant, proviso, or stipulation in a lease, or for non payment of rent the court may, on application by any person claiming as under-lessee any estate or interest in the property comprised in the lease or any part thereof ... make an order vesting, for the whole term of the lease or any part thereof in any person entitled as under-lessee to any estate or interest in such property upon such conditions as to execution of any deed or other document, payment of rent, costs, expenses, damages, compensation, giving security, or otherwise, as the court in the circumstances of each case may think fit, but in no case shall any such under-lessee be entitled to require a lease to be granted to him for any longer term than he had under his original sublease ...
(11) This section does not, save as otherwise mentioned, affect the law relating to forfeiture or relief in case of non-payment of rent.

Protection from Eviction Act 1977 s 2:

Where any premises are let as a dwelling on a lease which is subject to a right of re-entry or forfeiture it shall not be lawful to enforce that right otherwise than by proceedings in the court while any person is lawfully residing in the premises or part of them.

Supreme Court Act 1981 s 38(1):

In any action in the High Court for the forfeiture of a lease for non-payment of rent, the court shall have power to grant relief against forfeiture in a summary manner, and may do so subject to the same terms, and conditions as to the payment of rent, costs or otherwise as could have been imposed by it in such an action immediately before the commencement of this Act.

Rugby School (Governors) v Tannahill (1935) CA

The governors of RS leased premises to X, who, with the consent of the governors, sublet the property to T. The lease contained a covenant that the premises would not be used for illegal or immoral purposes and there was a proviso for re-entry on breach of covenant. T was convicted for knowingly allowing the premises to be used as a brothel, and the governors served notice to quit under s 146 of the LPA 1925 (see above). The notice, however, did not require the lessee to remedy the breach, nor did it require her to pay compensation for the breach. T argued that the notice was ineffective because it did not comply with s 146(1)(b) and (c). The judge at first instance found breaches of negative covenants to be incapable of remedy, and gave judgment for the governors. T appealed.

Held that the breach was incapable of remedy and that the landlords had no need to request compensation if they did not require it. Greer LJ doubted the judges assertion that all breaches of positive covenants are incapable of remedy. However, in this particular case, he could 'not conceive how a breach of this kind can be remedied. The result of committing the breach would be known all over the neighbourhood and seriously affect the value of the premises'.

Glass v Kencakes Ltd (1966)

K Ltd leased premises from G. The lease contained a covenant to use the premises for residential purposes only. K Ltd assigned the lease to WL Ltd, who sublet part of the premises to D. D allowed two of the flats to be used for prostitution, and G served notice to quit under s 146 (above) upon K Ltd, WL Ltd, and D. WL Ltd, who had no knowledge of the breach until the notice was served, themselves then served notice on D, who evicted the prostitutes. No evidence was produced to show that the property had depreciated in value or had acquired a bad reputation.

Held that WL Ltd's (and also K Ltd's) breach was innocent and had been remedied within a reasonable time. The notice served upon D, however, was effective because D's breach was incapable of remedy.

Billson v Residential Apartments Ltd (1992) HL

B were the landlords of premises which had been assigned to RAL. Despite the fact that the lease contained a covenant against alterations without the consent of the landlords, RAL began major works of reconstruction. B served notice on RAL under the Law of Property Act 1925 s 146(1) (see above), but RAL continued the work. Because RAL failed to remedy the breach, the landlords, exercising their right of re-entry, peaceably re-entered the premises and changed the locks. They then posted a notice on the door to the effect that the lease had been forfeited. Later the same day, RAL's workmen broke into the premises and regained possession for the tenants. B sought possession and the tenants counterclaimed for relief under s 146(2) (above).

At first instance the judge decided that the court did not have jurisdiction to grant relief because the landlord had already recovered possession, and was therefore not 'proceeding, by action or otherwise, to enforce such a right of re-entry or forfeiture' for the purposes of s 146(2). The Court of Appeal upheld the decision and RAL appealed.

Held, allowing the appeal, that until the landlord obtained an order for possession he was still 'proceeding' to enforce his rights. RAL's application for relief was remitted to the judge.

Distress for rent arrears

Note ——————————————————————————————————
Distress is the ancient right of a landlord to enter the demised premises and seize the tenant's goods in satisfaction of rent arrears. For an example, see *Walsh v Lonsdale* (1882) at 7.2.2. See also Kevin Gray, *Elements of Land Law* (Butterworths, 1993, 2nd edn) pp 839–43.

Action for arrears of rent

Note ——————————————————————————————————
The landlord may sue for a maximum of six years' rent. If the tenancy has been determined and the tenant remains in possession, the landlord may sue for *mesne* profits. See Gray, *op cit*, pp 844–5.

Action for damages

Note ——————————————————————————————————
This is available for breaches other than the non payment of rent. See Gray, *op cit*, pp 843–4.

Injunction

Note

This is a discretionary remedy and is not available to enforce covenants to repair.

7.8.7   Tenants' remedies for breach of covenant

Action for damages

Note

'The object of awarding damages against a landlord for breach of his covenant to repair is not to punish the landlord but, so far as money can, to restore the tenant to the position he would have been in had there been no breach' (*per* Griffiths LJ in *Calabar Properties Ltd v Stitcher* (1984)).

Injunction or specific performance

Note

The court has discretion to order an injunction to prevent a threatened breach of covenant by the landlord. Specific performance may be available for breach of a repairing obligation. See *Jeune v Queens Cross Properties* (1974), *per* Pennycuik V-C.

Retention of rent to pay for repairs or equitable set-off

Note

Although a tenant does not have a general right to withhold rent for breach of covenant, tenants have resorted to such action. Since *Lee-Parker v Izzet* (1971) it has been accepted that a tenant may undertake repair work himself and deduct the cost from the rent if the landlord is in breach of a repairing covenant. A receiver may also be appointed by the court if the property is neglected.

Eller v Grovecrest Investments Ltd (1995) CA

E complained of acts of nuisance and breach of covenant by the landlord, G Ltd. E then withheld rent and the landlord distrained on E's goods. The tenant signed a walking possession agreement and applied for an *ex parte* injunction to restrain the landlord on the grounds that he was entitled to set off his claim for damages and breach of covenant. At first instance, the injunction was granted, but the landlord's appeal was allowed in the High Court. E appealed.

Held, allowing the appeal, that the injunction should be restored. The tenant was entitled to set of the amount of the cross-claim for damages against the landlord's claim to levy distress for rent arrears.

7.9 Termination of leases

7.9.1 ... by effluxion of time

Note

A lease ends when the term of the lease expires. However, the tenant may have a right to renew the lease either by agreement or by virtue of rights conferred by statute (see 7.4).

7.9.2 ... by forfeiture

See 7.8.6.

7.9.3 ... by notice to quit

Note

This will terminate the tenancy at common law; if the tenancy is protected by statute a court order will be required to terminate the statutory tenancy. See 7.4, especially the Protection from Eviction Act 1977 s 5(1) with regard to the length of notice required for residential properties. The lease may also contain a break clause.

7.9.4 ... by surrender

Note

This occurs when a tenant surrenders his lease to the landlord, who accepts the surrender.

7.9.5 ... by merger

Note

Merger occurs when the tenant acquires the landlord's reversion or when a third party acquires both the lease and the reversion. The leasehold and freehold estates are merged into one.

7.9.6 ... by disclaimer

Note

Disclaimer occurs when the tenant denies his landlord's title and thereby disclaims the lease.

7.9.7 ... by enlargement

Law of Property Act 1925 s 153(1) and (8):
(1) Were a residue unexpired of not less than two hundred years of a term, which, as originally created, was for not less than three hundred years, is subsisting in land, whether being the whole land originally comprised in the term, or part only thereof ... the term may be enlarged into a fee simple in the manner, and subject to the restrictions in this section provided ...
(8) The estate in fee simple so acquired by enlargement shall be subject to all the same trusts, powers, executory limitations over, rights, and equities, and to all the same covenants and provisions relating to user and enjoyment, and to all the same obligations of every kind, as the term would have been subject to if it had not been so enlarged.

7.9.8 ... by frustration

National Carriers Ltd v Panalpina (Northern) Ltd (1981) HL
In 1974 NC leased to P a warehouse for a term of 10 years. In 1979 the local council closed the road which provided the only means of access to the warehouse, because the warehouse opposite was in a dangerous condition. The road was closed for a period of 20 months and the warehouse was, throughout this period, useless to P. P did not pay rent from the time that the road was closed, claiming that the lease was frustrated, and NC sued. At first instance it was thought that the doctrine of frustration could not apply to a lease. However, leave was given for P to appeal directly to the House of Lords under the Administration of Justice Act 1969 s 12.

Held, dismissing the appeal, that the lease was not frustrated. It was decided that the doctrine of frustration could apply to leases, but in this case a loss of under two years out of a total of 10 years, though severe for P, was not sufficient to frustrate the lease. The loss did not alter significantly the nature of the rights and obligations that had been contemplated by the parties at the time of the initial grant.

8 Easements and profits *à prendre*

8.1 Essential characteristics of an easement

Re Ellenborough Park (1956) CA

In 1855 D and W owned the White Cross Estate, which included Ellenborough Park. They divided up the estate into plots which were sold for building. To the purchasers of plots in Ellenborough Crescent, which adjoined the park, D and W granted rights which included, *inter alia*, rights of 'full enjoyment at all times hereafter in common with the other persons to whom such easements may be granted of the pleasure ground ... in the centre of the square called Ellenborough Park'. Similar rights were granted to purchasers of plots which did not adjoin the park but were within 150 yards of it. The rights were 'subject to the payment of a fair and just proportion of the costs and expenses of keeping in good order and condition the said pleasure ground'. In 1879, WHD purchased the unsold parts of the estate, including Ellenborough Park. He died in 1889 and his estate vested in the trustees of his will.

Between 1941 and 1946 the park was requisitioned by the War Office, who subsequently paid almost £2,000 compensation because of dilapidations. The trustees took out a summons asking, *inter alia*, whether the owners of the houses had any right to use the park, and whether they were therefore entitled to a share of the compensation awarded by the War Office. The trustees argued that the rights could not be easements because such rights did not accommodate the dominant tenements. The right was purely recreational and was akin to permission to use a zoological garden free of charge or to attend Lord's Cricket Ground without payment. It was also argued that the right was incapable of forming the subject matter of a grant. Danckwerts J found for the occupiers of the houses, and the trustees appealed.

Held, dismissing the appeal, that the plaintiffs were entitled to compensation. Evershed MR stated the four general characteristics of an easement from *Cheshire's Modern Real Property*, 7th edn. The characteristics are: (i) there must be a dominant and a servient tenement; (ii) the easement must accommodate the dominant tenement; (iii) the dominant and servient owners must be different persons; and (iv) the right must be capable of forming the subject matter of a grant. He considered that, although a right to use a park may be a mere personal licence, in this case the use of the park in common with the other residents created a 'garden (albeit [a] communal garden) of the houses to which its enjoyment is annexed'. Therefore it did accommodate the dominant tenements. Similarly, although a *jus spatiandi* (a right to wander at large) could not be granted as an easement, the right in question here was 'the provision for a limited number of houses in a uniform crescent of one single large but private garden'. There was no reason why it could not be the subject matter of a grant.

8.1.1 There must be a dominant and a servient tenement

Ackroyd v Smith (1850)
A and S owned two adjoining plots of land. A's predecessor in title had granted to one of S's predecessors in title a right to use a road across his land 'for all purposes' to the 'owners and occupiers' of the land, and to 'all persons having occasion to resort thereto'. S claimed to have an easement.
Held that the right was too 'ample' to be an easement, and was therefore a mere licence. Cresswell J said that 'a right unconnected with the enjoyment or occupation of the land cannot be annexed as an incident to it ... If a way be granted in gross (ie not appurtenant to land), it is personal only, and cannot be assigned.'

Note ──
Profits, on the other hand, may be either appurtenant to land or in gross.

Q Should it be possible to grant easements in gross?

London & Blenheim Estates Ltd v Ladbroke Retail Parks Ltd (1994) CA
In 1987 L Ltd transferred land to L&B together with any easements and other rights over retained land specified in a schedule to the transfer. Included was a right to park cars on any part of the retained land which had been set aside as a car park. The schedule provided that any land owned by L&B or which L&B had contracted to purchase could enjoy the benefit of the easements and other rights if notice was given within five years of the transfer. In 1988 L Ltd sold the retained land to W Ltd. Meanwhile, L&B had contracted to purchase additional land adjoining the retained land, and they served notice upon W Ltd that they wished to enforce the easement in favour of the land which they were about to acquire. W Ltd sold the retained land to LRP later in 1988, and L&B completed the purchase of the additional land in 1989. L&B sought a declaration that they were entitled to the benefit of the easements specified in the initial transfer of 1987. At first instance the judge, following the unreported case of *Newman v Jones* (1982), declared that a right to park cars could exist as a valid easement provided that the exercise of that right would not leave the servient owner without any reasonable use of any part of his land. However, he found for the defendants on the grounds that the

plaintiffs did not own the dominant tenement at the time of the grant. L&B appealed.

Held, dismissing the appeal, that the dominant tenement had to exist and be identified at the time of the grant. Peter Gibson LJ stated that 'I would hold ... that the grant of the right to nominate land as the dominant tenement did not create an interest in land which bound successors in title to the servient tenement and ... no interest in land binding successors in title to the servient tenement arose on the acquisition of the additional land by the plaintiff.'

8.1.2 The easement must accommodate the dominant tenement

Hill v Tupper (1863)

The proprietors of Basingstoke Canal Navigation leased premises on the banks of the canal to H. The lease gave him 'the sole and exclusive right or liberty to put or use boats on the said canal, and let the same for hire for the purposes of pleasure only'. T, the landlord of an inn on the canal bank, also put boats onto the canal. H claimed to have an easement.

Held that H was a licensee only. The right to put boats on to the canal did not accommodate the land. It was therefore a personal right which was binding only upon the proprietor of the canal.

Moody v Steggles (1879)

A house and an adjoining public house had once been owned by the same person. The house was eventually conveyed to S, and the public house was eventually acquired by M. There was a sign on the house which advertised the public house, and M claimed a right to keep it there. There was no express reservation of this right in the conveyance of the house, but evidence showed that the sign had been in place for over 40 years. S claimed that M had no right leave the sign on the house because such a right did not accommodate the land.

Held that M had an easement. The advertisement related to the business carried on in the public house. The public house was used for no other purpose, and therefore the sign did more than merely benefit the user of the public house for the time being. The right was more or less connected with the land and, as it had been used for 40 years, a grant of the easement by S's predecessor in title to M's predecessor in title must be assumed under the doctrine of lost modern grant.

Re *Webb's Lease* (1951) CA

W was the head lessee of three-storey premises. He had a butcher's shop on the ground floor and sublet the upper two storeys to the plaintiff. One side of the building contained an advertisement for W's business, and the other side contained an advertisement for Bryant & May's matches. There had been no express reservation of an easement. The plaintiff issued a summons to determine whether W had a right to use the walls for advertising purposes. At first instance Danckwerts J held that W had acquired an easement. The plaintiff appealed.

Held, allowing the appeal, that W had no right to an easement without an express reservation. Jenkins LJ stated that, in the absence of express terms, a reservation would only be implied in the event of necessity, or if it was the common intention of the parties at the time of the grant that such a right should be reserved. It was clearly not necessary for W to have the advertisement for his shop, and the advertisement for the matches did not accommodate the dominant tenement:

> it cannot in my view be contended that the maintenance during the term of the lease of his advertisement over the door was a necessary incident of the user so contemplated. This applies *a fortiori* to the 'Brymay' advertisement, the display of which on the outer wall of the demised premises ... was so far as I can see not related in any way to the to the use or occupation of the ground floor for the existing or any other purposes.

The right must not be purely recreational

Mounsey v Ismay (1865)

On one day of every year for over 20 years the freemen and citizens of Carlisle used land within the parish of Kingsmoor for the purposes of horse-racing. The plaintiff's land was damaged by the activities of the freemen and citizens, who claimed an easement under the Prescription Act 1832 (see 8.3.3).

Held that the freemen and citizens did not have an easement. There was no dominant tenement to benefit from such an easement and the right could not exist in gross. Martin B stated that, regardless of the existence of a dominant tenement, the right could not be an easement because it 'must be a right of utility and benefit, and not one of mere recreation and amusement'.

Note

1 The easement may of course include recreational purposes (see *Re Ellenborough Park*, above at 8.1) provided that it accommodates the dominant tenement and is not merely a personal right.

2 Rights in favour of the inhabitants of a particular locality may be enforced as customary rights provided that they are ancient, certain, reasonable and continuous (eg see *Wyld v Silver* (1963)).

8.1.3 The dominant and servient tenements must be owned by different persons

Roe v Siddons (1888) CA

Fry LJ stated that 'the owner of two tenements can have no easement over one of them in respect of the other. When the owner of Whiteacre and

Blackacre passes over the former to Blackacre, he is not exercising a right of way in respect of Blackacre; he is merely making use of his own land to get from one part of it to another.'

Note ──
It is now sufficient if the dominant and servient tenements are occupied (rather than owned) by different persons.

8.1.4 The right must be capable of forming the subject matter of a grant

There must be a capable grantor and a capable grantee

The right must be sufficiently definite

Note ──
For this reason there can be no easement of privacy (*Browne v Flower* (1911)) or of a right to a view (*Aldred's Case* (1610)). There is no general right to light; the right claimed must be through a defined aperture (*Wheeldon v Burrows* (1879)).

The right must be in the nature of rights traditionally recognised as easements

Dyce v Lady James Hay (1852) HL
D claimed that he and the other inhabitants of Aberdeen, together with the public generally, had enjoyed from time immemorial the right to use a footpath on the estate of the defendant.

Held that the right claimed did not accommodate a dominant tenement and therefore it was more in the nature of a public right. It could not be an easement. This does not mean that new categories of easement cannot be created, however. Lord St Leonards stated that 'the categories of servitudes and easements must alter and expand with the changes that take place in the circumstances of mankind'.

Phipps v Pears (1965) CA
O owned two adjoining houses. He demolished one house and rebuilt it before selling it to P. He sold the other house to D. D then demolished his house, causing rain to penetrate P's house through the exposed wall, which was not rendered. P claimed to have an easement.

Held that protection from the weather is not a right recognised as an easement. Lord Denning MR stated that there are two kinds of easements, positive easements and negative easements. A positive easement gives the dominant owner a right to do something on the servient land (eg a right of way, or a right to park a car), but a negative easement prevents the servient owner from doing something on his own land. Some negative easements have been recognised by law (eg easements of light), but negative rights are usually protected by means of restrictive covenants. He thought that 'a right to protection from the weather ... is entirely negative. It is a right to stop your neighbour pulling down his own house. Seeing that it is a negative easement it must be looked at with caution. Because the law has been very chary of creating new negative easements.'

Note ───

It is possible to have an easement of support for a building by adjoining buildings or land (see *Dalton v Angus*, below at 8.3.3). An action may also be brought in the tort of nuisance (see *Leakey v National Trust* (1980)).

8.1.5 The right must not amount to exclusive or joint user

Wright v Macadam (1949) CA

In 1940 Mrs W became the weekly tenant of a top-floor flat in M's house. In 1941 M gave Mrs W permission to use a garden shed for the storage of coal. M granted a new tenancy to Mrs W and her daughter by an unsealed document in 1943. No mention was made of the use of the shed, which Mrs W continued to use until 1947, when M suggested that she should pay 1s 6d per week for its use. Mrs W refused to pay and M denied her the use of the shed. Mrs W sought damages and an injunction restraining M's interference with her use of the shed. She claimed to have an easement under s 62 of the Law of Property Act 1925 (see 8.3.2). In the course of the hearing M pulled down the shed. At first instance the judge found in M's favour. Mrs W appealed.

Held that Mrs W had an easement to use the shed. Jenkins LJ found that Mrs W had a licence to use the shed in 1941. That licence became an easement upon conveyance in 1943 by virtue of s 62. He found that the unsealed document was a conveyance within the definition in s 205(1)(ii) of the Law of Property Act 1925. As the shed had been demolished, Mrs W was awarded damages.

Note ───

It has been questioned whether Mrs W's use of the shed for the storage of coal amounted to exclusive use. As Judge Paul Baker QC noted in *London & Blenheim Estates Ltd v Ladbroke Retail Parks* (1992) 1 WLR 1278 a 'small coal shed in a large property is one thing. The exclusive use of a large part of the alleged servient tenement is another'.

Q Was the unsealed document a conveyance for the purposes of s 62?

Copeland v Greenhalf (1952)

C owned a track which provided access to her orchard from her house. G was a wheelwright who lived opposite C. G and his father before him had stored vehicles and parts of vehicles on one side of the track for over 50 years. Sufficient room was always left for C to pass along the track, but the vehicles themselves could be left on the strip for years. C brought an action to restrain G from storing the vehicles on the strip. G claimed an easement by prescription.

Held that the right could not be an easement because it amounted to joint user of the land. Lord Upjohn stated that

> this claim ... really amounts to a claim to joint user of the land by the defendant. Practically, the defendant is claiming the whole beneficial user of the strip of land on the south-east side of the track there; he can leave as many or as few lorries there as he likes for as long as he likes; ... I am dealing solely with the question of a right arising by prescription.

Grigsby v Melville (1974) CA

H owned a property which he converted into a shop and a cottage. He conveyed the cottage to G's predecessor in title and then conveyed the shop to M. The original conveyance to G purported to reserve to the vendor all easements, rights and quasi-easements which may be enjoyed by the shop premises. There was a cellar under the cottage, but the only access to it was via the shop. When G discovered that M and her husband were using the cellar for storage purposes he sought to restrain M's use of the cellar. M claimed to have an easement of storage. At first instance Brightman J found that the use of the cellar for storage amounted to rights of exclusive user. M appealed.

Held that the right claimed could not be an easement because it amounted to rights of exclusive user.

8.1.6 The right must not involve the servient owner in expenditure

Crow v Wood (1971) CA

C and W were Yorkshire farmers. They had rights to allow their sheep to graze upon the moor. W's sheep trespassed upon C's land by passing through a hole in her fence. C claimed damages, but W claimed that he had an easement of fencing by which C was bound to keep her own fences in repair. The easement, he claimed, passed under s 62 of the Law of Property Act 1925 (see 8.3.2). C claimed that an easement should not involve her in expenditure.

Held that easements of fencing were exceptions to the rule that an easement must not involve the servient owner in expenditure. Diplock L J stated that 'it is now sufficiently established ... that a right to have your neighbour keep up the fences is a right in the nature of an easement which is capable of being granted by law so as to run with the land and to be binding upon successors'.

8.2 The extent of some common easements

8.2.1 Rights of way ...

Miller v Hancock (1893) CA

D owned a building, the different floors of which were let to various occupiers. Access to the floors was by means of a staircase which remained the property of D. The stairs were not kept in good repair and P, after visiting one of the tenants, fell while coming down the staircase and sustained personal injuries. P sued D for damages. The tenants claimed to have an implied grant of an easement to use the staircase, and the question arose as to who was responsible for maintaining the right of way. The jury awarded damages amounting to £200 to P. D appealed.

Held, dismissing the appeal, that, although maintenance of the right of way is normally the responsibility of the grantee, 'this is not the mere case of a grant of an easement without special circumstances' (*per* Bowen LJ). In this case it was deemed that 'it must have been intended by necessary implication' that the landlord should have a duty to repair and maintain the staircase.

... acquired by express grant

Gerrard v Cooke (1806)

A granted to P, his heirs and assigns a right of way over a strip of land. He granted him 'all other liberties, powers, and authorities incident or appurtenant, needful or necessary to the use, occupation or enjoyment of the said, road, way, or passage'. P, whose doorway opened on to the strip of land, placed a flagstone in front of his door. D took up the flagstone claiming that P had a right to repair but not to improve the right of way. He argued that he had exceeded the powers which had been granted to him.

Held that P's rights depended upon the construction of the original grant. The words 'needful' and 'necessary', though restrictive, did not preclude improvement of the way. Provided that such improvement did not cause any inconvenience to the grantor it should be allowed. Heath J asked 'if the plaintiff had repaired the way with gravel, it might in time have become a puddle; had he not, therefore, a right to lay this stone to repair it permanently?'

Note
Compare *Mills v Silver*, below.

Jelbert v Davis (1968) CA

J had a right of way over a strip of land belonging to D. The original conveyance stated that the land was conveyed to J with 'the right of way at all times and for all purposes over the driveway ... leading to the main road, in common with all other persons having the like right'. J obtained planning permission to use part of his land for a camping and caravan site for up to 200 caravans and/or tents. D and O, over whose land the right of way was exercised, objected to the change in use of the land, and they erected notices warning off the caravanners. J brought an action seeking removal of the notices, claiming that he had been granted a right of way for both pedestrian and vehicular traffic and that he was merely exercising that right. D counterclaimed that the proposed user was excessive and would be a nuisance. At first instance the judge found that J had established his right and that he was therefore free to use the right of way for 200 caravans. D appealed.

Held, allowing the appeal, that the contemplated user of 200 camping units was excessive. The question was one of fact and degree, but, 'no one of those entitled to a right of way must use it to an extent which is beyond that which is contemplated at the time of the grant' (*per* Lord Denning MR).

Note ────────────────────────────────

Compare *British Railways Board v Glass* (1965), below.

Graham v Philcox (1984) CA

In 1960, M, the owner of a large coach-house, let a first-floor flat to B for five years, together with a right of way for all purposes over the driveway to the house. In 1963 B assigned his lease to D. M's executors conveyed the house to W in 1975, subject to D's tenancy. In 1977 M's executors transferred to Mr and Mrs P land which included the land over which the right of way had been granted. W then sold the house to Mrs and Mrs G, subject to D's tenancy. D was now a tenant with a right of way over land belonging to Mr and Mrs P.

D then surrendered his tenancy to Mr and Mrs G, who then occupied the whole house and claimed to have a right of way over the land belonging to Mr and Mrs P. Mr and Mrs P argued that the easement was no longer valid because the original dominant tenement (ie the flat) no longer existed because it had been merged with the title of the house. They refused to allow Mr and Mrs G to use the right of way because the change in the dominant tenement increased the burden on the servient tenement.

Held that Mr and Mrs G were entitled to use the right of way. Purchas LJ stated that

in none of the judgments in any of the cases ... is there suggestion that a mere alteration of a dominant tenement to which a right of way is appurtenant is sufficient to extinguish it, or indeed to affect the entitlement to its use unless as the result of that alteration the extent of the user is thereby increased.

... *acquired by prescription*

Mills v Silver (1991) CA

In 1985 S purchased a hill farm, the only vehicular access to which was via a track across the land of M. The previous owner of the hill farm had used the path infrequently over a period of almost 60 years. Neither M nor M's predecessors in title gave permission for the path to be used, but they tolerated its use. Because the track was often waterlogged and impassable, S employed builders to lay a stone road so as to make the path passable in all weathers. M sought to prevent S from using the track with vehicles and sought damages for trespass. S claimed an easement by prescription. At first instance the judge found that the previous user's use of the track had been too infrequent to establish a prescriptive right, and the fact that the use of the track had been tolerated meant that it had not been used as of right. He held that S therefore did not have an easement and he awarded M damages for trespass. S appealed.

Held that mere toleration without objection by the servient owners did not prevent an easement from being acquired by lost modern grant. S therefore had an easement. However, as grantees of a prescriptive right of way, the defendants had a right to repair the way only. They had no right to improve it. By building the road S had increased the burden on the servient tenement beyond that which was authorised by the prescriptive right. M was therefore entitled to damages for trespass.

Note ———————————————————————————
Compare *Gerrard v Cooke*, above.

British Railways Board v Glass (1965) CA

In 1847 a railway company constructed a railway line close to a farm owned by A, G's predecessor in title. In order to construct the railway, the company purchased land from A, who reserved a right of crossing the railway track for himself and all manner of cattle. The company constructed a level crossing to enable A to cross the railway line. For many years part of the land had been used by campers and caravanners. In 1942 there were six caravans on the site, but by the time of the proceedings the number had grown to 28 or 29. BRB sought a declaration and an injunction to limit users of the crossing, claiming that the level of user was beyond the terms of the original grant. The defendant claimed that the original grant was not limited to agricultural purposes, and, even if it was, a prescriptive right had been acquired by the caravanners. At first instance Ungoed-Thomas J found in favour of the defendant. BRB appealed.

Held (Lord Denning MR dissenting) that the use of the crossing was not excessive. The right of way was not limited to agricultural purposes in the contemplation of the parties to the original conveyance. The prescriptive right of way acquired by the caravanners was not excessive because, in order for there to be excessive user of a prescriptive easement, the quality and not the quantity of user must change. The number of caravanners had increased from 6 to 29, but that was a change in quantity only. Lord Denning was of the opinion that the increase in quantity was effectively a change in quality because of the increased burden on the servient tenement. 'After all prescription is a presumed grant. No such grant for 30 caravans could ever be presumed from user for six.'

Note ————————————————————————————————
Compare *Jelbert v Davis*, above.

8.2.2 Easements of light

Colls v Home and Colonial Stores Ltd (1904) HL

H & C Ltd brought an action to restrain C from building on the opposite side of the road from one of their stores. At first instance the injunction was refused because the premises would be 'well and sufficiently lighted for all ordinary purposes of occupancy as a place of business'. The Court of Appeal reversed the decision and C appealed.

Held, allowing the appeal, that the injunction should be refused. Lord Lindley examined the conditions necessary for the acquisition of an easement of light under s 3 of the Prescription Act 1832 (below at 8.3.3). He accepted that H & C had enjoyed both access and use of light for a period of 20 years without interruption. They therefore had a right to the access and use of light which was absolute and indefeasible. However, there was no evidence that H & C's beneficial use and enjoyment of the premises had been affected. He stated that

> there is no rule of law that if a person has 45 degrees of unobstructed light through a particular window left to him he cannot maintain an action for a nuisance caused by the diminishing light ... But experience shews that it is, generally speaking, a fair working rule to consider that no substantial injury is done to him where an angle of 45 degrees is left to him, especially if there is good light from other directions as well.

Allen v Greenwood (1980) CA

P had used a greenhouse in his back garden for over 20 years. P's next-door neighbour, D, applied for planning permission for a two-storey extension, and P objected. D did not go ahead with the planned extension, but he parked a caravan alongside P's greenhouse. Shortly afterwards, D erected a fence which stood 18 inches above the eaves of the greenhouse and substantially reduced the amount of light. There was sufficient light for working but insufficient for growing plants. P sought an injunction and a declaration that he had acquired an easement under s 3 of the Prescription Act 1832 (below at 8.3.3). At first instance it was held that the greenhouse was a special use and, as there was no evidence that D knew of the special use, the injunction should be refused. P appealed.

Held, allowing the appeal, that the injunction should be granted. The greenhouse was being used for its normal use. The fact that it required a high degree of light did not prevent a right to such light from being acquired under s 3. D had knowledge that P required such a high degree of light and therefore the injunction should be granted.

Carr-Sauders v Dick McNeil Associates Ltd (1986)

In 1968, C-S purchased a property, the second floor of which was lighted naturally by two windows to the rear. The property situated opposite the windows was owned by DMA Ltd. The windows had been in position for more than 20 years and C-S claimed a prescriptive right to light under s 3 of the Prescription Act 1832 (below at 8.3.3). In 1976, C-S converted the second floor into living accommodation in which he lived until 1981, when he added two storeys for his own occupation. The second floor he converted into a suite of consulting rooms. The two consulting rooms at the rear were lighted by the two windows which faced the premises owned by DMA Ltd. DMA Ltd added two storeys to their premises and C-S claimed damages for obstruction of his right to light. DMA Ltd claimed that, although the windows in C-S's building had been in place for 20 years, the rooms behind those windows had not. They claimed that C-S should not therefore be entitled to claim a right to light under s 3. If the small rooms had not been constructed, they argued, the property would be adequately lit.

Held that the easement acquired by s 3 was a right to light to a building, and not to a particular room within it. C-S was entitled to such light as would leave his premises adequately lit for all ordinary purposes, including purposes to which the premises might be put in the future. This included subdivision of the internal space and alterations. As the rooms no longer received an adequate amount of light damages should be awarded.

Note ————————————————————————————————
See also *Wheeldon v Burrows* at 8.3.2.

8.3   Granting of easements and profits ...

8.3.1   ... by express grant

Formal grant

Note ————————————————————————————————
Formal grants must be by deed (see 1.5.1 for the formality requirements), and are usually incorporated into a transfer or conveyance of the legal estate. They must be created 'for an interest equivalent to an estate in fee simple absolute in possession or a term of years absolute' in order to be legal (see the Law of Property Act 1925 s 1(2)(a) at 1.4.2).

Informal grant

Note ───────────────────────────────
Easements may be created in a similar fashion to leases under the rule in *Walsh v Lonsdale* (see 7.2.2). The contract must comply with the necessary formalities (see 1.5.3) and it must be specifically enforceable. The easement so created will be equitable only.

Estoppel

Note ───────────────────────────────
Easements may be acquired by estoppel. See *Ives v High* at 2.2.3 and *Crabb v Arun DC* at 6.2.

Statute

Note ───────────────────────────────
Statutory easements are rare. They are usually granted in favour of public utilities.

8.3.2 ... by implied grant

Necessity

Wong v Beaumont Property Trust Ltd (1965) CA
In 1957 cellar premises were let by BPT's predecessors to a restaurateur who covenanted to use the premises as a restaurant, to control all smells and odours, and to comply with the health regulations. A ventilation duct should have been installed in accordance with the health regulations, but nether party was aware of this fact at the time of the grant of the tenancy. The duct was not installed. In 1961, W, another restaurant owner, bought the remainder of the lease. His business thrived until the other occupiers of the building complained to the public health inspector about the smells from the restaurant, and the inspector ordered a duct to be constructed. BPT refused to allow W to construct a ventilation duct because it would be fixed to the outside wall of their premises. W sought a declaration and damages. At first instance the judge found in W's favour. BPT appealed.

Held that W was entitled to an easement of necessity. Lord Denning MR thought that just as an easement of necessity should be implied when property is land-locked, because otherwise the owner of the land can obtain no benefit from it, in this case 'if ... the lessee is to have any benefit by the grant at all – he must of necessity be able to put a ventilation duct up the wall'.

Common intention

Pwllbach Colliery Co Ltd v Woodman (1915) HL

A tinplate company leased two adjoining plots of land. One plot was sublet to P Ltd, and the other was subsequently sublet to W, who was a butcher. W built a slaughter-house and sausage factory on the site, which was, according to the sublease, 'subject to all rights and easements belonging to any adjoining or neighbouring property'. P Ltd then erected screening apparatus which emitted coal dust and, when deposits of coal dust began to affect his factory, W sought an injunction to restrain P Ltd's actions. P Ltd claimed to have an easement to use the screening equipment. At first instance the judge found that P Ltd, though causing a nuisance, were conducting their operations without negligence in a manner which was usual in the district. The Court of Appeal reversed the decision, and P Ltd appealed.

Held that the grant of the lease to mine coal did not imply the grant of an easement to cause a nuisance. Although it might be desirable, it was not necessary for the purposes of mining coal for P Ltd to conduct the screening operation. In the absence of necessity, 'the law will readily imply the grant or reservation of such easements as may be necessary to give effect to the common intention of the parties to a grant of real property, with reference to the manner or purposes in and for which the land granted ... is to be used'. However,

> the business of coal mining ... appears to have been started by the defendants, and it is only recently that the defendants have commenced to use the screens which occasioned the dust. There appears, therefore, to be no room for any implication based upon common intention (*per* Lord Parker).

Q Was the easement in *Wong* (above) really one of necessity, or was it implied because of common intention?

The rule in Wheeldon v Burrows

Wheeldon v Burrows (1879) CA

T owned a large plot of land. In 1876 he sold one part of the land to W, the plaintiff's husband. Another adjoining part was sold to B the following month. On B's land there was a shed which was lighted by three windows which overlooked Mrs W's land. Mrs W erected hoardings facing B's shed, thereby reducing the amount of light in the shed. B, claiming to have an easement of light, knocked down the hoardings and Mrs W sought damages for trespass.

Held that B had no easement of light. If T had wanted to reserve an easement for the land which he later conveyed to B he should have expressly included the reservation in the conveyance to W. Thesiger J accepted that a landowner cannot have an easement which is enforceable against himself, but owners often tend to exercise rights akin to easements over one part of their land for the benefit of another part. These rights he termed 'quasi-easements'. He then considered the circumstances in which these quasi-easements should be implied into a conveyance. He stated that if the owner wished to reserve a quasi-easement over the land sold he must do so by express reservation. When the quasi-easement is over the land retained however 'on the grant by the owner of a tenement of part of that tenement as it is then used and enjoyed, there will pass to the grantee all those continuous and apparent easements (by which, of course, I mean quasi-easements), or ... all those easements which are necessary to the reasonable enjoyment of the property granted, and which have been and are at the time of the grant used by the owners of the entirety for the benefit of the part granted'.

Note ———

Since *Borman v Griffith* (1930) the rule in *Wheeldon v Burrows* has been applied to equitable as well as to legal grants.

Wheeler v JJ Saunders Ltd (1995) CA

The trustees of a pension fund [T] owned a large plot of land on the Mendip Plateau. They conveyed part of the plot to W, a veterinary surgeon specialising in pigs. The adjacent plot was retained in order that JJS could use it, under licence, as a pig farm. W, who was to manage the adjoining farm as a director of JJS, convenanted to use the outbuildings on his plot as holiday cottages, and for no other purpose. Unfortunately, before the pig farming could commence, W quarrelled with JJS and T, and another manager was appointed to run the farm.

There were two entrances to W's land, one of which was via a strip of land which had been retained by T. T and JJS blocked this entrance with a wall of breeze blocks, and W claimed to have an easement which had been acquired under the rule in *Wheeldon v Burrows*. He claimed that the right of way had been used when there was unity of seisin (ie it had been a quasi-easement) and that it was necessary for the reasonable enjoyment of his land. He also claimed, *inter alia*, damages and an injunction for the nuisance caused by the defendants, who had sited housing units for 40 pigs within 36 feet of W's holiday cottages. The judge at first instance awarded damages and an injunction in both cases. JJS and T appealed on the grounds that: i) they had obtained planning permission for the pig units; and ii) the right of way was not necessary for the enjoyment of W's property.

Held: i) dismissing the appeal, that planning permission cannot authorise a nuisance 'even if the nuisance was an inevitable consequence of the use of the relevant planning permission' (*per* Sir John May); ii) allowing the appeal, that the easement was not necessary for the reasonable enjoyment of W's land. Staughton LJ stated that 'even to a novice in the law of easements, it seems clear that the class of easements implied in favour of the grantee [under the rule in *Wheeldon v Burrows*] is wider than easements of necessity. The question is, how much wider?' Clearly, as W's plot was not landlocked, an easement of necessity could not be implied. However, the question was whether the right of way was necessary for the reasonable enjoyment of the land. It was decided that the alternative means of access was perfectly adequate, and therefore the easement was not necessary for the reasonable enjoyment of W's land.

Law of Property Act 1925 s 62

Law of Property Act 1925 s 62(1) and (4):

(1) A conveyance of land shall be deemed to include and shall by virtue of this Act operate to convey, with the land, all buildings, erections, fixtures, commons, hedges, ditches, fences ways, waters, watercourses, liberties, privileges, easements, rights, and advantages whatsoever, appertaining or reputed to appertain to the land, or any part thereof, or, at the time of the conveyance, demised, occupied, or enjoyed with, or reputed or known as part or parcel of or appurtenant to the land or any part thereof ...
(4) This section applies only and if and so far as a contrary intention is not expressed in the conveyance, and has effect subject to the terms of the conveyance and to the provisions therein contained.

Note
This section has been interpreted as being capable of turning a licence into an easement upon conveyance. For an example, see *Wright v Macadam* at 8.1.5, and *Crow v Wood* at 8.1.6.

8.3.3 Acquisition by prescription

Note
Prescriptive easements are really another form of implied grant. However, they are subject to their own separate rules. Abolition of this form of acquisition has been recommended (eg by the Law Reform Committee, 14th Report, Cmnd 3100, 1966). The category is far from obsolete, however, and disputes regarding prescriptive easements still occur (see *Mills v Silver* (1991) at 8.2.1).

Prescription at common law – user since 1189

Note
It is virtually impossible to acquire an easement by common law prescription because originally the right had to have been exercised since time immemorial, or 1189. The following five rules apply to all forms of prescription:
(i) the user must be a continuous user as of right;
(ii) the user must be a fee simple owner (see *Simmons v Dobson* (1991));

(iii) user *nec vi* – the user must not be forcible;

(iv) user *nec clam* – the user must not be surreptitious (see *Union Lighterage Co v London Graving Dock Co* at 8.4.2);

(v) user *nec precario* – the user must not be as a result of a licence or consent of the servient landowner.

The common law presumption – user for 20 years or within living memory

Note

Eventually the common law accepted that a prescriptive right should be enforced if the claimant could establish 20 years' user as of right, or user as of right within living memory. The presumption could still be rebutted if it could be shown that the particular user could not possibly have existed at all times since 1189.

Lost modern grant

Dalton v Angus & Co (1881) HL

P and D owned adjoining buildings, which gave each other mutual support. The buildings had stood for over 100 years when P removed the inside walls of his building and converted it into a factory. These alterations increased the burden of support on D's land. Twenty-seven years later D pulled down his building and began excavations. P's factory collapsed and he claimed a prescriptive easement of support either by virtue of lost modern grant or by the application of s 2 of the Prescription Act 1832. The case 'enjoyed the attention of no less than 18 judges and members of the House of Lords, perhaps embodying a greater variety of judicial opinion than any other leading case' (*Tehidy Minerals v Norman* (1971) *per* Buckley LJ – see 8.6.3). The judges in the lower courts were uncertain as to whether to apply s 2 or to imply a lost grant. The High Court decided that P did not have an easement of support. Lush J, dissenting, decided that P had an easement by virtue of 'the revolting fiction of a lost grant'. The Court of Appeal reversed that decision and D appealed.

Held in the House of Lords, that P could claim an easement by virtue of s 2 and also by the implication of a lost modern grant. It was held that, provided the user could show 20 years' uninterrupted enjoyment of an easement, the law will adopt the legal fiction of a lost grant. The court will adopt the fiction notwithstanding evidence to the contrary that no such grant was ever made. The right therefore becomes indefeasible unless it can be shown that it does not comply with the requirements for a prescriptive easement (ie those listed in 8.3.3 (i) – (v)), or that at the time of the purported grant there was no capable grantor (ie that the putative grantor lacked the legal capacity to make the grant).

Note ───────────────

See also *Moody v Steggles* at 8.1.2 and *Mills v Silver* at 8.2.1.

Prescription Act 1832

Prescription Act 1832 ss 1–4:

1. No claim which may be lawfully made at the common law, by custom, prescription, or grant, to any right of common or other profit or benefit to be taken and enjoyed from or upon any land of our sovereign Lord the King ... shall, where such right, profit or benefit shall have been actually taken and enjoyed by any person claiming right thereto without interruption for the full period of thirty years, be defeated or destroyed by showing only that such right, profit or benefit was first taken or enjoyed at any time prior to such period of thirty years, but nevertheless such claim may be defeated in any other way by which the same is now liable to be defeated; and when such right, profit or benefit shall have been so taken and enjoyed for the full period of sixty years, the right thereto shall be deemed absolute and indefeasible, unless it shall appear that the same was taken and enjoyed by some consent or agreement expressly made or given for that purpose by deed or writing.

2. No claim which may be lawfully made at the common law, by custom, prescription, or grant, to any way or other easement, or to any watercourse, or the use of any water ... when such way or other matter as herein last before mentioned shall have been actually enjoyed by any person claiming right thereto without interruption for the full period of twenty years, shall be defeated or destroyed by showing only that such way or other matter was first enjoyed at any time prior to such period of twenty years, but nevertheless such claim may be defeated in any other way by which the same is now liable to be defeated; and where such way or other matter as herein last before mentioned shall have been so enjoyed for the full period of forty years, the right thereto shall be deemed absolute and indefeasible, unless it shall appear that the same was enjoyed by some consent or agreement expressly given or made for that purpose by deed or writing.

3. When the access and use of light to and for any dwelling house, workshop, or other building shall have been actually enjoyed therewith for the full period of twenty years without interruption, the right thereto shall be deemed absolute and indefeasible ... unless it shall appear that the same was enjoyed by some consent or agreement expressly made or given for that purpose by deed or writing.

4. Each of the respective periods of years hereinbefore mentioned shall be deemed and taken to be the period next before some suit or action wherein the claim or matter to which such period may relate shall have been or shall be brought into question, and no act or other matter shall be deemed to be an interruption ... unless the same shall have been or shall be

submitted to or acquiesced in for one year after the party interrupted shall have had or shall have notice thereof, and of the person making or authorising the same to be made.

Note ───────────────────────────────────

For examples of cases on the Prescription Act 1832 see *Mounsey v Ismay* at 8.1.2; *Dyce v Lady James Hay* at 8.1.4; and the cases on the acquisition of rights to light at 8.2.2.

───────────────────────────────────

Davies v Du Paver (1953) CA

D purchased land in 1949 and he began to erect fencing in 1950. P and his predecessor in title had grazed sheep on D's land for over 60 years and he claimed a profit under s 1 of the Prescription Act 1832. P's solicitors then wrote to D objecting to the fencing, and D's solicitors wrote back on 2 August 1950. P took no further action until the issue of a summons in September 1951. D claimed that P could not have a profit because neither D nor his predecessors in title were aware of P's use of their land, and therefore such use could not be 'as of right'. Second, they argued that, even if P did have a profit, he had acquiesced in the interruption of his rights for over a year.

Held that, although silence and inaction could be interpreted as submission or acquiescence, in the present case there was obviously no acquiescence. However, as there was no evidence that either D or his predecessors in title had any knowledge of the user of their land, that user could not be 'as of right' and P's claim must therefore fail.

8.3.4 Access to neighbouring land

Access to Neighbouring Land Act 1992 s 1:

(1) A person –

(a) who, for the purpose of carrying out works to any land (the 'dominant land'), desires to enter upon any adjoining or adjacent land (the 'servient land'); and

(b) who needs, but does not have, the consent of some other person to that entry ...

may make an application to the court for an order under this section ('an access order') against that other person.

(2) On an application under this section, the court shall make an access order if, and only if, it is satisfied –

(a) that the works are reasonably necessary for the preservation of the whole or any part of the dominant land; and

(b) that they cannot be carried out, or would be substantially more difficult to carry out, without entry upon the servient land ...

Note ────────────────────────────────
The right acquired under the above Act is not an easement at all. It is really only a statutory licence to enter the servient land in order to carry out works of maintenance or renovation. Once the work has been completed the dominant occupier has no right of access. The order may impose conditions upon the right of access and compensation may be payable to the servient owner or occupier (see ANLA 1992 ss 2 and 3).

8.4 Reservation of easements and profits

8.4.1 Express reservation

Note ────────────────────────────────
In the event of doubt or ambivalence the terms of the express grant are to be construed against the grantor (ie the purported reserver of the right). Any reservation must be carefully drafted.

8.4.2 Implied reservation ...

Necessity

Union Lighterage Co v London Graving Dock Co (1902) CA
X owned a dock and a wharf. He secured the side of the dock by laying tie-rods under the ground. The tie-rods encroached about 15 feet on to the wharf but, as they were underground, only the nuts on the ends of the rods were visible. X conveyed the wharf to P and then later conveyed the dock to D's predecessor in title. P discovered the tie-rods while excavating his land. D claimed to have an easement either by way of prescription or by an implied reservation of necessity.

Held that D's use of the tie-rods was surreptitious and therefore prescriptive rights could not be acquired. Romer LJ considered that 'a prescriptive right to an easement should only be acquired when the enjoyment has been open'. Stirling LJ stated that in *Wheeldon v Burrows* (above at 8.3.2) the lights were necessary for the enjoyment of the workshop but no reservation was implied: 'So here it may be that the tie-rods ... are reasonably necessary to the enjoyment of the defendants' dock in its present condition; but the dock is capable of use without them, and I think that there cannot be implied any reservation in respect of them.'

Q In what circumstances do you think a reservation will be implied because of necessity?

Common intention

Re *Webb's Lease* (1951) CA
See 8.1.2.

Q Will a common intention ever be implied when the reservation is not one of necessity?

8.5 Protection of easements and profits ...

8.5.1 ... in unregistered land
- Legal easements and profits are rights *in rem* and bind the whole world.
- Equitable easements and profits created after 1925 are registrable as class D (iii) land charges (see 2.2.2).
- Equitable easements created before 1926 are subject to the doctrine of notice.
- Easements by estoppel are subject to the doctrine of notice (see *Ives v High* at 2.2.3).

8.5.2 ... in registered land
- Most legal easements will be entered on the register against the title affected. Those which are not will be overriding interests under the Land Registration Act 1925 s 70(1)(a) if created before first registration. All profits are similarly protected.
- Equitable easements should be entered as minor interests, although if they are 'openly exercised and enjoyed' they may be protected under s 70(1)(a) by virtue of the decision in *Celsteel v Alton* (1986) (see 3.6.1).
- Easements by estoppel may be entered as minor interests or they may be overriding under s 70(1)(a). Alternatively, they may not bind subsequent purchasers. Their status is still uncertain. See Kevin Gray, *Elements of Land Law* (Butterworths, 1993, 2nd edn) pp 364-7.

8.6 Extinguishment of easements ...

8.6.1 ... by unity of possession and ownership

Note —————————————————————————————
Unity of possession and ownership will obviously extinguish the easement because nobody can have an easement enforceable against themselves. If the unity occurs as a result of the servient owner acquiring a lease of the dominant land, however, the easement is only suspended for the duration of the lease.

8.6.2 ... by express release

Note —————————————————————————————
In the case of a legal easement or profit such release must be by deed.

8.6.3 ... by implied release or abandonment

Moore v Rawson (1824)

M's predecessor in title enjoyed easements of light and air in respect of certain windows facing R's house. M pulled down the wall facing R's house and built a stable. A wall without any windows now faced R's land. Fourteen years later, R placed a building opposite M's blank wall. Three years after that M opened a window in the formerly blank wall and brought an action for obstruction, claiming to have an easement of light.

Held that M did not have an easement. He had abandoned his rights by demolishing the original wall. Holroyd J thought that 'when the house and the windows were destroyed by his own act, the right which he had in respect of them was also extinguished. If, indeed, at the time when he pulled his house down, he had intimated his intention of rebuilding it, the right would not then have been destroyed with the house'.

Gotobed v Pridmore (1971) CA

G claimed a right of way over a lane on P's land. An easement had been granted by an enclosure award in 1819. G's predecessors in title had ploughed the land at the end of the lane from 1919 until 1964, during which time there was a fence between the ploughed land and the lane. The lane itself had been cultivated by P's predecessor in title since 1942 and was surrounded by barbed wire. At first instance it was held that the right of way had been abandoned. G appealed.

Held, allowing the appeal, that in order for a right of way to be extinguished it must be shown not only that the right had been abandoned, but also that there was an intention to abandon it permanently. Buckley LJ stated that 'to establish abandonment the conduct of the dominant owner must have been such as to make it clear that he had at the relevant time a firm intention that neither he nor any successor in title should thereafter make use of the easement'.

Tehidy Minerals Ltd v Norman (1971) CA

The defendants established that they had a right to graze cattle on a down, until 1940, when the Ministry of Agriculture requisitioned the land. The Ministry fenced off the down and farmed it until 1954. Between 1954 and 1960 the defendants exercised their grazing rights by licence of the Ministry. The defendants claimed common rights of grazing on the down, but they could not assert their rights under Prescription Act 1832 because the activities of the Ministry constituted an interruption for the purposes of the Act. The question was whether they could assert their rights by common law prescription and/or lost modern grant, or whether the requisitioning of the down by the Ministry, together with their permission to graze, meant that the rights had been abandoned.

Held that the rights had been suspended but not abandoned. Buckley LJ stated that:

abandonment of an easement or of a profit *à prendre* can only ... be treated as having taken place where the person entitled to it has demonstrated a fixed intention never at any time thereafter to assert the right himself or to attempt to transmit it to anybody else.

Benn v Hardinge (1992) CA

B had been the owner of a farm for over 20 years. His predecessors in title had been granted a right of way over a track by an enclosure award in 1818. Mrs H was an adjoining landowner who had used the track as a private carriageway. Neither B nor his predecessors in title had ever used the track because they had an alternative means of access. When part of his land became waterlogged B sought to use the track and Mrs H objected. At first instance the judge found that the enclosure award conferred no rights upon B and he appealed.

Held, allowing the appeal, that the enclosure award conferred a right of way upon B's predecessors in title. Dillon LJ stated that abandonment of the right could not be presumed merely because nobody had occasion to use it. This applied even if, as in this case, the period of non-user amounted to 175 years. No evidence was produced to show that there was ever any intention to abandon the right and therefore B was entitled to use the carriageway.

Note

For the intention required to abandon an easement see Christine Davis [1995] Conv 291.

9 Freehold covenants

9.1 Enforcement of covenants by the original parties

Note ────────────────────────────────────

There are usually few problems when the original parties wish to enforce a covenant because they may sue each·other on the contract. However, it is possible for a third party to sue on the covenant if it was expressed in the conveyance that the third party was intended to benefit from the covenant.

────────────────────────────────────

Law of Property Act 1925 s 56(1):

A person may take an immediate or other interest in land or other property, or the benefit of any condition, right of entry, covenant or agreement over or respecting land or other property, although he may not be named as a party to the conveyance or other instrument.

White v Bijou Mansions (1938) CA

In 1887 the owners of an estate sold part of it to F, who covenanted that he would build a house which would be used only as dwelling house. The vendors covenanted that every future sale would include a similar covenant from the lessee or purchaser. F later sold his land to W. In 1890 a nearby plot was sold to N, who entered into a similar covenant for himself, his heirs, executors, administrators and assigns. N sold the plot to P, who granted a lease of the property for 28 years. The lease contained a covenant that the house would only be used as a private dwelling or for private flats. The lease was assigned to BM, who used the house for flats, and W sought to restrain the use by enforcing the covenant originally given by N. He claimed to have the benefit by virtue of s 56.

Held that the original covenant in 1890 was between N and the owners of the estate. The conveyance did not imply that F or W were to benefit. Therefore W was not entitled to the benefit of the covenant given by N: 'The mere fact that somebody comes along and says: "it would be useful to me to if I could enforce that covenant" does not make him a person entitled to enforce it under section 56. Before he can enforce it he must be a person who falls within the scope and benefit of the covenant according to the true construction of the document in question' (*per* Sir Wilfrid Greene MR).

9.2 Running the benefit of a covenant to the successors of the covenantee ...

9.2.1 ... at common law

Law of Property Act 1925 s 78:
(See 7.8.1.)

Prior's Case (1368)
A prior covenanted by deed for himself and his successors to sing in the chapel of a manor for the benefit of the lord of the manor and his successors in title. The question was whether subsequent tenants in tail could enforce the covenant against the prior's successors notwithstanding the fact that the latter held no estate in land which could be burdened by the obligation.

Held that the covenant could be enforced against the prior's successors. The covenantee must hold some estate in the land in order to claim the benefit, but the covenantor does not need to hold an estate in land in order to be burdened.

Smith and Snipes Hall Farm Ltd v River Douglas Catchment Board (1949) CA
RDCB covenanted under seal with freehold owners of surrounding land that, in return for the freeholders contributing to the cost, they would maintain the banks of a brook. Mrs S, one of the original covenantees, sold her land expressly with the benefit of the covenant to the first plaintiff, S. S then granted a yearly tenancy of the land to his company, SHFL. The brook burst its banks and the plaintiffs sought damages for breach of covenant. RDCB claimed that anybody seeking to enforce the covenant must have the same legal estate in the land as the original covenantee, and as SHFL were lessees they did not possess the same freehold estate as Mrs S, the original covenantee.

Held that the plaintiffs were entitled to damages. Tucker LJ stated that all the necessary conditions were satisfied for running the benefit of the covenant: the covenant touched and concerned the land; both the original covenantee and the person seeking to enforce the covenant held a legal estate in the land; and the deed demonstrated an intention that the covenant was to run with the land because 'its object was to improve the drainage of land liable to flooding and to prevent future flooding'. Denning LJ stated that 'it has always been held ... at common law that, in order that a successor in title should be entitled to sue , he must be of the same estate as the original owner ... This limitation ... has been removed by [s 78 of] the Law of Property Act 1925 ...'.

Note ——
1 For Lord Oliver's test of whether a covenant 'touches and concerns' the land, see *P & A Swift Investments v Combined English Stores Group* (1989) at 7.8.1
2 If the benefit runs at law, it does not matter that the burden will only run in equity. The covenant may still be enforced.
——

9.2.2   ... in equity ...

... by annexation

Rogers v Hosegood (1900) CA
In 1869 a vendor conveyed a plot of land to the Duke of Bedford, who entered into a covenant that no more than one dwelling house may be erected on the plot 'with intent that the covenants ... might ... bind the premises thereby conveyed and every part thereof and might enure to the benefit of [the vendors] ... their heirs and assigns and others claiming under them to all or any of their lands adjoining or near to the said premises'. The same vendor then sold a nearby plot, which was eventually conveyed to Sir John Millais in 1873. Sir John had no knowledge of the Duke's covenant. The Duke's successor in title proposed to erect a block of residential flats, and Sir John's executors sought to enforce the covenant. Farewell J thought that in order to touch and concern the land a covenant 'must either affect the land as regards mode of occupation, or it must be such as *per se*, and not merely from collateral purposes, affects the value of the land'. He found that the covenant in question satisfied this test. He therefore considered that the covenant was intended to run with the land and gave judgment for the executors. The developers appealed.

Held that the executors could enforce the covenant. Collins LJ stated that the words of the original covenant entered into by the Duke demonstrated an intention that the covenant was to run with the land and that it should be enforceable by successors in title for the benefit of the land. The fact that Sir John Millais had no knowledge of the covenant did not prevent him or his successors from taking advantage of it, provided that it had been annexed to the land. The benefit 'runs, not because the conscience of either party is affected, but because the purchaser has bought something which inhered in or was annexed to the land bought'.

Federated Homes Ltd v Mill Lodge Properties Ltd (1980) CA
MH Ltd wished to develop a large plot of land. The plot was to be divided into three, and planning permission was obtained, but the overall density of houses to be built on the area was restricted. MLP Ltd purchased one of the plots of land subject to a covenant with the vendor that they would not build more than 300 dwellings on the plot. If they were allowed to build more than 300 it would limit the density of dwellings which could

be built upon the other two plots because of the terms of the planning permission. The other two plots were sold and were eventually purchased by FH Ltd. FH Ltd wanted to enforce the covenant against MLP Ltd. With regard to one of the plots of land acquired by FH Ltd, there was a complete chain of the assignment of the benefit of the covenant (see 9.2.2 below). With regard to the other property, however, there was no such chain. MLP Ltd argued that the covenant with MH Ltd was a personal covenant and that the express language was not sufficient to demonstrate an intention that it was to run with the land. As it was not annexed to the land FH Ltd could not claim the benefit of the covenant.

Held that FH Ltd were entitled to the benefit of the covenant in respect of both plots of land. For one plot because there was a complete chain of assignment, and for the other because, although there was no express annexation, s 78(1) had the effect of annexing the benefit of the covenant to all or any part of the land of the covenantee.

... by assignment

Union of London and Smith's Bank Ltd's Conveyance, Miles v Easter (1933) CA

X purchased a plot of land in 1908. The conveyance contained covenants which were made with the purchasers, their heirs and assigns or other owners or owner for the time being of the land. These covenants were held to be validly annexed to the retained land and could be enforced. However, the conveyance also contained another covenant which was made with the vendors and their successors and assigns only; the conveyance did not specify the land to be benefited. M subsequently acquired the property originally purchased by X, and E acquired part of the retained land. The benefit of the second covenant had not been expressly assigned in the original conveyance to E, but two subsequent conveyances purported to assign the benefit to him. E sought to enforce the covenants against M.

Held that covenants were unenforceable. The original conveyance to E did not assign the benefit as no land to benefit from the covenant had been defined. The chain had therefore been broken and subsequent conveyances could not assign what no longer existed. X could not subsequently assign the covenants because he no longer owned the land to be benefited. Romer LJ stated the requirements for a valid assignment of the benefit in equity: (i) the covenant must have been taken for the benefit of the land of the covenantee; (ii) the land must be indicated with reasonable certainty; (iii) the land must be retained in whole or in part by the plaintiff; (iv) the land must be capable of benefiting from the covenant; (v) the assignment of the covenant and the conveyance of the land must be contemporaneous.

Newton Abbot Co-operative Society Ltd v Williamson & Treadgold Ltd (1952)

Mrs M was the owner of two properties. She conducted her business as an ironmonger from one of the properties, and sold the other one, on the opposite side of the same street, to X, who covenanted not to use the premises for the business of an ironmonger. The deed did not specify which land was to be benefited by the covenant, although Mrs M's address was given on the deed. In 1941, Mrs M died and the property passed by will to her son, M. In 1947 X sold the property opposite the ironmonger's shop to W&T Ltd. In 1948 M assigned the ironmongery business, together with the benefit of the covenant, to NACS Ltd for 21 years. W&T Ltd began to trade as ironmongers and NACS Ltd sought to rely upon the covenant. W&T Ltd claimed that the plaintiffs could not rely upon the covenant because it was a personal covenant with Mrs M. The land to be benefited was not expressly defined in the covenant.

Held that NACS Ltd were entitled to an injunction to prevent W&T Ltd from trading as ironmongers. Upjohn J considered that the covenant did concern the land because it enhanced the value of it. The covenant had not been annexed to the land because the land to be benefited was not defined. However, it was possible to ascertain the land to be benefited from the deed and the benefit was capable of assignment. If M had the benefit of the covenant he had assigned it to NACS Ltd. The problem was that the benefit of the covenant had not been expressly assigned to him by his mother's will. Upjohn J decided that Mrs M's executors held the benefit of the covenant on trust for M, who was therefore capable of assigning the benefit.

Note
See also the *Federated Homes* case above at 9.2.2.

Roake v Chadha (1984)

W Ltd sold a number of plots of land, each of which reserved rights that were to be enforceable by W Ltd 'and their assigns'. In 1934 L purchased a plot of land from W Ltd, and the land was subject to a covenant that he would not build anything other than a single dwelling house. The deed stated that 'the covenant shall not enure for the benefit of any owner or subsequent purchaser of any part of the estate unless the benefit of this covenant shall be expressly assigned'. C, the successor in title to L, proposed to build another house on the plot of land, and R, W Ltd's successor in title, sought to rely upon the covenant. R claimed that the covenant had been annexed to the land by virtue of s 78 of the Law of Property Act 1925, or, alternatively, that the benefit of the covenant passed under s 62 (see 8.3.2).

Held that R could not rely upon the covenant. Judge Paul Baker QC stated that s 78, unlike s 79 (see 7.8.1) could not be excluded by contrary intention. However, the covenant as a whole needs to be considered, and, as the covenant expressly stated that the benefit was not to run with the land unless expressly assigned, the benefit had not been annexed to the land. 'As to whether the benefit of a covenant not annexed can ever pass under s 62, I share the doubts of Farewell J [in *Rogers v Hosegood* above at 9.2.2] that the rights referred to under s 62 are confined to legal rights rather than equitable rights which the benefit of a restrictive covenant is. It cannot be described as a right appertaining or reputed to appertain to land when the terms of the covenant itself would seem to indicate the opposite.'

Note ———————————————————————————————
See also the comments regarding s 62 by Browne-Wilkinson V-C in *Kumar v Dunning* (1989).
————————————————————————————————————

Q In the unlikely event that s 62 can be applied to restrictive covenants, was there not a contrary intention expressed in this case? See s 64(4) at 8.3.2.

... by a scheme of development (building scheme)

Elliston v Reacher (1908) CA
The owners of a large area of land divided it up into plots and sold two plots to E's predecessor in title and two plots to R's predecessor in title. All of the conveyances were in identical terms and contained the same covenants. R began to use the buildings on his land as a hotel in breach of covenant. E, relying upon the covenant, sought an injunction.

Held that an injunction should be granted to restrain the breach of covenant. Parker J, at first instance (1908) 2 Ch 374, stated the four conditions for a scheme of development:

it must be proved (1) that both the plaintiffs and defendants derive title under a common vendor: (2) that ... the vendor laid out his estate ... for sale in lots subject to restrictions intended to be imposed on all the lots ... (3) that these restrictions were intended by the common vendor to be and were for the benefit of all the lots intended to be sold ... and (4) that both the plaintiffs and defendants, or their predecessors in title, purchased their lots from the common vendor on the footing that the restrictions subject to which the purchases were made were to enure for the benefit of the other lots included in the general scheme.

Reid v Bickerstaff (1909) CA
Cozens-Hardy MR added a fifth requirement to those listed in *Elliston v Reacher*. He stated that 'in my opinion there must be a defined area within which the scheme is operative. Reciprocity is the foundation of the idea of the scheme'.

Baxter v Four Oaks Properties (1965)
Lord C sold part of his land to X. In the conveyance X promised to observe certain covenants regarding building upon the land. The covenant was made by X, his heirs, assigns and all persons deriving title under him. On

the same day, X and Lord C covenanted on behalf of themselves and all other persons who might thereafter purchase lands on the estate to use the buildings on the estate only as private dwelling houses. Subsequent purchasers signed conveyances in the same terms and also signed a deed of covenant. B and FOP Ltd succeeded to land on the estate. When FOP Ltd erected a block of flats the plaintiffs sought to rely upon the covenant and claimed to be entitled to an injunction. They claimed the benefit of the covenant because a building scheme had been established. FOP Ltd claimed that the covenant could not be part of a building scheme because Lord C had not laid out the estate in plots before selling it, thereby failing to comply with the second requirement in *Elliston v Reacher* (above).

Held that a building scheme existed despite the fact that the land had not been laid out in plots. Cross LJ held that the intention of the parties to be bound by mutually binding covenants was the conclusive factor. He awarded damages rather than grant an injunction, however.

Re Dolphin's Conveyance (1970)
A 30-acre estate became the property of two sisters, A and M, as tenants in common. They sold four plots of land in 1871 to four different purchasers, each of whom covenanted to build only detached dwelling houses on plots of no less than one quarter of an acre. Each purchaser covenanted to obtain similar covenants from subsequent purchasers of any part of the estate. A died in 1873, leaving her share to her nephew, W, who, in 1876, acquired the remainder of the estate from M by deed of gift. He sold off the remainder of the estate in six parcels, obtaining similar covenants from the purchasers of each apart from the last parcel. Birmingham Corporation acquired a plot of land which had once belonged to the estate, and wished to build in breach of the covenants. Part of the land which the Corporation held had been originally acquired from A and M in 1871, and part of it had been acquired from W in 1877. They claimed that the covenants were not binding because there could be no building scheme. The land had never been divided into plots before sale and there was no common vendor.

Held that the land was subject to a building scheme and that the covenants were binding upon the Corporation. Stamp J cited the principle in *Baxter v Four Oaks Properties* (see above) that mutual obligation and reciprocity were the characteristic features of a building scheme. He defined a building scheme as 'the common intention to lay down a local law involving reciprocal rights and obligations between several purchasers'.

Note
In *Jamaica Mutual Life Assurance Society v Hillsborough Ltd* (1989) the Privy Council were of the opinion that the only relevant factors in establishing a building scheme are a system of 'local laws' involving reciprocal rights and duties, and a common intention that the covenants are to be enforced.

Elias & Co Ltd v Pine Groves Ltd (1993) PC

In 1938 land was divided into five lots. Lots 1–4 were sold to different purchasers. Lot 5 was conveyed to the person who purchased lot 4, but it was not shown on the plans annexed to the conveyances of lots 1–3. The purchasers of lots 1, 4 and 5 entered into covenants with the vendor and its assigns, including a covenant not to erect any building other than one dwelling house. The purchasers of lots 2 and 3 entered into a similar covenant with the vendor not to erect more than one dwelling house, but they also entered into other covenants which were different from those made by the purchasers of lots 1, 4 and 5. E & Co subsequently became the owner of lot 3, and PG Ltd became the owner of lot 1. PG Ltd began to build more than one house on its land and E & Co sought to enforce the covenant. The judge held that a building scheme had not been created and his decision was upheld by the Court of Appeal of Trinidad and Tobago. E & Co appealed.

Held that E & Co could not enforce the covenant because there was no building scheme. Lord Browne-Wilkinson found that there could not be a building scheme, for two reasons. First, the area of the scheme was not defined: lot 5 was not shown on the conveyances of lots 1–3, and there was no evidence that the purchasers of lots 1–3 were aware of any scheme involving that plot of land. Second, the covenants by which the lots were bound were not uniform. Some lots were subject to a covenant restricting the use of the land, and others were not; some were subject to a covenant not to cause a nuisance to occupiers of neighbouring land, and others were not: 'This disparity again militates against the finding of any intention to create a mutually enforceable local law based on reciprocity.'

9.3   Running the burden of a covenant to the successors of the covenantor ...

9.3.1   ... at common law

Austerberry v Corporation of Oldham (1885) CA

E conveyed part of his freehold land to X Ltd in order that they could build a toll road over his land. X covenanted with E, his heirs and assigns to make up the road and to keep it in good repair. In 1868 A bought E's land, and Oldham Corporation took over the road in 1880. The Corporation claimed that it was A's responsibility to maintain the road under the Public Health Act 1875, whereas A claimed that maintenance was the responsibility of the Corporation by virtue of the covenant. Both parties had notice of the covenant when they purchased their respective plots of land.

Held that A could not enforce the covenant. Lindley LJ found that the benefit of the covenant had not passed to A because it conferred a benefit on the general public rather than on A as a landowner. It therefore did not touch and concern the land. The burden of the covenant could not run at law because no party can be made liable upon a covenant unless he was a party to it. Because the covenant was positive in nature (ie it involved the covenantor in expenditure) it could not run in equity under the rule in *Tulk v Moxhay* (see below at 6.3.2).

Q Should the burden of positive covenants run with the land? See, for example, Law Commission Report No 127 (1985)

Law of Property Act 1925 s 79(1) and (2):
(See 7.8.1.)

Tophams Ltd v Earl of Sefton (1967) HL
T Ltd were the owners of Aintree Racecourse. They covenanted with the E of S that they would not cause or permit the land to be used for purposes other than horse-racing. The agreement stated that T Ltd were not to be liable for any breach of the covenant which occurred after they had parted with their interest. The E of S did not own any land in the vicinity of the racecourse and the benefit of the covenant was accordingly not expressed to be for the benefit of any land. T Ltd contracted with X Ltd to sell the racecourse for housing development. The E of S sought an injunction against T Ltd. At first instance the injunction was granted, and the decision was affirmed by the Court of Appeal. T Ltd appealed claiming that sale of the land was not in breach of the covenant, which merely restricted T Ltd's use of the land. It was expressly stated that the covenant would not bind X Ltd. The E of S argued that sale of the racecourse for housing development was 'permitting' the land to be used for purposes other than horse racing, and, even should that not be the case, the covenant was binding upon T Ltd's successors in title by virtue of s 79 of the Law of Property Act 1925.

Held that T Ltd were not in breach of covenant. The sale of the property was not a breach *per se* and once the property was sold T Ltd had no control over X Ltd's use of the property. It was not possible for T Ltd to 'permit' what they could not control. It was common ground that the burden of the covenant could not pass in equity under the rule in *Tulk v Moxhay* (at 9.3.2) because the E of S held no land which could be benefited by the covenant, and the covenant itself expressly stated that the burden was not to run with the land. Section 79 was seen as a mere word-saving provision which did not affect the status of the covenant.

Q Is this interpretation of s 79 correct? See, for example, Kevin Gray, *Elements of Land Law* (Butterworths, 1993, 2nd edn) p 1133, n 17.

Rhone v Stephens (1994) HL
In 1960 the owner of a large freehold house divided it up into two parts. He retained the larger dwelling, the house, and sold the smaller dwelling, the cottage, to X. Part of the roof of the house lay above one of the

bedrooms in the cottage. The owner covenanted for himself and his successors in title 'to maintain to the reasonable satisfaction of the purchasers and their successors in title such part of the roof ... as lies above the property conveyed in wind and watertight condition'. When the roof of the cottage began to leak, R, who had purchased the property from X, sued S, the executor of the original owner's successor in title. At first instance the judge, applying *Halsall v Brizell* (1957) (see 2.2.3), found that the roof belonged to the defendant and, as the maintenance of the roof also benefited her property, that the covenant should be enforced. The Court of Appeal allowed the appeal on the grounds that a positive covenant could not run with freehold land. The benefit which the defendant derived from the maintenance of the roof was seen as *de minimis*. R appealed, contending, *inter alia*, that the rule that positive covenants could not run with freehold land had been reversed by s 79 of the Law of Property Act 1925.

Held that R could not enforce the covenant. Lord Templeman stated that the rule that positive covenants could not run with freehold land was still good law. The rule has been much criticised, most notably by the Law Commission, but any reform is a matter for Parliament. The burden of the covenant could not run at law because a person cannot be made liable on a contract to which he is not a party; it could not run in equity because it is a positive obligation; it could not run under s 79 because that section is a mere word-saving provision – it does not have similar effect to that which s 78 has on the benefit of a covenant; and for the doctrine of mutual benefit and burden to apply the burden must in some way be related to the benefit enjoyed. 'It does not follow that any condition can be rendered enforceable by attaching it to a right, nor does it follow that every burden imposed by a conveyance may be enforced by depriving the covenantor's successor in title of every benefit which he enjoyed thereunder. The condition must be relevant to the exercise of the right.' In this case there existed reciprocal benefits and burdens of support, but the obligation to repair the roof was 'an independent provision' and could not be enforced.

Methods of enforcing positive obligations
● The land may be leased rather than sold so as to run covenants which touch and concern the land when there is privity of estate between the parties. See 7.8.1.

Note ──────────────────────────────────────
This has traditionally been the chosen method of enforcing positive covenants between flat owners who require positive covenants for the upkeep of common parts, mutual support etc. If the government's proposals for the introduction of commonhold are enacted it will ensure that the owners of freehold flats can enforce positive covenants between themselves.
──────────────────────────────────────

● Identical covenants may be taken by each successive purchaser, thereby forming a chain of indemnity. The chain may be broken, however.

- The doctrine of mutual benefit and burden may apply. See *Halsall v Brizell* at 2.2.3; *Ives v High* at 2.2.3; and *Rhone v Stephens* (above).
- The right may be enforceable as an easement of fencing. See *Crow v Wood* at 8.1.6.
- A long lease may be granted which is then enlarged into a fee simple estate. See Law of Property Act 1925 s 153(1) and (8) at 7.9.7.
- An estate rentcharge may be created for the maintenance of property. See the Rentcharges Act 1977 s 2(3)(c).
- A right of re-entry may be reserved. See *Shiloh Spinners v Harding* at 2.2.3.
- In registered land a developer of a newly developed estate may enter a restriction on the register prohibiting the sale of plots on the estate without his consent. See the Land Registration Act 1925 s 58 at 3.5.4.

9.3.2   ... in equity

Tulk v Moxhay (1848)

In 1808 T sold a plot of land in Leicester Square to E, who covenanted for himself his heirs and assigns with T his heirs and assigns that the land would at all times be kept, at his own expense, 'in an open state, uncovered with any buildings, in neat and ornamental order'. The property was sold on a number of occasions before being conveyed to M. M's conveyance contained no covenant but he did have notice of the covenant in the deed of 1808. He proposed to build on the site, and T sought an injunction to restrain the breach of covenant. The injunction was granted by the Master of the Rolls, and M appealed.

Held, dismissing the appeal, that the injunction should be granted. Lord Cottenham stated that 'the question is, not whether the covenant runs with the land, but whether a party shall be permitted to use the land in a manner inconsistent with the contract entered into by his vendor, and with notice of which he purchased'. M had knowledge of the covenant when he purchased the land, and he probably acquired it at a lower price because of the covenant. It would be inequitable for M to build upon the land and then to sell it free of the covenant.

Note ───────────────────────────────────────

The doctrine of *Tulk v Moxhay* was originally based upon the doctrine of notice and was initially interpreted very widely by the courts. The doctrine has since been restricted by the following conditions precedent.

The covenant must be negative in nature

Note ───────────────────────────────────────

It is the substance not the form which must be negative or restrictive. The test to be applied is whether the covenant involves the covenantor in expenditure.

The covenantee must at the time of the creation of the covenant and afterwards own the land for the protection of which the covenant is made

London County Council v Allen (1914) CA

A applied for permission from LCC to lay out certain land for building purposes. LCC gave permission subject to a covenant which A made on behalf of himself, his heirs and assigns, and other persons claiming under him not to build upon that part of the land which LCC required for road building. In 1911, A mortgaged the land to W, who conveyed it on redemption to A's wife. Mrs A mortgaged the land to N and built three houses on the plot which was required by LCC. LCC sought to enforce the covenant against Mrs A and N.

Held that the covenant was binding neither upon Mrs A nor upon N because LCC held no land which could take the benefit of the covenant.

The covenant must touch and concern the dominant land
(See *Rogers v Hosegood* at 9.2.2.)

It must be the common intention of the parties that the burden of the covenant shall run with the land of the covenantor

Note ───
This will usually be presumed unless a contrary intention is shown. See the Law of Property Act 1925 s 79 at 7.8.1. This does not mean that s 79 enables the burden of a covenant to run at law – see *Tophams Ltd v Earl of Sefton* at 9.3.1 and *Rhone v Stephens* at 9.3.1.
───

9.4 Protection of covenants ...

9.4.1 ... in unregistered land
- If created before 1926 restrictive covenants are subject to the doctrine of notice.
- Restrictive covenants created after 1925 must be registered as Class D (ii) Land Charges (see Land Charges Act s 2 (5) at 2.2.2).

9.4.2 ... in registered land
- Restrictive covenants must be entered as minor interests under the Land Registration Act 1925 s 20.

9.5 Modification and discharge of covenants ...

9.5.1 ... by unity of seisin

Texaco Antilles Ltd v Kernochan (1973) PC

In 1925 developers proposed to sell off a large area of land in lots. The lots were sold in two groups. The lots in the first group were subject to a covenant, which was expressly annexed to the land, that no public garage should be built on the land. The lots in the second group were not conveyed subject to the same express covenants but the attached plan had a note stating that the property was 'restricted to residence except where otherwise indicated'. O was the original purchaser of the second group of lots. C Ltd eventually acquired lots from both the first and the second group. They sold two lots in the first group to K, and two from the first group and four from the second group to T Ltd, who proposed to build a service station. K sought and obtained an injunction restraining the breach of covenant at first instance. The order was affirmed by the Court of Appeal for the Bahamas Islands, and T Ltd appealed. T Ltd claimed: (i) that a service station is not a public garage; (ii) that the lots in the second group were bought by O, who were purchasers for value without notice of the covenant; and (iii) that both K's lots and T Ltd's lots had been owned by C Ltd and that therefore the covenants had been extinguished by unity of seisin.

Held, dismissing the appeal: (i) that in 1925 the term 'public garage' would have included a service station; (ii) that O had constructive notice of the covenant because of the words which were written on the plan; and (iii) that the rule that covenants are extinguished by unity of seisin does not always apply to a building scheme. The building scheme created a system of 'local laws' which could still be enforced by (or against) O Ltd against (or by) the owner of any other property within the scheme. O Ltd could obviously not enforce the covenant against themselves during the period of unity of seisin, and the covenant was suspended during that period; it revived when the lots were separated.

9.5.2 ... by release

Chatsworth Estates Co v Fewell (1931)

F's predecessor in title had covenanted with CEC's predecessor in title not to use the land 'otherwise than as a private dwelling house'. Other people in the locality who had purchased property subject to the same covenant from CEC's predecessor in title had been allowed, with the consent of CEC or their predecessors, to use their properties as a school, as flats, and (in four cases) as boarding houses. F opened a guest house and CEC sought an injunction and damages. F argued that the covenant should not be enforced because: (i) there was a change in the character of the neighbourhood; and (ii) he had been impliedly released from the burden of the covenant because six properties had been released expressly from the covenant and there were other cases in which CEC had acquiesced in similar breaches.

Held that CEC were entitled to an injunction. Farwell J found that, as 'there were still a large number of private dwelling houses in the area', the character of the neighbourhood had not changed sufficiently to render the covenant unenforceable. He stated that it was possible for release to be implied from the acts and omissions of the covenantee or his assignees. When the covenantee acquiesces in past breaches the situation is 'analogous to the doctrine of estoppel and I think that it is a fair test to treat it in that way and ask, "Have the plaintiffs by their acts and omissions represented to the defendant that the covenants are no longer to be enforceable and that he is therefore entitled to use his house as a guest house?"'

9.5.3 ... by application to the Lands Tribunal

Law of Property Act 1925 s 84(1):

(1) The Lands Tribunal shall ... have power from time to time, on the application of any person interested in any freehold land affected by any restriction arising under covenant or otherwise as to the user thereof or the building thereon, by order wholly or partially to discharge or modify any such restriction on being satisfied –

(a) that by reason of changes in the character of the property or the neighbourhood or other circumstances of the case which the Lands Tribunal may deem material, the restriction ought to be deemed obsolete; or

(aa) that in a case falling within subsection (1A) below the continued existence thereof would impede some reasonable user of the land ...

(b) that the persons of full age and capacity for the time being or from time to time entitled to the benefit of the restriction ... have agreed, either expressly or by implication, by their acts or omissions, to the same being discharged or modified; or

(c) that the proposed discharge or modification will not injure the persons entitled to the benefit of the restriction ...

and an order discharging or modifying a restriction under this subsection may direct the applicant to pay to any person entitled to the benefit of the restriction such sum by way of consideration as the Tribunal may think it just to award under one, but not both, of the following heads, that is to say, either –

(i) a sum to make up for any loss or disadvantage suffered by that person in consequence of the discharge or modification; or

(ii) a sum to make up for any effect which the restriction had, at the time when it was imposed, in reducing the consideration then received for the land affected by it.

(1A) Subsection (1) (aa) above authorises the discharge or modification of
a restriction by reference to its impeding some reasonable user of land in
any case in which the Lands Tribunal is satisfied that the restriction, in
impeding that user, either –

(a) does not secure to persons entitled to the benefit of it any practical
benefits of substantial value or advantage to them; or

(b) is contrary to public interest ...

and that money will be an adequate compensation for loss or disadvantage if any which any such person will suffer from the discharge
or modification.

(1B) In determining whether a case is one falling within subsection (1A)
above, and in determining whether ... a restriction ought to be discharged
or modified, the Lands Tribunal shall take into account the development
plan and any declared or ascertainable pattern for the grant or refusal of
planning permission in the relevant areas, as well as the period at which
and context in which the restriction was created or imposed and any other
material circumstances.

(1C) It is hereby declared that the power conferred by this section to modify a restriction includes power to add such further provisions restricting
the user of or building on the land affected as appear to the Lands Tribunal
to be reasonable in view of the relaxation of the existing provisions, and as
may be accepted by the applicant; and the Lands Tribunal may accordingly refuse to modify a restriction without some such addition.

Re Bass Ltd's Application (1973) LT

Bass Ltd acquired a site which had previously been owned by another
brewery company. The site was subject to a restriction that it would only
be used for dwelling houses. Bass Ltd wished to use the site to load and
unload articulated lorries. They claimed that 180 lorries per day were
already being loaded and unloaded at their nearby brewery, and that this
development would merely increase the numbers to 228 per day. The area
was already zoned as being for industrial use in the development plan and
planning permission had been obtained. Bass Ltd sought discharge of the
covenant under ss 1 (aa) and (1A). Over 200 protesters objected to the proposals because of the dangers caused by the increased traffic.

Held that the covenant should not be discharged. J Stuart Daniel QC
dealt with the matter by asking the following questions:

1. Is the proposed user reasonable? He held that Bass Ltd's application
was reasonable.

2. Do the covenants impede that user? He held that they did.

3. Does impeding the proposed user secure practical benefits to the
objectors? He held that it did.

4. Are those benefits of substantial value or advantage? He held that the
advantages were substantial with regard to the noise, fumes, vibrations,
and increased risk of accidents.

5. Is impeding the proposed user contrary to the public interest? He held that it was not contrary to the public interest even though planning permission had been obtained and the area had been zoned as industrial.

6. If the answer to question 4 had been negative, would money have been an adequate compensation?

7. If the answer to question 5 had been affirmative, would money have been an adequate compensation?

On the issue of planning permission he stated that 'a planning permission only says, in effect, that a proposal will be allowed; it implies that such a proposal will not be a bad thing, but it does not necessarily imply that it will be positively a good thing.'

Re Beech's Application (1990) LT

B purchased his council house under the right-to-buy provisions of the Housing Act 1985. He covenanted not to use his house other than as a private dwelling. The house was part of a terrace of four houses adjoining a solicitor's office. B wanted to convert his house into office accommodation for the use of the adjoining solicitors, and he applied for, and obtained, planning permission. He sought discharge of the covenant, claiming that the covenant conferred no substantial benefit on the council. The council claimed that using the property for commercial purposes would make the neighbouring council houses more isolated and therefore less desirable. The use of the garden as a car park would have adverse environmental impact.

Held that, although the change in use would have little impact upon the adjoining properties themselves, it would have an adverse effect upon the area generally. If this application were allowed it would be more difficult to resist future applications.

Re Lloyd's and Lloyd's Application (1993) LT

Mr and Mrs L purchased a large house in 1981. Since 1935 the house had been subject to a restrictive covenant forbidding any trade or business from being conducted from the house. The carrying on of professions, a school, or a boarding house was not forbidden. Mr and Mrs L obtained planning permission in 1989 for a change of use to a community care home for 10 psychiatric patients. They contended that the covenant should be discharged or modified because of the change in the residential character of the neighbourhood. The house next door was used for business purposes by a builder, and another was used in breach of covenant as a residential home for 41 elderly people. As it was already permitted to use the property as a school or as a boarding house, they argued that the change in use would not be detrimental to the neighbourhood.

The objectors claimed that the proposed change in use could not be equated with use as a school or boarding house. They argued that the proposed use was inappropriate in a residential area, and that property values would fall. The residents themselves could not be compensated with money for the feelings of apprehension and unease which would be caused to them.

Held that the restriction should be modified. The proposed user was reasonable and impeding that user was contrary to public policy. The local council have a statutory duty to provide accommodation for the mentally ill, and there was a grave shortage of such accommodation within the region. The covenant conferred no substantial benefit upon the objectors because there was no evidence to show that a house for occupation by 10 psychiatric patients would be any more or less objectionable than a boarding house occupied by 10 residents from the community at large.

10 Mortgages

10.1 Creation of mortgages

10.1.1 Creation of legal mortgages ...

Law of Property Act 1925 s 85(1):
A mortgage of an estate in fee simple shall only be capable of being effected at law either by a demise for a term of years absolute, subject to a provision for cesser on redemption, or by a charge by deed expressed to be by way of legal mortgage ... Provided that a first mortgagee shall have the same right to the possession of documents as if his security included the fee simple.

Law of Property Act 1925 s 86(1):
A mortgage of a term of years absolute shall only be capable of being effected at law either by a subdemise for a term of years absolute, less by one day at least than the term vested in the mortgagor, and subject to a provision for cesser on redemption, or by a charge by deed expressed to be by way of legal mortgage; and where a licence to subdemise by way of mortgage is required, such licence shall not be unreasonably refused ... Provided that a first mortgagee shall have the same right to the possession of documents as if his security had been effected by assignment.

... by demise

Law of Property Act 1925 s 85(2):
Any purported conveyance of an estate in fee simple by way of mortgage made after the commencement of this Act shall ... operate as a demise of the land to the mortgagee for a term of years absolute, without impeachment for waste, but subject to cesser on redemption, in manner following, namely –
  (a) A first or only mortgagee shall take a term of three thousand years from the date of the mortgage;
  (b) A second or subsequent mortgagee shall take a term ... one day longer than the term vested in the first or other mortgagee whose security ranks immediately before that of the second or subsequent mortgagee ....

Law of Property Act 1925 s 86(2):

Any purported assignment of a term of years absolute by way of mortgage made after the commencement of this Act shall ... operate as a subdemise of the leasehold land to the mortgagee for a term of years absolute but subject to cesser on redemption, in the manner following, namely –

(a) The term to be taken by a first or only mortgagee shall be 10 days less than the term expressed to be assigned;

(b) The term to be taken by a second or subsequent mortgagee shall be one day longer than the term vested in the first or other mortgagee whose security ranks immediately before that of the second or subsequent mortgagee, if the length of the last mentioned term permits, and in any case for a term less by one day at least than the term expressed to be assigned ...

... by charge by way of legal mortgage

Law of Property Act 1925 s 87(1):

Where a legal mortgage of land is created by a charge by deed expressed to be by way of legal mortgage, the mortgagee shall have the same protection, powers and remedies ... as if –

(a) where the mortgage is a mortgage of an estate in fee simple, a mortgage term of three thousand years without impeachment of waste had been thereby created in favour of the mortgagee; and

(b) where the mortgage is a mortgage of a term of years absolute, a sub-term less by one day than the term vested in the mortgagor had been thereby created in favour of the mortgagee.

10.1.2 Creation of equitable mortgages ...

... by a contract to create a legal mortgage

Note

The contract must be capable of specific performance and must comply with the formalities necessary for a valid contract (see 1.5.3). The contract takes effect as a mortgage because of the rule in *Walsh v Lonsdale* (see 7.2.2).

... by equitable charge

Note

Equitable charges are now rare. They are created by an agreement to charge land with an obligation, such as the repayment of a debt. The chargee has a right to realise his assets by seeking an order for sale or the appointment of a receiver.

... by deposit of title documents

United Bank of Kuwait plc v Sahib (1994)

S and his wife held the matrimonial home as joint tenants. In 1991 UBK obtained a judgment against S for £229,815. In October 1992 they obtained a charging order *nisi* against S's interest in his freehold property. The order was subsequently made absolute. The question of priority arose between UBK and SoGenAl, who had made an advance of £130,000 to S in 1990. S's solicitor held the land certificate of his house to the order of SoGenAl in order to secure the £130,000, and SoGenAl therefore claimed to have an equitable charge on the property by deposit of title documents. SoGenAl further claimed that, even if the deposit of the title documents was insufficient to create a mortgage, S had effected a disposition of his equitable interest in the house, and he had thereby mortgaged his equitable interest.

Held that SoGenAl did not hold any equitable interest or charge over S's undivided share in his property. Chadwick J gave three reasons for the decision: (i) the rule that a deposit of title deeds was sufficient to secure a debt no longer applied since the coming into force of s 2 of the Law of Property (Miscellaneous Provisions) Act 1989 (see 1.5.3); (ii) in order to charge Mr S's share in the property, notice should have been given to Mrs S under the rule in *Dearle v Hall* (1823) (see 10.4.3 below) (in any case, it is doubtful whether the rule should be applied to judgment creditors who have been content to give credit without taking a security); and (iii) SoGenAl's claim that in the absence of a valid contract the deposit of title documents constituted a disposition of S's share cannot be correct because any disposition of his equitable interest must comply with s 53(1)(c) of the Law of Property Act 1925 in order to be valid (see 1.5.2).

> Note ———————————————————————
>
> Before this case the status of an equitable mortgage by deposit of title deeds was uncertain. It now appears that it has not been possible to create a mortgage in this manner since 27 September 1989.

Mortgage of an equitable interest

> Note ———————————————————————
>
> A mortgage of an equitable interest is created by assigning the equitable interest to the mortgagee subject to a proviso for reassignment on redemption. The assignment must comply with s 53(1)(c) of the Law of Property Act 1925, however. See *United Bank of Kuwait plc v Sahib*, above.

10.2 The mortgagor's equity of redemption – 'once a mortgage, always a mortgage'

10.2.1 'There should be no clogs or fetters on the equity of redemption' – the right to redeem must not be excluded

Reeve v Lisle (1902) HL

L granted a mortgage over a ship in favour of R. R advanced £3,000 and promised to lend a further £2,000 over two years. Ten days later L granted R an option to purchase the mortgaged property. The question was whether the option was void because it deprived L effectively of his equity of redemption.

Held that the option was valid. Had the option been granted at the same time as the mortgage, L would have been vulnerable to unconscionable conduct. However, as the option was granted ten days later it was seen as an independent transaction.

Samuel v Jarrah Timber and Wood Paving Corporation Ltd (1904) HL

J Ltd mortgaged debenture stock valued at £30,000 to S in order to secure a loan of £5,000. The principal to be payable, plus interest at 6%, at 30 days' notice on either side. S was also granted an option to purchase the stock at any time within twelve months. S attempted to exercise the option and J Ltd claimed that it was void because it excluded their right to redeem the mortgage.

Held that the option was void. The Earl of Halsbury LC reluctantly agreed that J Ltd should be allowed to redeem the mortgage free from the option even though the option was made by two parties dealing at arm's length:

> A perfectly fair bargain made between two parties to it, each of whom was quite sensible of what they were doing, is not to be performed because at the same time a mortgage arrangement was made between them. If a day had intervened between the two parts of the arrangement, the part of the bargain which the appellant claims to be performed would have been perfectly good and capable of being enforced; but a line of authorities going back for more than a century has decided that such an arrangement ... is contrary to a principle of equity.

10.2.2 There should be no unreasonable postponement of the right to redeem

Fairclough v Swan Brewery Co Ltd (1912) PC

F took out a mortgage with S Ltd in order to finance the purchase of his 17-year lease. The terms of the mortgage stated that he could not purchase beer from anybody else during the term of the mortgage and that he could not redeem the mortgage until six weeks before the end of the term. F wished to redeem the mortgage early in order to obtain beer from elsewhere. He claimed that the postponement of the right to redeem was void.

Held that the postponement was a clog on F's equity of redemption. He could not redeem until six weeks before the end of the term, by which time the lease would be virtually worthless. Lord Macnaughten thought that 'for all practical purposes this mortgage is irredeemable. It was obviously meant to be irredeemable'.

Knightsbridge Estates Trust Ltd v Byrne (1940) HL

K Ltd owned a considerable amount of property, which they mortgaged to the Prudential Assurance Co for £300,000 at 6% per annum. They negotiated a loan of £310,000 at 5% per annum from the Royal Liver Friendly Society and they transferred the mortgage in order to take advantage of the lower rate of interest. The terms of the mortgage stated that it could be neither redeemed nor called in for 40 years. A few years later K Ltd attempted to redeem the mortgage on giving six months notice.

Held that the mortgage could not be redeemed. Sir Wilfrid Greene MR (in the Court of Appeal) was of the opinion that the agreement was made 'between two competent parties, acting under expert advice and presumably knowing their own business best'. K Ltd negotiated the best terms possible at the time and then, because of falling interest rates, attempted to claim that the rates were unreasonable, 'but equity does not reform mortgage transactions because they are unreasonable'. In the absence of fraud or inequality of bargaining power the agreement should stand. 'Any other answer would place an unfortunate restriction on the liberty of contract of competent parties who are at arm's length.'

10.2.3 There should be no unfair collateral advantages

Biggs v Hoddinott (1898) CA

H, the owner of a public house, took out a mortgage with B, a brewer. The terms of the mortgage stated that H should purchase liquor only from B throughout the term of the mortgage, and that the mortgage should be neither redeemed nor called in for five years. Two years later H began to purchase liquor from another supplier and B sought an injunction. The injunction was granted at first instance and H appealed.

Held, dismissing the appeal, that the injunction should be granted. Lindley MR found that the agreement was a perfectly fair one and 'to say that to require such a covenant as that now in question is unconscionable is asking us to lay down a proposition which would shock any business man ...'.

Noakes & Co Ltd v Rice (1902) HL

R purchased the lease of a public house with the aid of a mortgage loan from N & Co. The mortgage contained a covenant by which R agreed not to sell any liquor other than that purchased from N & Co for the term of the lease. R sought to repay the loan and redeem his mortgage free from the covenant.

Held that the covenant was a collateral advantage and could not be enforced after redemption of the mortgage. Lord Davey asserted that 'a mortgage cannot be converted into something else; and when once you come to the conclusion that a stipulation for the benefit of the mortgagee is part of the mortgage transaction, it is but part of his security, and necessarily comes to an end on the payment off of the loan'.

Kreglinger v New Patagonia Meat and Cold Storage Co Ltd (1914) HL

K lent £10,000 to NP Ltd. K agreed not to call in the principal loan for five years, but NP Ltd managed to repay the loan after just over two years. Clause 8 of the mortgage agreement granted K an option to purchase sheepskins from NP Ltd for five years 'so long as the lenders are willing to purchase the same at a price equal to the best price ... offered ... by any ... other person'. NP Ltd were to pay K 1% commission if they sold sheepskins to anybody else. NP Ltd disputed K's right to carry on exercising their option after the mortgage had been redeemed because it was seen as a collateral advantage and a clog on the equity of redemption. K sought an injunction to restrain the sale of the sheepskins to other persons. The injunction was refused by the Court of Appeal and K appealed.

Held, allowing the appeal, that K were entitled to an injunction. Lord Parker of Waddington thought that the agreement was perfectly fair because it was a separate agreement, notwithstanding the fact that it was contained within the mortgage agreement. The mortgage could be paid off but the option would run for five years, and K had agreed to give a fair price for the skins: 'My Lords, after the most careful consideration of the authorities I think it is open to this House to hold ... that there is now no rule in equity which precludes a mortgagee ... from stipulating for any collateral advantage, provided such collateral advantage is not either (1) unfair and unconscionable, or (2) in the nature of a penalty clogging the equity of redemption, or (3) inconsistent with or repugnant to the contractual and equitable right to redeem.'

Solus agreements

Esso Petroleum Co Ltd v Harper's Garage (Stourport) Ltd (1968) HL

H owned two garages. He entered into a solus agreement with Esso to sell only their petrols and oils in the first garage for a period of four years and five months. H took out a mortgage for £7,000 with Esso for the second garage. The terms of the mortgage required H to purchase all his oils and petrols from Esso until the mortgage was repaid. H was not allowed to redeem the mortgage for 21 years, and in return for prompt payments and keeping open during working hours H received a discount on the price of petrol. When cut-price petrol began to be offered, H obtained his supplies from elsewhere, and Esso sought to enforce the agreement. H claimed that the terms of the mortgage were in restraint of trade and therefore void.

Held that the agreement for 21 years was void for restraint of trade. It was held that the agreement was different from the 'tied house' agreements where a new landlord of a public house takes out a mortgage in order to purchase the property. In this case, H was giving up a right that he already possessed (ie the right to purchase petrol from whomsoever he should choose). The tie for four years and five months was seen as being reasonable, but the 21-year agreement was not. The mortgage itself could be redeemed free from the solus agreement.

See also *Alec Lobb (Garages) Ltd v Total Oil (GB) Ltd* (1985).

10.2.4 There should be no oppressive or unconscionable terms

Cityland and Property (Holdings) Ltd v Dabrah (1968)

D took out a mortgage with his landlord, C&P Ltd. The landlord charged a monthly 'premium' over and above the capital repayments and reserved the right to demand in full the outstanding balance for any default. The 'premium' payable represented an effective annual rate of interest of 19%, and if the entire capital sum was to be paid immediately in the case of default the premium would amount to 57% of the sum lent. When D defaulted, C&P sought possession and repayment of the arrears.

Held that possession should be ordered, but that the amount repayable should be reduced to the principal plus 7% interest, minus the repayments already made by D. Goff J found the interest rate to be 'unfair' and 'unconscionable'. There had been a great disparity of bargaining power between the parties. D was a sitting tenant of limited means who had been threatened with eviction upon expiry of his lease. C&P, on the other hand, were a property company who were well aware of the effect of the transaction, and they should not be allowed to take advantage of D's circumstances.

Multiservice Bookbinding Ltd v Marden (1979)

MB Ltd took out a mortgage from Marden after obtaining legal advice. The terms of the mortgage were: (i) that interest be payable at 2% above bank rate on the full capital for the full duration of the mortgage; (ii) that arrears of interest be capitalised after 21 days; (iii) that the loan be neither redeemed nor called in for 10 years; and (iv) that the value of the capital and interest be index-linked to the Swiss franc. Unfortunately for MB Ltd, there were 12 Swiss francs to the pound in 1966, when the mortgage was taken out, but only just over four francs to the pound at the end of the 10-year period. Because of this fact an amount in excess of £130,000 was owed at the end of the term in order to repay an original loan of £36,000. MB Ltd claimed that the terms were unconscionable.

Held that the terms were enforceable. Browne-Wilkinson J found that the mortgage was valid because 'the test is not reasonableness. The parties made a bargain which the plaintiffs, who are businessmen, went into with their eyes open, with the benefit of independent advice, without any sharp practice by the defendants. I cannot see that there was anything unfair or oppressive or morally reprehensible in such a bargain entered into in such circumstances'. The value of the property had more than doubled during the term of the mortgage and MB Ltd's growth had been considerable.

Extortionate credit bargains

Consumer Credit Act 1974:

138. (1) A credit bargain is extortionate if it –
(a) requires the debtor or a relative if his to make payments ... which are grossly exorbitant; or
(b) otherwise grossly contravenes ordinary principles of fair trading.
(2) In determining whether a credit bargain is extortionate, regard shall be had to such evidence as is adduced concerning –
(a) interest rates prevailing at the time it was made;
(b) the factors mentioned in (3) to (5); and
(c) any other relevant considerations.
(3) Factors applicable under subsection (2) in relation to the debtor include –
(a) his age, experience, business capacity and state of health; and
(b) the degree to which, at the time of making the credit bargain, he was under financial pressure, and the nature of that pressure.
(4) Factors applicable under subsection (2) in relation to the creditor include –
(a) the degree of risk accepted by him, having regard to the value of any security provided;
(b) his relationship to the debtor; and
(c) whether or not a colourable cash price was quoted for any goods or services included in the credit bargain.
(5) Factors applicable under subsection (2) in relation to a linked transaction include the question how far the transaction was reasonably required for the protection of the debtor or creditor, or was in the interest of the debtor.
139. (1) A credit agreement may, if the court thinks just, be reopened on the ground that the credit bargain is extortionate –
(a) on an application for the purpose made by the debtor or any surety to the High Court, county court or sheriff court; or
(b) at the instance of the debtor or a surety in any proceedings to which the debtor and creditor are parties, being proceedings to enforce the credit agreement, any security relating to it, or any linked transaction; or
(c) at the instance of the debtor or a surety in other proceedings in any court where the amount paid or payable under the credit agreement is relevant.

(2) In reopening the agreement, the court may, for the purpose of relieving the debtor or a surety from payment of any sum in excess of that fairly due and reasonable, by order –

(a) direct accounts to be taken ...

(b) set aside the whole or part of any obligation imposed on the debtor or a surety by the credit bargain or any related agreement;

(c) require the creditor to repay the whole or part of any sum paid under the credit bargain or any related agreement by the debtor or a surety, whether paid to the creditor or any other person;

(d) direct the return to the surety of any property provided for the purposes of the security; or

(e) alter the terms of the agreement or security instrument.

Note ───────────────────────────────────

Most of the this Act applies only to regulated agreements. It does not apply to loans over £15,000, building society mortgages, or local authority mortgages (see ss 8-9). However, ss 137-9 apply to extortionate credit bargains of any amount (see ss 137 and 140).

A Ketley Ltd v Scott (1981)

Mr and Mrs S required a loan at very short notice in order to complete the purchase of their flat at a temporary bargain price. S had already charged the property to secure a bank overdraft, but he did not inform K Ltd of this fact. Mr and Mrs S obtained the loan from K Ltd at an interest rate of 12% over three months (an annual rate of 48%). They sought to have the bargain reopened or set aside.

Held that the agreement should not be altered or set aside. Foster J thought that the nature of the transaction justified the imposition of a rate of interest well in excess of that offered by banks and building societies. S was advised by his own solicitors and 'judging by his earnings and business experience knew exactly what he was doing'.

Woodstead Finance Ltd v Petrou (1986) CA

P charged her home to W Ltd in an effort to stave off her husband's bankruptcy. The amount of the loan was £25,000 for a period of six months. Her husband had a very bad record in relation to payments and the finance company imposed an interest rate equivalent to 42.5% per annum.

Held that, considering the risk taken by the lender, the interest rate was not extortionate. Browne-Wilkinson V-C considered that the bargain was harsh but, in view of P's 'appalling record' of repayments and the financial circumstances of Mr and Mrs P, it is unlikely that they could have received a loan elsewhere. The interest rate was 'normal for a risk of this kind'.

Q Does this mean that the Consumer Credit Act 1974 does not protect those debtors who are most in need of protection?

10.2.5 There should be no misrepresentation or undue influence

Note ───

Obviously a transaction procured by undue influence will be unenforceable by the party who has exerted the undue influence (for a recent example see *Cheese v Thomas* (1994)). It is rare for mortgagees themselves to exert undue influence, but they may be unable to enforce the mortgage if either they have actual or constructive notice of undue influence exerted by a third party, or if the third party is deemed to have been acting as the agent of the mortgagee.

───

Lloyds Bank Ltd v Bundy (1975) CA

B, an elderly farmer, and his son were customers of Lloyds Bank. The son founded a company and obtained overdrafts from the bank in order to finance the activities of the company. In 1966 the father, after taking advice, stood guarantor for the overdraft and allowed the bank to place a charge on his farm. In May 1969 B executed a further guarantee and charge. In December 1969 B's son visited his father with the assistant manager of the bank and B duly signed a further guarantee for £11,000 and a further charge for £3,500. The assistant manager did not advise B to obtain independent advice, and he was aware that B had no assets other than the farm. When the son defaulted the bank sought possession, which was granted by the judge. B appealed.

Held, allowing the appeal, that the guarantee and legal charge of December 1969 should be set aside for undue influence. B had relied implicitly upon the assistant manager of the bank, and the assistant manager was aware of that fact. He should have ensured that B received independent advice. Lord Denning MR thought that 'it is not right that the strong should be allowed to push the weak to the wall', and that this was a case 'where there has been inequality of bargaining power such as to merit the intervention of the court'.

National Westminster Bank plc v Morgan (1985) HL

Mr and Mrs M purchased a house with the aid of a building society mortgage. When M defaulted, the building society initiated possession proceedings. Mr M then arranged for a short-term bridging loan with the plaintiff bank in order to keep the house and finance his business. The bank insisted upon M and his wife executing a legal charge in their favour. M signed the charge and the bank manager went to M's house in order to obtain the signature of Mrs M. Mrs M described the atmosphere of their meeting as 'tense', and she expressed doubts about the effect of the charge, but she signed it. The loan was not repaid and the bank sought possession. Mrs M claimed that undue influence had been exerted by the bank manager. The judge at first instance found that the transaction had not been manifestly disadvantageous to Mrs M; she would have lost the house in any case had she not consented to the charge. The Court of Appeal allowed Mrs M's appeal on the grounds that the bank manager should have ensured that she received independent advice. The bank appealed.

Held, allowing the appeal, that, before a transaction can be set aside for undue influence it had to be shown that it was manifestly disadvantageous to the party seeking to avoid it. There was no such evidence in this case, and the relationship of banker and client is not sufficient, by itself, to raise the presumption of undue influence. Lord Scarman thought that the charge was 'an ordinary banking transaction'. It was also held *per curiam* that more than mere inequality of bargaining power was required to raise the presumption of undue influence. The dictum of Lord Denning in *Bundy* (above) was disapproved.

Kings North Trust Ltd v Bell (1986) CA

Mr B was the sole legal owner of the matrimonial home, in which his wife had an equitable interest. In order to finance his business, he arranged a second mortgage of his house with K Ltd. K Ltd sent the mortgage deed to B's solicitors who entrusted B with obtaining Mrs B's signature. B misrepresented the scope and purpose of the loan in order to obtain his wife's signature. When B defaulted, K Ltd sought possession, and Mrs B claimed that her signature had been procured by her husband's false representation and undue influence. She had not received independent advice. The judge ordered possession because, although she had been misled as to the purpose of the mortgage, Mrs B had been aware that she was creating a charge on her home when she signed the mortgage deed. Mrs B appealed.

Held that when Mr B made the fraudulent misrepresentation to his wife, he was acting as the agent of the mortgagee. K Ltd had left it to Mr B to procure his wife's signature by any method he should choose. Mrs B should have been advised to seek independent advice and the mortgage was therefore void as against her.

Bank of Credit and Commerce International v Aboody (1990) CA

Mr and Mrs A were directors and shareholders of a family company. Mr A took all of the decisions and Mrs A relied upon his judgment. The company's overdraft was secured by three charges on Mrs A's house. BCCI's solicitors had been asked to ensure that Mrs A received independent advice before execution of the last charge. They accordingly arranged for another firm of solicitors, F Ltd, to give Mrs A advice. The solicitor at F Ltd attempted to propose alternative arrangements to Mrs A, but she refused to accept them. Mr A burst into the interview between Mrs A and the solicitor and ordered his wife to sign the charge. There followed an argument between Mr A and the solicitor, and, under pressure, Mrs A signed the charge document. The solicitor's attendance note stated that 'Husband is a bully. Under pressure and she wants peace.' When the company collapsed, BCCI sought to enforce the securities, and Mrs A claimed that her signature had been procured by undue influence. The judge held that Mr A had undoubtedly exerted undue influence over his wife but, as the charge was not manifestly disadvantageous to her, the husband's undue influence did not affect the bank. Mrs A appealed, her counsel contending that it is unnecessary to establish manifest disadvantage when there has been actual, rather than presumed, undue influence.

Held that the transaction was not manifestly disadvantageous to Mrs A because she probably would have signed the charge in the absence of any undue influence. It was also stated *per curiam* that, had the charge been manifestly disadvantageous to Mrs A, the bank could possibly have been affected by the undue influence on two grounds: if Mr A was deemed to be their agent; or if they had notice of the undue influence.

Barclays Bank plc v O'Brien (1994) HL

Mr and Mrs O agreed to execute a second mortgage of the matrimonial home in order to secure overdraft facilities for Mr O's company. The branch manger sent the necessary documents to another branch for execution, along with instructions that the parties were to be made fully aware of the nature of the transaction and that if in doubt they were to seek independent legal advice. The instructions were not complied with, and the effect of the documents was not explained to Mrs O. Mr O assured her that the loan was limited to £60,000 and that it would last only three weeks. In fact, the amount of the charge was unlimited. Mrs O signed the documents without reading them. When the company's overdraft exceeded £154,000 the bank sought possession, and Mrs O claimed that her signature had been procured by undue influence. The judge found that, as there was no evidence that the husband was acting on behalf of the bank, the charge was enforceable against Mrs O. The Court of Appeal allowed the appeal, holding that the charge was only enforceable against Mrs O to the extent of the £60,000 to which she had consented. The bank appealed.

Held, dismissing the appeal, that the charge should be set aside. Lord Browne-Wilkinson took the opportunity 'to consider a problem which has given rise to reported decisions of the Court of Appeal on no less than 11 occasions in the last eight years and which has led to a difference of judicial view'. He looked at the different types of undue influence, as identified in *Aboody* (above), namely: Class 1, actual undue influence; Class 2 (A), undue influence which is presumed because of a special relationship, for example solicitor and client; and Class 2 (B), undue influence which is presumed because of a *de facto* relationship of trust and confidence. He decided that the relationship of husband and wife was not a special relationship for the purposes of Class 2 (A) undue influence, but that the trust and confidence which Mrs O placed in her husband with regard to their financial affairs brought their relationship into Class 2 (B). The fact that undue influence may be presumed does not necessarily mean that the undue influence will affect the bank. How, therefore, does the undue influence of the husband affect the bank? 'Although there may be cases where, without artificiality, it can properly be held that the husband was acting as the agent of the creditor in procuring the wife to stand as surety, such cases will be of very rare occurrence.' The doctrine of notice 'provides the key' in such circumstances. The bank were put on inquiry when Mrs O offered to stand surety for her husband's debts when: (a) she herself gained no financial advantage from the transaction; and (b) there was a 'substantial risk' that the husband would commit a legal or equitable wrong which could entitle the wife to have the order set aside. The bank should have taken 'reasonable steps' to satisfy themselves that Mrs O's consent had been properly obtained. The bank were quite well aware of the steps to be taken: they should have insisted that the wife attend a private meeting (in the absence of her husband) with a representative of the bank at which she would be told the extent of her liability and the nature of the transaction. She should have been urged to take independent advice. The bank had not complied with these rules and it was therefore fixed with constructive notice of the undue influence.

Q Does this decision reintroduce the doctrine of notice into registered land? Of what did the bank have constructive notice? Was it Mrs O's rights in the property, or of the nature of the transaction? See Martin Dixon (1994) Conv 421.

CIBC Mortgages plc v Pitt (1994) HL

Mr and Mrs P owned the matrimonial home jointly. In 1986 Mr P proposed to remortgage the house in order to purchase shares on the stock market. The couple were offered £150,000 by CIBC on condition that the money was used for the purchase of a second property. The second property was never purchased. Both Mr and Mrs P signed the charge, but Mrs P did so without reading any of the documents. She had been reluctant to sign but gave her consent after pressure from Mr P. CIBC sought possession of the property when Mr P defaulted after the stock market crash of 1987. Mrs P claimed that the charge was not binding upon her because of undue influence and misrepresentation. At first instance it was held that there had been no misrepresentation and that, although there had been actual undue influence, CIBC were not affected by that undue influence. The Court of Appeal upheld the decision, and Mrs P appealed.

Held that the charge could be enforced against Mrs P. In cases of actual undue influence it was unnecessary to prove manifest disadvantage (thereby overruling *Aboody* on this point) in order to have the transaction set aside. However, in this case, Mr P was not acting as the agent of CIBC, nor did CIBC have notice of the undue influence. Unlike the O'Brien case, where the wife stood surety for her husband's debts, in this case the transaction appeared to be a normal advance to husband and wife for their joint benefit. CIBC could not be fixed with constructive notice.

Massey v Midland Bank plc (1995) CA

M owned her own house. She had a long-standing relationship with P, who had previously persuaded her to stand surety for a loan for a business venture. That venture failed, leaving M liable to pay £25,000. P then persuaded M to grant a further legal charge over her property in order to finance another business venture. He told her that the financial position of the company was excellent and he assured her that the previous charge would be repaid. Both statements were untrue. The bank required M to take independent advice and P arranged for her to visit his solicitors, who explained the nature of the charge to her in P's presence. When P's business failed, the bank sought possession, and M claimed that the bank was affected by P's misrepresentation and undue influence. At first instance the judge found that P had not acted as the agent of the bank and ordered possession. M appealed, relying upon the doctrine of constructive notice.

Held that the charge was enforceable against M. The nature of the transaction, M standing surety for P, put the bank on inquiry. However, the bank, by insisting that M took independent advice, had taken reasonable steps to ensure that M's consent had been properly obtained. The bank was entitled to rely upon the quality of the advice given, which was a matter for the professional judgment of the solicitor, and therefore they were not fixed with constructive notice.

Banco Exterior Internacional v Mann (1995) CA

BEI were prepared to lend M £175,000 for his business, provided that a second charge was granted over the matrimonial home. The bank stated that Mrs M should receive independent advice from her solicitor and required that the solicitor should sign the charge document to that effect. M took Mrs M to the company's solicitor, where she signed the charge in the presence of her husband and the solicitor. Mrs M said that she told the solicitor that she had no choice but to sign the charge. When M defaulted, the bank sought possession. The judge at first instance, applying *O'Brien*, found that the circumstances raised the presumption of undue influence and that the presumption had not been rebutted. The bank appealed.

Held that the bank had taken reasonable steps to avoid being fixed with constructive notice. The bank was entitled to assume that the solicitor was honest and competent, and that he was aware of the purpose of the advice he was asked to give.

TSB Bank plc v Camfield (1995) CA

C was a partner in a vehicle leasing business. He and his partner agreed an overdraft facility with the TSB for £30,000, provided that a charge was executed over their houses. The bank stipulated that the wives should receive independent legal advice, and wrote to the solicitors acting for the husband, requesting that advice should be given to all parties by a separate person within the firm. The firm agreed to do this. C innocently misrepresented the extent of the charge, believing liability to be limited to £15,000, when in fact liability was unlimited. The legal executive, who advised Mrs C in the presence of her husband, was aware of the mistake but did not disillusion Mrs C. The legal executive wrote to the bank that 'they [ie the wives] were ... under the impression that their commitment was limited to £15,000 each, whereas of course as far as the partnership is concerned the amount would in fact be £30,000'. Two further advances were made to the partnership and, when the business failed, the bank sought possession. At first instance the judge gave judgment against C for £47,000, but limited Mrs C's liability to the £15,000 to which she had consented. Mrs C appealed.

Held that the charge should be set aside in its entirety as against Mrs C. The nature of the transaction, together with the husband's innocent misrepresentation, put the bank on inquiry, and the advice given was not sufficient to prevent the bank being fixed with constructive notice. The Court of Appeal in *O'Brien* found that the charge was enforceable against Mrs O to the extent of the £60,000 to which she had consented, and that £60,000 had already been satisfied. The House of Lords upheld the decision without declaring whether the charge should be set aside in full or in part, though Lord Brown-Wilkinson indicated that the charge should be set aside in its entirety. Roch LJ decided that, under the terms of s 2(2) of the Misrepresentation Act 1967, Mrs C had the right to rescind the contract if it was induced by misrepresentation. She would not have entered into the contract at all had she been aware of its true nature. 'Mrs Camfield is entitled to be placed in the position she would have been in had the misrepresentation not been made and had she been made aware of the true nature of the legal charge.' As Nourse LJ observed, there was no question of unjust enrichment. Mrs C gained no benefit from the charge, and therefore 'there is nothing for the wife to give back, and no cause for her to provide compensation'.

Q Why were the bank not entitled to rely upon the quality of the advice given by the legal executive? Did the bank take reasonable steps to avoid being fixed with constructive notice? Were the solicitors, rather than the bank, negligent?

Note ───────────────────────────────

1 See the cases at 3.6.3 for problems when a mortgagee advances money and a third party claims to have a prior interest in the security.

2 On the issue of subrogation when there are numerous charges, some of which have been obtained by fraud and/or undue influence see *Castle Phillips Finance v Piddington* (1995).

Q What is the difference between the cases in 10.2.5 and 3.6.3?

Q Why was Mr Prestidge's charge only partially set aside as against Mrs Bown (in *Equity & Law Home Loans Ltd v Prestidge* at 3.6.3), but Mr Camfield's charge set aside in its entirety as against Mrs Camfield?

10.3 The rights of mortgagees

10.3.1 The right to sue on the covenant

Limitation Act 1980 s 20:

(1) No action may be brought to recover –
   (a) any principal sum of money secured by a mortgage or other charge on property (whether real or personal); or
   (b) proceeds of the sale of land ...
after the expiration of twelve years from the date on which the right to receive the money accrued.

(5) ... no action to recover arrears of interest payable in respect of any sum of money secured by a mortgage or other charge or payable in respect of proceeds of the sale of land, or to recover damages in respect of such arrears shall be brought after the expiration of six years from the date on which the interest became due.

10.3.2 The power of sale

Law of Property Act 1925 s 91(2):

In any action, whether for foreclosure, or for redemption, or for sale, or for the raising and payment in any manner of the mortgage money, the court, on the request of the mortgagee, or of any person interested either in the mortgage money or in the right of redemption, and, notwithstanding that –
   (a) any other person dissents; or
   (b) the mortgagee or any person so interested does not appear in the action ...
and without allowing any time for redemption or for payment of any mortgage money, may direct a sale of the mortgaged property, on such terms as it thinks fit, including the deposit in court of a reasonable sum fixed by the court to meet the expenses of sale and to secure performance of the terms.

Law of Property Act 1925 ss 101 and 103:

101. (1) A mortgagee, where the mortgage is made by deed, shall, by virtue of this Act, have the following powers, to the like extent as if they had been in terms conferred by the mortgage deed, but not further (namely):
   (i) A power, when the mortgage money has become due, to sell, or to concur with any other person in selling, the mortgaged property, or any part thereof, either subject to prior charges or not, and either together or

in lots, by public auction or by private contract, subject to such conditions respecting title, or evidence of title, or other matter, as the mortgagee thinks fit with power to vary any contract for sale, and to buy at an auction, or to rescind any contract for sale, and to re-sell, without being answerable for any loss occasioned thereby ...

103. A mortgagee shall not exercise the power of sale conferred by this Act unless and until –

(i) Notice requiring payment of the mortgage money has been served on the mortgagor or one of two or more mortgagors, and default has been made in payment of the mortgage money, or of part thereof for three months after such service; or

(ii) Some interest under the mortgage is in arrear and unpaid for two months after becoming due; or

(iii) There has been a breach of some provision contained in the mortgage deed or in this Act, or in an enactment replaced by this Act, and on the part of the mortgagor, or of some person concurring in making the mortgage, to be observed or performed, other than and besides a covenant for payment of the mortgage money or interest thereon.

Note

Sections 101 and 103 refer to mortgages by deed. A registered chargee of an equitable mortgage also has the power of sale. An equitable mortgagee without the power of sale may apply under s 91(2) above.

Palk v Mortgage Services Funding plc (1993) CA

Mr and Mrs P borrowed £300,000 on a joint mortgage in 1990. In order to raise money, the Ps took out two further mortgages on the property. Mr P went bankrupt shortly afterwards and Mrs P attempted to sell the property in 1991. She negotiated a sale for the purchase price of £283,000, but the outstanding mortgage debt was £360,000. The second and third mortgagees agreed to the sale because they had no hope of recovering their loan, but MSF refused their consent to a sale. They wished to retain the property until the market improved, rather than sell during a time of recession. MSF obtained a possession order (see 10.3.3), which was suspended pending Mrs P's application under s 91(2) (above) for an order for the sale of the property. At first instance Mrs P's request was refused because it was held that a sale could only be ordered without the consent of the mortgagee if the proceeds would be sufficient to redeem the mortgage. Mrs P appealed.

Held, allowing the appeal, that sale should be ordered. Sir Donald Nicholls V-C thought that postponing sale would be very unfair to Mrs P. She would be forced to retain property which she neither wanted nor enjoyed while her debts mounted. Even though the sum outstanding at the date of the hearing was £409,000, 'it is just and equitable to order a sale because otherwise unfairness and injustice will follow'.

Sale of the mortgaged property and application of the proceeds of sale

Law of Property Act 1925 s 105:

The money which is received by the mortgagee, arising from the sale, after discharge of prior incumbrances to which the sale is not made subject, if any, or after payment into court under this Act of a sum to meet any prior incumbrance, shall be held by him in trust to be applied by him, first, in payment of all costs, charges, and expenses properly incurred by him as incident to the sale or any attempted sale, or otherwise; and secondly, in discharge of the mortgage money, interest, and costs, and other money, if any, due under the mortgage; and the residue of the money so received shall be paid to the person entitled to the mortgaged property, or authorised to give receipts for the proceeds of the sale thereof.

Cuckmere Brick Co Ltd v Mutual Finance Ltd (1971) CA

CBC purchased a plot of land with planning permission for up to 100 flats. They borrowed £50,000 from MFL. Because they were short of capital, CBC decided to apply for planning permission to build 33 houses on part of the site. The planning permission was granted but work did not commence. Five years after the initial advance, MFL decided to call in the loan, and, as CBC were unable to repay the money, they took possession of the plot of land. MFL decided to sell the plot of land by auction and they advertised the land together with the planning permission for the 33 houses. They made no mention of the planning permission for 100 flats. CBC informed MFL that the land was worth approximately £75,000 with planning permission for 100 flats, but that it was worth much less if sold with permission for only 33 houses. MFL ignored CBC's advice and sold the plot for £44,000. CBC brought an action claiming that MFL had failed to take reasonable care in exercising their power of sale, and that they should be made to account for the shortfall. At first instance the judge found that MFL had failed in their duty by ignoring the planning permission for the flats and by refusing to postpone the auction at CBC's request. MFL appealed.

Held that 'a mortgagee, in exercising his power of sale, does owe a duty to take reasonable precaution to obtain the true market value of the mortgaged property at the date on which he decides to sell' (*per* Salmon LJ). MFL were in breach of this duty.

Parker-Tweedale v Dunbar Bank plc (1991) CA

Mr and Mrs P-T purchased a farm with the aid of a mortgage from DB. Mrs P-T was the sole legal owner and mortgagor, though Mr P-T had agreed that he would make no claim against the mortgagee with regard to his beneficial interest. In 1988, when Mrs P-T defaulted on the mortgage, DB sold the property in exercise of their power of sale, with Mrs P-T's consent. The property had been valued at between £380,000 and £450,000 but was eventually sold for £575,000. A week later the property was sold to a property developer for £700,000. Mr P-T brought an action claiming that DB had failed to take reasonable care in obtaining a proper price.

Held that DB owed no duty to Mr P-T, the mortgage agreement being between themselves and Mrs P-T. The duty is one of beneficiary and trustee; it does not arise independently by the tort of negligence. Even had DB owed a duty to Mr P-T, the evidence showed that the price obtained was a fair price. It was in excess of the valuation. The fact that the property was sold for a considerably higher price one week later was unfortunate for Mr P-T but it was not, by itself, evidence of lack of care on the part of DB, especially at a time of rising property prices.

10.3.3 The right to possession

Administration of Justice Act 1970 s 36:
(1) Where the mortgagee under a mortgage of land which consists of or includes a dwelling house brings an action in which he claims possession of the mortgaged property, not being an action for foreclosure in which a claim for possession of the mortgaged property is also made, the court may exercise any of the powers conferred on it by subsection (2) below if it appears to the court that in the event of its exercising the power the mortgagor is likely to be able within a reasonable period to pay any sums due under the mortgage or to remedy a default consisting of a breach of any other obligation arising under or by virtue of the mortgage.
(2) The court –
    (a) may adjourn proceedings; or
    (b) on giving judgment, or making an order, for delivery of possession of the mortgaged property ... may –
        (i) stay or suspend execution of the judgment or order; or
        (ii) postpone the date for delivery of possession ...
for such period or periods as the court thinks reasonable.

Four-Maids Ltd v Dudley Marshall (Properties) Ltd (1957)
The terms of a legal charge stated that the principal would not be called in as long as the interest repayments were paid punctually. When the interest payments were late, the lender sought possession. The debtor then paid off all the arrears and challenged the claim to possession.

Held that the mortgagee was entitled to possession. Harman J stated that 'the right of the mortgagee to possession in the absence of some contract has nothing to do with default on the part of the mortgagor. The mortgagee may go into possession before the ink is dry on the mortgage unless there is something in the contract, express or by implication, whereby he has contracted himself out of that right'.

Note
An equitable chargee has no right to possession of the property unless the right is specifically given by the contract.

Target Home Loans Ltd v Clothier (1994) CA

C borrowed £225,000 by way of mortgage from T Ltd. C became incapable of repaying the mortgage instalments and T Ltd sought a possession order when no repayments had been made for two years. C proposed to repay the mortgage by selling part of the garden to a neighbour and borrowing the balance from a relative. The judge adjourned proceedings for four months on the grounds that C was likely to be able to repay the mortgage within a reasonable period (see Administration of Justice Act 1970 s 36, above). When it became apparent that C's proposed method of payment was no longer possible, T Ltd appealed, seeking an order for immediate possession. C claimed that he had put the property up for sale and that an offer of £450,000 had been made to the estate agents. The question was whether the court had jurisdiction under s 36 to suspend proceedings pending a sale by the mortgagor. Section 36 is usually used to suspend proceedings in order that the mortgagor may find the means to repay the arrears and remain in the property.

Held that possession should be postponed for three months. Nolan LJ thought that it was in the interests of both parties to suspend the order if there was a prospect of an early sale. The mortgagors in occupation were in a better position to sell the property than a mortgagee in possession.

10.3.4 The right to appoint a receiver

Law of Property Act 1925 ss 101 and 109:

101. (1) A mortgagee, where the mortgage is made by deed, shall, by virtue of this Act, have the following powers ...

(iii) A power, when the mortgage money has become due, to appoint a receiver of the income of the mortgaged property, or any part thereof ...

109. (1) A mortgagee entitled to appoint a receiver under the power in that behalf conferred by this Act shall not appoint a receiver until he has become entitled to exercise the power of sale conferred by this Act, but may then, by writing under his hand, appoint such persons as he thinks fit to be a receiver.

(2) A receiver appointed under the powers conferred by this Act or any other enactment replaced by this Act, shall be deemed to be the agent of the mortgagor; and the mortgagor shall be solely responsible for the receiver's acts or defaults unless the mortgage deed otherwise provides.

Supreme Court Act 1981 s 37(1):

The High Court may by order (whether interlocutory or final) grant an injunction or appoint a receiver in all cases in which it appears to the court to be just and convenient to do so.

The right to appoint a receiver is only available if the mortgage has been created by deed. Other equitable mortgagees may apply under s 37(1) of the Supreme Court Act 1981 above.

10.3.5 The right to foreclose

Law of Property Act 1925 ss 88 and 89:
88. (2) Where any such mortgagee [of freehold land] obtains an order for foreclosure absolute, the order shall operate to vest the fee simple in him (subject to any legal mortgage having priority to the mortgage in right of which the foreclosure is obtained and to any money thereby secured), and thereupon the mortgage term, if any, shall thereby be merged with the fee simple, and any subsequent mortgage term or charge by way of legal mortgage bound by the order shall thereupon be extinguished.
89. (2) Where any such mortgagee [of leasehold land] obtains an order for foreclosure absolute, the order shall, unless it otherwise provides, operate ... to vest the leasehold reversion affected by the mortgage and any subsequent mortgage term in him, subject to any legal mortgage having priority to the mortgage in right of which the foreclosure is obtained and to any money thereby secured, and thereupon the mortgage term and any subsequent mortgage term or charge by way of legal mortgage bound by the order shall, subject to any express provision to the contrary contained in the order, merge in such leasehold reversion or be extinguished.

Note ——————————————————————————————————————
1 In any action for foreclosure the court may exercise its discretion under s 91(2) (at 10.3.2 above) to order sale instead of foreclosure.
2 An equitable mortgagee has the same right of foreclosure as a legal mortgagee. An equitable chargee, on the other hand, has no right of foreclosure.

10.3.6 The right to consolidate

Note ——————————————————————————————————————
If a mortgagor has mortgaged more than one property to the same mortgagee, that mortgagee's right to insist that one loan is not redeemed without redeeming the others has been restricted by s 93 of the LPA 1925.

Law of Property Act 1925 s 93:
(1) A mortgagor seeking to redeem any one mortgage is entitled to do so without paying money due under any separate mortgage made by him, or

by any person through whom he claims, solely on property other than that comprised in the mortgage which he seeks to redeem.

(3) Save as aforesaid, nothing in this Act, in reference to mortgages, affects any right of consolidation or renders inoperative a stipulation in relation to any mortgage made before or after the commencement of this Act reserving a right to consolidate.

10.4 Protection of mortgages ...

10.4.1 Mortgages of the legal estate in unregistered land

Legal mortgages

Note
Legal mortgages protected by deposit of title deeds bind the world and do not need further protection. If they are not protected by deposit of title deeds they should be registered as a class C (i) land charge in the Land Charges Register (see 2.2.2)

Equitable mortgages
- Equitable mortgages protected by the deposit of title deeds created before 27 September 1989 are subject to the doctrine of notice.
- Equitable mortgages created under the rule in *Walsh v Lonsdale* must be registered as class C (iv) land charges (see 2.2.2).
- General equitable charges should be registered as class C (iii) land charges (see 2.2.2)

10.4.2 Mortgages of the legal estate in registered land

Legal mortgages

Note
Legal mortgages should be registered and entered in the charges register against the title to be charged. Until registration, all mortgages are equitable, even if created by deed. See *Mortgage Corporation Ltd v Nationwide Credit Corporation Ltd* at 10.5.1.

Equitable mortgages

Note
All equitable mortgages should be entered as a minor interest on the register (see 3.5).

10.4.3 Mortgages of equitable interests

Dearle v Hall (1823)

B had a life interest in a fund under his father's will. The income from the fund amounted to £93 per annum. He sold to D an annuity of £37 to be paid out of (and be charged upon) his life interest. He then sold another annuity of £27 to S. S's annuity was similarly charged upon the life interest. B then sold his life interest in its entirety to H. H's solicitors made proper enquiries regarding B's title but had no notice of the annuities granted to D and S. H gave notice to the executors of B's father's will of the assignment of B's interest to him. The executors later found out about the annuities, and sought guidance regarding payment of the income from the fund. D and S claimed that their interests should take priority because they were created first.

Held that the assignment to H should take priority over the annuities in favour of D and S. Plumer MR stated that the equitable rule that the first in time prevails does not apply to the legal estate. In order to affect the legal estate notice should be given to those who hold that legal estate, which in this case was the executors, or trustees. 'They say, that they were not bound to give notice to the trustees; for that notice does not form part of the necessary conveyance of an equitable interest. I admit, that, if you mean to rely on contract with the individual, you do not need to give notice; from the moment of the contract, he, with whom you are dealing, is personally bound. But if you mean to go further, and to make your right attach upon the thing which is the subject of the contract , it is necessary to give notice.' Neither D nor S had given notice to the executors. H had given notice and therefore his interest took priority.

Note ──
The rule in *Dearle v Hall* applies to both registered and unregistered land.
──

Law of Property Act 1925 s 137(3):
A notice, otherwise than in writing, given to, or received by, a trustee after the commencement of this Act as respects any dealing with an equitable interest in real or personal property, shall not affect the priority of competing claims of purchasers in that equitable interest.

10.5 Priority of mortgages

10.5.1 Mortgages of the legal estate ...

... in unregistered land
● A legal mortgage which is protected by deposit of title deeds will have priority over all subsequent mortgages.

- A legal mortgage not protected by deposit of title deeds will have priority over all subsequent mortgages from the date of registration as a class C (i) land charge (see 10.4.1).
- An equitable mortgage protected by the deposit of title deeds is subject to the doctrine of notice. The fact that the mortgagee is in possession of the deeds will usually be sufficient to fix subsequent mortgagees with notice.
- An equitable mortgage not protected by deposit of title deeds should be entered either as a class C (iii) or as a class C (iv) land charge (see 10.4.1). The relevant date for the purposes of priority is the date of registration.

... in registered land

- A mortgage cannot be legal until the chargee is registered as the proprietor of the charge. Once registered, the mortgage will have priority over all subsequent mortgages.
- A unregistered 'legal' charge takes effect in equity only, and ranks as an equitable mortgage (see s 106 of the LRA 1925, below).
- An equitable mortgage which has been entered as a minor interest will have priority over all subsequent mortgages whether they are legal or equitable.
- The order of priority between equitable charges is determined by the maxim 'where the equities are equal the first in time prevails'. An earlier equitable mortgage will take priority over a later equitable mortgage regardless the date of registration.

Land Registration Act 1925 s 106:

(1) The proprietor of any registered land may, subject to any entry to the contrary on the register, mortgage by deed or otherwise, the land or any part of it in any manner which would have been permissible if the land had not been registered, and, subject to this section, with the like effect.

(2) Unless and until the mortgage becomes a registered charge –

    (a) it shall take effect only in equity; and

    (b) it shall be capable of being overridden as a minor interest unless it is protected as provided by subsection (3) below.

(3) A mortgage which is not a registered charge may be protected on the register by –

    (a) a notice under section 49 of this Act ...

    (b) any other such notice as may be prescribed; or

    (c) a caution under section 54 of this Act.

Mortgage Corporation Ltd v Nationwide Credit Corporation Ltd (1994) CA

L borrowed £367,500 from M Ltd and he executed a legal charge in their favour on 10 July 1989. On 31 July, L executed a further legal charge in favour of N Ltd in order to raise £60,000. On 14 August, N Ltd entered a notice on the register in order to protect their charge. M Ltd did not make any application either to register their charge or to protect it by entering a notice or a caution on the register. When L defaulted on both mortgages M Ltd obtained a possession order and sold the property for £300,000. N Ltd agreed to withdraw their notice in order that the property could be sold, and they agreed to allow the court to determine the issue of priority. At first instance the judge decided in M Ltd's favour. N Ltd appealed.

Held that M Ltd's charge should take priority. N Ltd's charge, though entered as a notice, took effect in equity only (see LRA 1925 s 106, above). Therefore M Ltd's charge, being first in time, should prevail. The effect of the notice was to protect the charge from subsequent purchasers; it did not affect priority in relation to earlier charges (see LRA 1925 s 52, at 3.5.1). Dillon LJ, after referring to s 52, stated that 'notice is indeed notice, but it does not give priority which would not, apart from the 1925 Act, have been there. Therefore the plaintiff's charge has priority to the defendant's charge.'

10.5.2 Mortgages of an equitable interest

Note ───
Priority depends upon the order in which notice was given to the trustees under the rule in *Dearle v Hall* (see 10.4.3).

10.5.3 The right to tack further advances ...

...in unregistered land

Law of Property Act 1925 s 94:
(1) After the commencement of this Act, a prior mortgagee shall have a right to make further advances to rank in priority to subsequent mortgages (whether legal or equitable) –
(a) if an arrangement has been made to that effect with the subsequent mortgagees; or
(b) if he had no notice of such subsequent mortgages at the time when the further advance was made by him; or
(c) whether or not he had such notice as aforesaid, where the mortgage imposes an obligation on him to make such further advances.
This subsection applies whether or not the prior mortgage was made expressly for securing further advances.
(2) In relation to the making of further advances after the commencement of this Act a mortgagee shall not be deemed to have notice of a mortgage merely by reason that it was registered as a land charge if it was not so registered at the time when the original mortgage was created or when the last search (if any) by or on behalf of the mortgagee was made, whichever last happened.
This subsection only applies where the prior mortgage was made expressly for securing a current account or other further advances.

(3) Save in regard to the making of further advances as aforesaid, the right to tack is hereby abolished.

... in registered land

Land Registration Act 1925 s 30:

(1) When a registered charge is made for securing further advances, the registrar shall, before making any entry on the register which would prejudicially affect the priority of any further advance thereunder, give to the proprietor of the charge at his registered address, notice by registered post of the intended entry, and the proprietor of the charge shall not ... be affected by such entry, unless the advance is made after the date when the notice ought to have been received in due course of post ...

(3) Where the proprietor of a charge is under an obligation, noted on the register, to make a further advance, a subsequent registered charge shall take effect subject to any further advance made pursuant to the obligation.

Index